ADVANCE PRAISE

Max Friedman's *Painful Joy* dutifully fulfills the biblical mandate to honor one's father and mother. Sensitively and lovingly written, compelling and at times poetic, it reminds us all that the tragedy of the Holocaust lies not in grand historical events, political or military, but in the broken lives of real human beings, both those who did not survive and those who did, and, all-too-often, communicated that brokenness to their children and grandchildren. Frieda and Sam Friedman survived, made their way into the world of the foreign land of the United States, birthed two children, and bequeathed to them – and us – the power not only of love despite all, but perseverance and resilience as well. *Kol hakavod*! [Hebrew for "A job well done!"]

– Rabbi Dr. Steven Leonard Jacobs is Professor of Religious Studies and Emeritus Aronov Endowed Chair of Judaic Studies at The University of Alabama, Tuscaloosa

Max opens a door for us to enter a shared world; a world touched by his family's pain, longing, love, sorrow and hope. His gentle, respectful and caring writing style will leave a mark upon you after you close the book for the last time – inviting you to open the door again. You will re-open this book!

– Rabbi Steven Silberman, Congregation Ahavas Chesed, Mobile, AL

Painful Joy, A Holocaust Family Memoir is dedicated to and in memory of Salomon and Frieda Friedman, cherished parents of Max. The reader feels the love, appreciation and respect the author holds for his parents as he grapples with the incomprehensible acts of inhumanity they endured and endeavors to understand the indelible mark the Holocaust left upon them and the trauma he inherited through their DNA and as the child of Holocaust survivors. Factual content, precise descriptions of environs, explanations of customs and mores, definitions of non-English words as well as personal musings are beautifully woven within the memoir. Friedman's command of the English language is superb, and the reader will be immersed in the narrative, almost able to utilize one's senses to hear, see, smell and touch that which is described in this well-crafted memoir. The reader becomes acquainted with the richness of his parents' and grandparents' lives and the Jewish communities in which they lived. Information about the villages and cities is presented to the reader through meticulous research, bringing us back as far as the 13th century so that we can understand more fully how these communities evolved. We reflect how pain and hardship define our very being, as does love. Like Salomon and Frieda, we can feel joy after knowing sorrow.

– Millie Jasper is Executive Director, Holocaust & Human Rights Education Center, White Plains, NY

Although eight decades have passed since the beginning of the Holocaust, the horrors inflicted upon survivors left painful scars that continue to shape life for younger generations today. In this compelling and beautifully written memoir, *Painful Joy* takes us on the journey of the author's parents, Sam and Frieda, who met in Sweden after surviving the Holocaust. It explores how this family learned to overcome pain, demons, death and mental illness while finding justice in celebrating life. This story offers a stark reminder of why it's important to keep the memories of those lost in the Holocaust alive and powerfully shows that in order to move forward, our darkest moments in history can only be met with love, hope, faith and family.

– Lisa Sherman-Cohen is Communications Manager, World Jewish Restitution Organization (WJRO)

This powerful and poignant book tells of two interweaving journeys. As the son of two Holocaust survivors, Max sought to discover the story of his parents' lives before, during and after the Holocaust and thus his own story. Meticulously researched over several years, he makes discoveries that help give meaning to both their and his experiences. Given what we now know about the effects of trauma and PTSD, attachment theory, epigenetics and the physiological effects of trauma on the next generation, Max re-explores his relationships with his parents from childhood through adulthood. This makes for a fascinating and compelling journey and a testimony to the complexity, resilience and ultimately love that can prevail despite the most devastating and tragic of circumstances.

– Ronald Garson, M.D., is a psychiatrist in the Washington, DC area

---

Painful Joy is like no other Holocaust story I have read. It is mostly biography, the pieced-together stories of the lives of Friedman's parents. But it is also memoir, recollecting Friedman's life with his parents and his sister, and autobiography: Friedman's account, albeit incomplete, of his own life story, all told against the backdrop of a once vibrant Jewish life in Poland, the Holocaust, and immigrant life in the United States. His parents, Szlama/Salomon and Frimet/Frieda, were Holocaust survivors. When Max Friedman asks himself the question, "What allowed some small fraction of the Jews to survive?" he begins his answer with the word luck. Salomon and Frieda were lucky during their six years of torture under the Nazis, and they remained lucky even after their deaths. How many Holocaust survivors had a child who possessed the talent, the time, the resources, and the determination to dig into archives, libraries, and other sources of records in at least half a dozen countries so that their stories of survival could be brought to light in vivid detail? I suspect not many. Salomon and Frieda are lucky. Thanks to their son, their story is seeing the light of day.

Salomon and Frieda met in Sweden after their liberation from Bergen-Belsen, one of the most horrible of the Nazi concentration camps. Salomon's journey to Bergen-Belsen took him through the Będzin ghetto, several years of slave labor in at least three different camps, and a six-week death march covering 310 miles in harsh winter conditions. Frieda's journey took her through the Kraków Ghetto, the Płaszów concentration camp and Auschwitz. During those years they experienced starvation, beatings, physical torture and humiliation. They also lost their first spouses and children, along with most of their extended families. The Holocaust experience left them psychologically damaged. Max and his sister Rachel, hearing Salomon and Frieda scream in their sleep, would wake them to try to make their nightmares go away. "They never did," Max writes. The author himself does not "scream" as he describes his parents' Holocaust sufferings. His account is simply factual, with no moralizing or ideological judgments. This matter-of-fact approach creates a powerful effect in us readers, who are left to deal as we can with a camp constructed on the grounds of two former Jewish cemeteries and a ghetto enclosed by a wall made of stones designed to look like tombstones.

Friedman tells his parents' stories with love and understanding. Through all the daytime arguing and nighttime screaming, the forced Yeshiva school and piano lessons, the dramas involving food and dress and social outings, we are shown two people who survived unimaginable attacks on their humanity and were now trying their best to raise a second family after the first had been stolen from them. Friedman writes of his father, "He wanted to get it right. And at the end of the day, he did." Friedman had a more complicated relationship with his mother, who had been crushed by three of the worst Holocaust killing-sites: Płaszów, Auschwitz, and Bergen-Belsen. Nevertheless, the description of the day he pushed her around the parking lot in her wheelchair is the most touching scene in the entire book. In the process of describing his parents' immigrant life in New York and Mobile, Alabama, Friedman reveals something of his own life and that of his sister. The details are sketchy, but we get a glimpse into what it must be like to be the child of a Holocaust survivor.

This is a book about the Holocaust experience, Holocaust survival and the children of Holocaust survivors. It is also a book about the struggle for one's humanity in the face of extreme adversity. *Painful Joy* is well-researched and well-crafted and will appeal to a broad readership.

– Gerald Darring is Co-Director, Gulf Coast Center for Holocaust and Human Rights Education, Mobile, AL

Memory and its profound effects on all it encounters vividly come to life in *Painful Joy*, Max Friedman's compelling and painstakingly researched memoir honoring the legacy of his parents, Sam and Frieda. Stitching together a quilt from disparate pieces of evidence, including first-hand accounts, letters and recently discovered records from Poland, Sweden and the US, Friedman completes his parents' story from before, during and after the Holocaust. In a narrative unique to second-generation Holocaust survivors' experiences that searches to understand "beyond the ghosts that haunted them," this account invites the reader to learn who Sam and Frieda wholly were, beyond their surviving "when most others they knew were murdered." Their lives as eyewitnesses to genocide changed them forever. In turn, their memories shaped all of those whom they touched, particularly their children, in a remarkably complex way. Refugees, immigrants, "always strangers in a strange land," Sam and Frieda's love story is marked by unfathomable pain, resilience and even moments of joy. Their lived experiences remind us how inhumanity can define both those who survive and those who surround survivors. They remind us as well, in an increasingly divided world, of the fragility of humankind and how hatred, cruelty and unchecked evil can easily spiral into the unthinkable, unspeakable and unimaginable.

When establishing the United States Holocaust Memorial Museum, Elie Wiesel declared, "A museum unresponsive to the future violates the memory of the past." Similarly, Sam and Frieda's story compels us to recognize the egregious crimes perpetrated during the Holocaust, their lasting impact and the ongoing need to give meaning to that otherwise empty phrase "Never again." Max Friedman not only honors his parents, sister, children and grandchildren by telling a more complete story of their lives, but also calls us to action, to do whatever can be done to ensure that these heinous acts of inhumanity that defined the Friedman family's lives beyond measure never happen again.

– **John Heffernan has devoted his career to the advancement of human rights including directing the Genocide Prevention Initiative at the United States Holocaust Memorial Museum. He is currently president of the Foundation for Systemic Change.**

PAINFUL JOY

A HOLOCAUST FAMILY MEMOIR

MAX J. FRIEDMAN

ISBN 9789493231832 (ebook)

ISBN 9789493231825 (paperback)

ISBN 9789493231849 (hardcover)

Publisher: Amsterdam Publishers, The Netherlands

info@amsterdampublishers.com

Painful Joy is part of the series Holocaust Survivor True Stories

Cover Design by Rick Rawlins, Principal and Design Director, Rick Rawlins/Work

Cover image: Szlama and Frieda Frydman in Halmstad, Sweden, 1946.

Finalist at the 2023 Next Generation Indie Book Awards in the category Autobiography / Biography.

CONTENTS

This memoir honors the memory and lives of my parents, Salomon and Frieda Friedman, and of all the members of their families who were lost forever. It seeks to tell their story. It is also dedicated to the family that today still carries these memories in our hearts.

With all our love and respect,

The Friedman/Borak Family, April 2022.

The family my parents would have loved, July 2019. Seated, from left: Jackson Borak, Baylis Borak, Haiden Borak, Emma Friedman, Finley Borak, Jacob Friedman, Sarah Borak, Elissa Borak. Standing, from left: Greg and Jennifer Borak, Beth and Hugh Borak, Yanqing and Noah Friedman, Eric Friedman, Max and Jennifer Friedman, Rachel and Elliot Borak, Sam Borak, Becky and Jeremy Borak, Joshua Borak.

PREFACE

A Painful Joy

It is a fearful thing to love
what death can touch.
A fearful thing to love,
hope, dream: to be -
to be, and oh! to lose.
A thing for fools this, and a holy thing,
a holy thing to love.
For your life has lived in me,
your laugh once lifted me,
your word was gift to me.
To remember this brings a painful joy.
'Tis a human thing, love, a holy thing,
to love what death has touched.[1]

He was a stranger in a strange land, but that had been his life for some time. Because of what had happened to him and to those he loved, nothing would ever be the same again. He knew that. It was late at night on February 2, 1946, and my father, Szlama[2] Frydman, 34 years old, had just finished washing the dishes at the only job a

Swedish refugee agency called *Kristidsstyrelsen* (literally, the Crisis Time Organization) could get for him back then. For his efforts, he received 121 kronor[3] a month, plus room and board. He was the kind of man who thanked God for any work because he believed every blessing he received came from his God. Most days, he remained thankful just to be alive after what he had seen, lost and endured for the nearly six years that had just passed. Sitting in the small room he shared with three other Polish Jewish refugees from the concentration camps, he started to compose a letter.

That day had been special because he had received an extra bonus: a voucher to get a new set of everyday "walking" clothes to wear in place of the threadbare shirt and pants he had received back in Celle, the displaced persons staging camp in Germany from which he had come to Sweden in late June 1945 after his liberation from the notorious Bergen-Belsen concentration camp that April.

As on virtually every other day since then, he remained preoccupied with efforts to learn for certain what had become of his wife Chaja and their two little girls, Ada and Feigla. Over the intervening months he had come to accept that the worst was likely and nothing pointed to any hope of ever finding them alive. Months before, he had met someone who said he saw them taken to the gas chambers in Auschwitz. There was no official confirmation, so perhaps a miracle was still possible. Yet each new day brought its share of the pain that loomed like a dark cloud above his head, creating a gaping hole in his heart whether he was awake or asleep. He was also beginning the complicated bureaucratic process of trying to apply to emigrate to the United States, where several of his first cousins had lived for some years. Here he was, in Sweden of all places, free at last, safe at last, but still not free to live the life he had once known and cherished.

A few months earlier, though, something that had happened gave him a new measure of comfort and a glimpse of the possibility of a better future: he had met someone. Now he was trying to help her return to the world, as he sought to do himself. Maybe she would become a part of his world as well.

Midway through my research, I discovered a letter my father had composed shortly after meeting my mother. Written in Yiddish, it was found among the papers that the Swedish National Archives kept in a special Jewish refugee repository of materials relating to survivors who were brought to Sweden after their liberation from several different concentration camps. This collection also held many other letters written by my father. I'd had them translated; most of them were in Yiddish but some were in German or Polish. This particular note, the most surprising one, was about love.

Perhaps one of the most startling things I learned about my parents through this journey of trying to reconstruct the facts about the arc of their lives before I knew them was that despite their ordeals and terrible losses, they had retained the capacity to love once again. I'm not just talking about loving my sister Rachel and me or the grandchildren we produced. We always felt our parents' love, even though we never really understood where it came from since they so often were sad or angry, at odds with each other or with the world. I'm talking about their love for each other. It was a side of them I saw rarely, if ever. The narrative I had written in my head about my parents was that they had met in a refugee camp in Sweden where coincidence and pure chance, convenience and opportunity led them to decide that fate had brought them together to restart their lives. Starting over seemed to be almost a transactional or even practical arrangement. They married, had two children and somehow found a new path toward living again, though not at all from where they had left off – a kind of fresh start. Too often, however, it became a rocky and desperate journey. When we were young and even later, their relationship seemed unhinged, perhaps untenable.[4]

I no longer believe my original narrative was all that accurate. It was too simplistic. It gave them too little credit as humans and ultimately, too much of it wasn't even the whole story. It took me more than 70 years to figure it out. If only they could have told me all of it when I was a little boy. They could have told me not just what their real stories were, but also what gave them joy, along with the pain they mostly wore on their sleeves. Maybe then, or later as I grew older, I would have been able to see more clearly through their mental instabilities, know who they once had been and look beyond it all to the love that lay beneath. Maybe then I would have understood them better and better appreciated the nature of their love in the face of unbearable pain, hardship and loss.

Is this a love story? In a way, yes: a love story complicated by many different kinds, faces and stages of love and loss.

The letter my father was writing was to Willhelm Michaeli, a lawyer who helped many refugees with their problems, supported at that time by the Jewish Community in Stockholm.[5] Szlama wrote it in the same formal, honest, earnest, simple way he had learned throughout life, in a sense reflecting the way he tried to live his entire life. In this touching letter filled with both pain and hope, he wrote about his newfound love for another human being. This love was still tenuous and uncertain, dependent on whether each of them could come to terms with having lost their families. Maybe they both finally found a valid reason to have survived. Anyway, what was most startling to me was that he could write this letter at all. Clearly, it came from deep inside his heart. This was someone whose formal schooling had ended after sixth grade. It was someone who had been beaten around his head and everywhere else over the course of many days, weeks, months and years in the recent past. It was someone who had been starved and brought to the breaking point again and again. All that no longer mattered so much. This letter was about Frieda Friedmann, who later that year became his wife and eventually my mother.

I admired the way the letter was penned in Yiddish, the language that represented the culture and traditions that were familiar to my father and gave him comfort, but a language that also, very recently, had been nearly extinguished forever. I could imagine him lingering on each word, every sound, symbol and syllable, each seeming to ignite a cascade of painful and joyful memories, perhaps all at the same time. It was a past that was lost. Now he was determined instead to consider the future and even build a future anew, if at all possible.

Here is a translation of some of what he wrote as he pleaded for help and advice. I am certain it does not do justice to the original in Yiddish.

"As I begin writing to you, I am asking that you give me the wise answer, not only for myself, but also for a woman who endured the worst suffering in the camps. It was only a matter of a few days or she would have also been a victim like all the others. Certainly it was fate that she survived and she is once again a human being like everyone else.

"My name is Friedman and the woman I mentioned is also a Friedman. She was married eight months before the war. Up to now she has not located her husband. When I came to Mölle on December 10, I made her acquaintance. After only several days, we began to fall in love with one another and we spent our time together. We have decided to remain together if we do not find our spouses. We would actually cohabit until people in these circumstances will be permitted to marry."

His question for Counselor Michaeli was how to help Frieda make it to America if he himself was fortunate enough to get permission to emigrate.

He continued: "What should I do about the woman I am seeing? I love her and she loves me. She has suffered enough. She is alone and has no one who might take an interest in her. I would gladly bring her to America with me." He wanted to know if Michaeli could help make that happen. "If you will help me in this matter," he concluded, "then two people who have endured so much will be happy because of you. Perhaps it is too soon for me to be thinking about her. Unfortunately, things don't go the way a person would like."

"Things don't go the way a person would like." This was certainly an understatement of what they both had endured all too recently at the time when my father penned this note: a love letter I never expected to find, hidden amidst the ashes of lives gone up in the smoke and fires of the concentration camp crematoria. They had consumed not just his first wife and children but also her first husband and her parents, along with many, so many, beloved others. Yet in many ways, this letter seemed the perfect embodiment of what the Brooklyn-born poet Chaim Stern called "a painful joy."

In a meditation or prayer meant to accompany the traditional recitation of the mourner's *kaddish* (prayer for the dead), Stern, who authored the official *Siddur* (prayer book) of Reform Judaism, describes how aspects of the human condition sometimes accompany love. How when we love, we should expect to be challenged by the pain and grief we may also sometimes experience. Maybe, he proposes, this is the riddle of our lives: How does joy, even painful joy, exist alongside love, if love is what helps us survive at the most difficult of times, especially when we also experience the touch of death that came with that love? It is the human condition.

"'Tis a human thing, love," Stern wrote, "a holy thing, to love what death has touched." He seems to say that there is a beginning and an end to all love. Never pure or unvarnished, it is instead a complicated affair fraught with pain and sometimes loss and death. That is true of love, and it is true of our lives.

A painful joy. A complex series of emotions, much more than love, that touch the human experience and sometimes, for some, reach out to notions of the Divine. This painful joy often came to define the subjects of this memoir: my parents, Sam and Frieda Friedman.

The title of this book is *Painful Joy*. The joy refers to aspects of my parents' lives that were filled with pleasures they experienced thanks in large measure to their families, both first and second, nuclear and extended, spread across generations and geographies. Of course they endured painful times, sometimes in ways we or they could hardly have imagined. Painful joy may describe many dimensions of many other lives lived, not just those of my parents. Yet to my ear, the phrase describes their particular dimensions in a way that seems to fit better than any other description I could come up with myself.

To begin, I will offer some definitions of the terms I use and their origins. We should probably start with *holocaust*, since at some level the Holocaust is a defining feature of this story. The word is derived from the Greek *holokauston*, a translation of the Hebrew word *olah*, meaning a burnt sacrifice offered whole to God. This word was chosen and gained wide usage because in the extermination camps, which were the ultimate manifestations of the Nazi killing program, the bodies of the victims were consumed whole in the open fires of the crematoria.

One description I found in the *Encyclopedia Britannica*[6] is worth sharing:

"Human history has few tragedies that rival the magnitude and moral bankruptcy of the Holocaust, the systematic state-sponsored killing of six million Jewish men, women, and children and millions of others by Nazi Germany and its collaborators during World War II. For the antisemitic Nazis who met at the Wannsee Conference in Berlin on January 20, 1942 to discuss the implementation of a policy decision made by Hitler and his senior leaders sometime the year before, the mass murder of Jews would eventually represent the 'Final Solution' to the so-called Jewish question. The deliberate and systematic destruction of a group of people because of their ethnicity, nationality, religion or race was given a name, 'genocide,' by Raphael Lemkin, a Polish-born jurist who served as an adviser to the US Department of War during World War II. Subsequently, genocide was made a crime by the United Nations General Assembly in December 1946, punishable under international law."

Still, how did this most infamous of genocides become known as the Holocaust?

"In the years immediately after World War II, Yiddish-speaking Jews and survivors of Nazi persecution called the murder of the Jews the 'Ḥurban' ('Destruction'), the same word used to denote the destruction of the First Temple [also called Solomon's Temple, where the Hebrew Ark of the Covenant was housed] in Jerusalem by the Babylonians in 586 BC and the destruction of the Second Temple by the Romans in 70 AD.

"In Israel and France, *Sho'ah*, a biblical Hebrew word meaning 'catastrophe,' became the preferred term for the event, largely in response to Claude Lanzmann's influential nine-and-a-half-hour 1985 motion picture documentary of the same name (*Shoah*). *Sho'ah* emphasizes the annihilation of the Jews – not the totality of Nazi victims, which also included Germans deemed intellectually, physically or emotionally unfit, as well as the Roma and Sinti, homosexuals and Jehovah's Witnesses."

Indeed, about three million Soviet prisoners of war, as well as millions of Poles, Russian civilians and other Slavic peoples who were not Jewish, were also to become victims of the Nazi reign of terror.[7]

Thus, the Holocaust or *Sho'ah* is certainly the centerpiece of this story, but as you will see and can easily imagine, it is not the whole story, which in essence is about the lives of two people who were born before this tragedy, survived it and then were determined to start their lives again, with new partners and a second family.

If ever there was a couple who seemed mismatched, it was Sam and Frieda. My father was a quiet man and mostly just wanted to be left alone to pray, work, father children and find the time and energy to be proud of them. He wanted to find a life after having lost everything, possibly including his soul. My father was also a thinker, a peacemaker, a problem solver and a religious man. He liked to laugh and smile and eat sweets. He enjoyed listening to Yiddish radio and reading the *Jewish Daily Forward*. He was devoted to the idea of Israel and its continued existence. And in trying to simplify his life, he deferred to others, perhaps too often. He may once have been ambitious, but after the war he was more interested in just being.

My mother was the opposite. She would never go gentle into any good night. She would fight everything and everyone, whether it was her one surviving sister, her devoted husband or a past filled with unbearably vivid demons that haunted her every day and night. For her there was no escape. When she screamed at us or at my father, she was shouting at those demons, the voices that never went away. The screams were embedded in her very being. My mother was always looking for what was wrong, rather than what could possibly be right. She lived in another universe, one of her imagination, of being a young girl again, of living a life filled with pleasure, dancing, dressing up and experiencing the delights she thought she deserved. It was not her real world. It was a world she had imagined for herself.

Each of them began a family that was then interrupted by the war. And while their lives before the war were surely full of serious challenges and compromises, they were also filled with the pleasures of belonging to a large extended family, life amidst a resurgent Jewish culture and the promise of a better economic and social future. Much was possible, if only for a brief period in the interwar years. Though born in the past of the shtetl, these two people grew up aware of the possibilities of the cosmopolitan future to be had in large, vibrant cities and cultures. All that ended when they encountered a new reality that also came close to ending their lives: a new universe from which there was no escape, no exit, except death.

Having survived the unsurvivable, the question they both faced was whether either of them could, in the face of the nightmares and vanished worlds that sometimes still beckoned as a result of years of torment, sustain the good experiences they had enjoyed in their lives before the war.

Chaim Stern's poetry and that letter from my father seem as good a way as any to begin to understand this very complicated story, which tries to present memories of my parents' lives before we came to the United States in 1952. Some of these recollections seem to have actually happened, some probably did, and a few I have had to guess at or imagine. The stories come from the times and places in which my parents were born, from shtetls in Poland before World War I to larger towns and cities where they had hoped to start families. Their tale continues through the Holocaust years, when they lost almost everything and everyone they had ever known as death occupied their souls intimately and forever in occupied Poland and then in Germany. It also offers a long look after their liberation into starting anew in the postwar era, first in Sweden and then in the United States.

Their stories, which sometimes were only fragments pieced together with lots of poetic license and conjecture on my part, have too long been hidden, though little pieces of the worst of them, probably representing the greatest of their losses, revisited them in frequent nightmares. When we were still very young, we would go to their bedsides at night as they screamed in terror. Frightening though it was for young children like us, we would waken them from their beds by shaking them, trying to chase away their demons. Freud once wrote something to the effect that our psychological health depends on our ability to constantly revise and fashion memory to allow for growth and change. The absence of this process, certainly in my mother and perhaps in my father too, and the stagnation of memories as their brains' treatment of them became fixed, led to a range of pathologies, some of which they also experienced – sadly, as you will learn.

My mother compared everything in her life after the war to the war years themselves and sometimes found the present to be even worse than the worst of her past. My father, however, rarely went back willingly into that same dark night, which never disappeared until the last few years of his life, when his memory of everything and everyone evaporated into thin air.

Five years ago, I took it upon myself to go back and revisit what had been, to consider who they were and ultimately, through this memoir and considerable research, to paint a picture of what they were like and what the times in which they lived meant for them. I hoped thereby to help restore their humanity in some small way. Of all the things I imagined this memoir would be, I never imagined it as a love story. But as Stern insists, "It is a fearful thing to love what death can touch. A fearful thing to love, hope, dream; to be – to be and oh! To lose. A thing for fools this, and a holy thing, a holy thing to love."

I also started to think of this collection of memories, facts and guesses about who my parents were as a holy thing as well: a strange kind of love story that they alone could share because they had shared so intimately the deaths and losses that came with their first loves, as well as what followed. Maybe that's why I ultimately felt driven to uncover their past and share it with those they knew, those who knew of them and those I know and love. I hope to give something of their lives and their memories back to the Sam and Frieda we knew, or might have known, to honor them and those they lost and to share all of that as best I can with family and friends and eventually with a wider group of readers.

To strangers who didn't know them, their story could be revealing, given the lessons it offers about survival in a world that is still too full of hate, desperation and hopelessness. Resurrecting the past can be painful, but it also holds potential for joy, reconciliation and forgiveness. The question remains: How do we deal with the pain while discovering the joy? How, when we encounter people like Sam and Frieda and their stories, can we better understand the human condition and how it reflects on each of us? Finally, given all that is now known and having read other stories of survival and renewal, difficult and heartbreaking though they sometimes are, what do we do with the emotions they elicit and the insights gained? Can they help us change ourselves or others? Can they give us new perspectives on what survival is really all about, or about the nature of love and hope, despair and defeat? I hope so.

Empathy implies that we can place ourselves into the shoes of another. I can't possibly do full justice to that aspiration, but I can consider other emotions that arise: compassion, sympathy, forgiveness, love, gratitude, kindness, sadness. Though we lose love throughout our lives, we can still find love again. This story, Sam and Frieda's, is certainly about love lost, hope devoured and survival in the darkest worlds imaginable. Yet it is also about the pleasures of a "normal" life and love that can be reimagined. Perhaps it teaches us that we need to remember both the pain and the joy that love and hope, even if once lost, can bring once more. Through this memoir of my family I intend first and foremost to recognize these two souls and in time learn more about them, so that the reader comes away honoring who they once were and who they eventually became. As for everyone else, I hope that readers of this book will connect it to identifiable emotions and situations that challenge the strongest amongst us to learn from these two people about what to do, and maybe what not to do, in the face of unspeakable challenges.

By discovering the love that emerged in all its complicated forms, we can realize how measures of kindness, when shared – even in the face of great cruelty or even greater despair – can benefit us all. On too many days, Sam and Frieda were challenged by life and had to choose a path to take and then deal with the consequences of their choices. I hope readers will come to realize that no path is always the right one. The important thing is to choose and then move ahead, not looking back in anger or recrimination, but instead looking forward with hope and possibility.

PART I

QUESTIONING SURVIVAL

INTRODUCTION

I once heard the Israeli writer Amos Oz talk about trying to write a book about his parents. Like mine, his didn't talk very much about what their lives were like before they became his parents. One day he decided to conjure up everyone who knew them in the past: uncles, aunts, grandparents and his parents themselves. They all were gone, but he still had questions that remained unanswered, so he invited their ghosts into his living room for a *bissel* (little, in Yiddish) cake and coffee and conducted a grand and imaginary Jewish séance, interviewing them and then, after considering their responses, sending them on their way. He also decided what made sense and what didn't, using his knowledge of who they were from his own experiences with them while they were alive.

With this memoir, I have tried to do something similar in my own more modest way. The last five years have found me harvesting the treasures and mysteries of the internet, archives and other documentation, seeking answers to sometimes unanswerable questions and attempting to better understand how my parents directly and indirectly affected who I am today and how I became that person. In this endeavor, I have been aided by a host of talented and selfless researchers, experts, other writers and translators, as well as other people doing largely what I have tried to do here through a process of searching for their own family truths. In so doing, I have traveled to Poland, Sam and Frieda's homeland; to Israel, to meet a previously unknown relation; to Sweden, my birthplace, where my parents first met after the war, and back in time to my own memories and Rachel's. In all of this, I have benefited from the wise counsel, patience and companionship of my loving wife Jennifer. What follows is my reporting on, and in some cases imagining, their lives and times as best I could.

Throughout this memoir, one central fact must be recognized: When I was growing up, I knew virtually nothing about Sam and Frieda, beyond the fact that as they were Holocaust survivors, my sister and I too often saw them as tragically damaged human beings. They also seemed very different from pretty much everyone else I encountered as a child, a teenager, an adolescent and even as an adult. Living with them was sometimes a challenge. Discovering or surmising just who they were before tragedies befell them has been a considerable challenge as well. I've given it my best, always keeping in mind not only the sadness I saw but also the love that often came with it.

For too much of their lives, my parents seemed to be eternally wrestling with and reliving past tragedies. My mother especially bemoaned missed opportunities. She often looked for others to blame for the totality of her life. My father, however, simply sought to move on. Sadly, her demons would add to his own tragic experiences. But that's not to say there weren't times when we all laughed together. Despite the seemingly pervasive stress and tension, we always felt their devotion and love for us and for each other too, as much as was possible. That was especially true once we had our own families. Our children, who were not their direct responsibilities, were able to help Sam and Frieda bridge their lives toward a better place and a happier present.

My parents showered their love on us and on our children as best they could. It varied from day to day, moment to moment, sometimes from nightmare to nightmare. At least at the beginning of their relationship, when they needed to rekindle the love that had been drained from their beings, they were able to bestow love once more, on each other. The darker side reappeared when they unmasked their anger at the world and often at each other for somehow disappointing them, and for the unfairness of it all. Yet our family functioned better than one would have thought possible, despite that undercurrent of sadness and pain.

When our parents did lock horns, which was quite often, their fights raged and continued for what seemed like hours. They only argued in Yiddish, which unfortunately, at least when it came to these fights, we had come to understand too well. Today, when recollecting those early years, my sister, who as the older sibling knew and understood more, admits that she was terrified. When the ceaseless screaming would drive my father to storm out of our little apartment, she feared he wouldn't come back. As for me, I feared the toll all this would take on him. Sometimes, when he slept during the day (just to escape the recriminations and memories, I now understand), I would go into the bedroom and watch his chest rise and fall as his breath went in and out, certain that one day his breath would just stop and he would die as a result of all the anger and sadness in him and surrounding him. Such scenes would repeat themselves on an all-too-regular basis. We tried to hug our parents, to hold them and ask them to stop. When we couldn't block the inevitable drama as it unfolded, we felt utterly powerless.

Sam and Frieda had come together as survivors of the Holocaust, looking for and believing they had found love once more. The tragedy of that is twofold. First, they may have been looking for love, hope and happiness in all the wrong places and people, and for some of the wrong reasons. Second, they probably couldn't manage any better than they did as they alternated between the joys of love and the terrors that inevitably accompanied their love and the pervasive sense of its loss.

I have focused a great deal on the difficult times, as they surely were. Because of that, this story sometimes seems quite negatively charged.

The facts and my memories tilt that way. Still, it is of course true that in their lives, especially their younger lives, they had each found time and things to laugh about, as well as opportunities to revel in a distant innocence, the experience of a world of mutually supportive siblings and a Jewish culture and tradition that sought to provide some comfort and security in their universe. My task was to discover their past, including and beyond the tragedies. In their early lives they often faced the challenges of growing up poor in a larger world that was tough and even hostile, especially to Jews. Ultimately, much of their lives remained anonymous and unknown for too long. Thanks to prodding from others, late in my own life I finally determined to attempt to honor my parents by relating as complete a story as I could, about them and for them.

Many years after they were gone, I came to understand this effort initially as an obligation, but later as an opportunity that I would appreciate wholly and eventually embrace with all my heart. To those who knew them or will come to know them here, it will be apparent that these were two complicated people who in many ways led challenging lives that took me years to start to unravel and seek to explain. Being their children was not easy or generally enjoyable. Still, I suppose it was never boring or without challenge either. It taught us what they already had to learn the hard way: resilience, tenacity, perseverance and of course, survival.

These past years of intensive research have opened my eyes to what can be learned, but also to what is unknowable and can only be guessed at. With this awareness in mind, I have made assumptions throughout based on what I discovered and what I could only surmise. Another set of facts or a different person might arrive at other conclusions. This memoir contains lots of endnotes, some of which point to alternative spellings, alternative sets of facts and therefore sometimes alternative conclusions about what was and what was not, or indeed, what is still unknown and unknowable. Sometimes these notes simply provide a much more detailed explanation of a statement or fact, placed as an endnote to avoid interrupting the flow of the story while still allowing readers to pursue any family member's story further if they wish. Please forgive my need to include them as a kind of historical or genealogical record. This is not an academic accounting of two people's lives. Instead, I hope you will discover a loving reconstruction and reinterpretation of two lives that would otherwise have remained unexamined, as the details of their survival would have been lost forever. They deserved more than that. Most of us do.

The project did give me the opportunity to take a broader view and sit down with my parents, so to speak, pushing the pain of the past aside and getting to know them better, this time without the noise and emotional undercurrents of living with them, and with only a few intrusions by my own history. For the first time, I was able to stand outside their lives and my own and see them in a fresh way, hopefully with greater objectivity but also certainly with greater empathy and compassion than was possible in the moments when we actually experienced their lives at their sides. Still, understandably, what you will read here is only an incomplete version of what they experienced, that is, only what I have been able to piece together years later.

While filming a documentary in Israel, the prize-winning journalist Bill Moyers, with whom I had the good fortune to work for several years, was struck by the words attributed to the Baal Shem Tov and inscribed at the entrance to the Yad Vashem World Holocaust Remembrance Center: "Remembrance is the secret to redemption." Similarly, I hope this story, their story, also serves as at least a measure of redemption for their suffering and even for their too-painful joys.

My father almost never spoke about the war until I insisted he do so when I was already 20 years old. My mother, on the other hand, talked again and again about certain of her concentration camp experiences, but said almost nothing else about any other part of her younger life. Why?

Ultimately, I think Sam and Frieda lived with different faces of love. My father found love when he was still young and lost it too quickly and tragically. He never wanted that to happen to him again. He would endure anything, as long as he could find peace from his torments, many of which seemed tied to his lost loves. As for my mother, she continued to relive each day focused on survival alone, as though it were her last day. She fought everything and everyone, struggling against demons and enemies both real and imagined. Hers seems to have been a life in which she had to compete for love, and when she did discover it she still found it imperfect, seeing herself as settling for less than she had hoped. Finding love, whether in her youth or later, existed alongside a seeming inability to find happiness.

Was it always so? Did it have to be this way for both of them? One can only imagine, and I hope that upon reading this you can judge for yourself.

Did any of it change when Frieda met Sam? I'm not sure.

Nevertheless, these questions and more remain. Who were they before the camps? And did their most horrific experiences affect not only themselves, but the genetic code they passed on to the next generation and the one after that, and even one more, for better or for worse? I sought some answers as well for my own sake and that of our family. How satisfying those answers are remains for the reader to judge.

Ultimately, the overriding aim of my effort is to restore humanity to Sam and Frieda and come to terms with how they are to be remembered. I admit that I always defined them, especially when they embarrassed, frustrated, angered or saddened me, by their experiences of loss and the traumas they suffered in the camps and ghettos of World War II. After all, I would tell myself, they were survivors. That was a good thing. But with survival came great harm and torturous, inescapable recollections. I ignored their normalcy, their lives beyond the Holocaust, their own DNA and the times and cultures in which they lived. I overlooked that they had sometimes thrived with the support of their large families – a reality I never knew, since most of them had perished. Theirs were large families that extended not only through many individuals, but also into the past and potentially on to the future. Had I stopped to consider it, I would have realized such a family was what I longed for most. Still, my parents couldn't give me any of it. Through no fault of their own, they too had lost that great anchor of history, and they missed the people in those big families even more than I ever could imagine.

What about their accomplishments beyond the war: their resiliency, their creativity, their strengths, their native intelligence, their cunning, their perseverance? How did all that fit into my definition of being a survivor? How did it define them? After all, there had to be more to their lives before the war than just surviving them. Even during the war they were more than just survivors, and after the war they sought to become more than that. Throughout this project I have had to come to terms with the nature of survival. My task now is to communicate who they were, other than people who stayed alive when most others they knew were murdered. They also were more than struggling, flawed human beings deserving of pity. I wanted to introduce them, not only through this research but also by reliving my memories of them, as multidimensional, complex, precious human beings who were tragically scarred and, as we all are, imperfect. I have tried, if only in a limited way, to reexamine the points of light and darkness in their lives in order to learn what to forgive and also what to celebrate, what to forget or ignore, and how to recognize human imperfection and what it is, as well as what we will never know about what was.

Sam and Frieda have both been gone for about a quarter of a century. Sam died first, in 1993; Frieda, five years later.

When I first began this project, I had just finished helping create two separate memoirs of two other people who, like all of us, had lives worth recording, exploring and examining. From there I turned to my own life and the people who largely shared the responsibility for who I became. It was then that I began to confront the many unanswered questions about the people who gave me life. The simple truth is that neither my sister nor I wanted to press them beyond what they were willing to tell us about their past while they were still alive. Dredging up so many memories seemed too upsetting for them, and for us as well. We didn't want to add to their pain, or possibly to ours, by digging further or knowing anything more.

Both my parents would mention, sometimes offhandedly, their times in the *Lagers*, as they called the camps where they were imprisoned. There seem to be several different translations of the German word *Lager*, such as a place where soldiers rest or a temporary dwelling, but one definition that seems particularly relevant is that of *Lagers* as warehouses or storerooms. After all, that was more or less how the Nazis saw the ghettos, slave labor camps (sometimes called forced labor camps) and concentration camps: as temporary solutions, holding pens in which to warehouse Jews until it was their turn to be wiped from the face of the earth forever.

More than once, my mother recalled to us that when she and her sister, my Aunt Genny, tumbled out of the cattle car that brought them to Auschwitz, it was the so-called Angel of Death, Dr. Josef Mengele himself, who oversaw their selection on the train ramp. They would either live now and die later, or they would die right away. I always regarded this as an apocryphal story, another example of my mother's reimagining of her life to give it more drama than it already had. In this case, though, I have come to believe her. And with that, I am also struck by something a colleague of Mengele's once said, when asked how the doctor had been able to take on so horrific a task as choosing who should live and who should die. "Mengele alone accepted that all the Jews were already dead upon arrival," the colleague observed. "He was sorting out ghosts, not people."[1]

My task here is therefore to make my parents into people again, people visible beyond just surviving, beyond the ghosts that haunted them, and bring them back to the living and once again into our lives. Please forgive some of my judgments and interpretations. They may sound arbitrary, even harsh, but I don't mean them as such. I mean them to show that these were human beings capable of pain and joy, both their own and others. Like us all, they were far from perfect, but they had a clear right to their humanity. I hope to restore that humanity once more.

Not everyone gets to experience life the way my sister and I did as their children. Our childhoods were not necessarily any worse or better than those of many other children. Because of what Sam and Frieda lived through, though, I am impelled to share what I have discovered and sometimes what I have concluded or surmised, right or wrong, for better or worse, ordinary or startling, sad or joyous. Maybe those who knew Sam and Frieda will gain some new insights. Maybe my discoveries will help Rachel and me resolve our own doubts or fears. Perhaps, thanks to this memoir, our children and grandchildren, and with luck our great-grandchildren, will better appreciate where they came from. In the process they might learn more about who they are and what can be achieved in the face of great odds, increasing their understanding of love and joy in the process. Such lessons can be universally applied, so any reader might benefit from knowing their story, its origins and its unfolding.

The reason I am so energetically compelled to offer explanations, to relate so much of my parents' story to others and to ask so many questions, is that there is something about Sam and Frieda's lives that can teach us about values, assumptions and secrets, what matters and what may not, the sacrifices we knowingly or otherwise make for others and the consequences that can arise from them. For me, maybe I can better begin to put myself in their shoes and consider what I might have done, given the choices they had to make. Such consideration is the essence of empathy. The stories of others can give us a broader view of ourselves, moving us beyond the self-centeredness of our own lives.

Several other forces brought me to this memoir. I would like to acknowledge them briefly.

In the fall of 2016, I had just completed the two memoirs mentioned earlier when my sister received an email from Jerry Darring, who had taught at McGill-Toolen Catholic High School and Spring Hill

College, a Jesuit institution, both in Mobile, Alabama. He asked Rachel and then me to tell him more about our parents. He and a few of his colleagues sensed that for most high school students in Mobile and similar places, the Holocaust was virtually unknown or forgotten, distant and foreign in every possible way. Eventually, when my father became seriously ill we moved our parents closer to my sister in Mobile, who was in a better position than I was to oversee their care. Rachel was willing, and to this day I remain grateful to her for the selfless generosity and loving care she provided.

Jerry, full of faith and determination, made it his mission to try to help address the loss of a necessary memory of evil in his small part of the world. In an attempt to expose students to stories about people who in fact were once their neighbors, if sometimes only briefly, he and his colleagues had decided to research my parents and other Mobile residents who had survived or otherwise been touched by the Holocaust. My sister and I helped as best we could and were delighted to learn more from their early research efforts.

We already knew one thing: as I have indicated, our parents, for better or worse, left their psychic fingerprints all over us and possibly some of their DNA imprints as well. In ways big and small, it all translated into my sister and me taking on many of the marks of survivorship, some of which we then passed on to our children and even our grandchildren.

After spending four years developing memoirs for other people, I realized that I had let my own parents down. For too long I had failed to do what those teachers in Mobile, in their generosity of spirit, had attempted to do: to tell my parents' stories. They had gone online and collected information about my parents that I had never seen before and frankly had never even imagined trying to uncover.

I felt embarrassed and ashamed. Yet certainly some part of me had always been averse to learning more and avoided revisiting our parents' horrors, especially now that they were gone. What use would it serve to relive that painful past? My sister felt that way too. But then it struck me that if Jerry could do this voluntarily, I too must also feel some obligation to tell their stories and learn more about them, for my sister's children and grandchildren as well as my own. Perhaps our parents' story would even resonate with people outside our immediate family, reaching friends, acquaintances or even strangers. After all, antisemitism was a big part of the forces that affected our parents' lives. Its close partners racism, xenophobia and extreme nationalism likewise had a big impact, as did anti-immigrant and anti-refugee movements. Haven't these forces and worse reemerged of late? And don't they seem to be growing, not only in other parts of the world but here in the US as well? In the end, as Jerry Darring emphasized, the Holocaust has receded from too many people's memories. For many young people in the US, the admonition "Never Forget" has become "I hardly even know." I now have an opportunity to help return what the Holocaust took from my parents and an obligation to restore some measure of their identity and worth, extending their story into something even larger.

Thus, I decided to start finding out more. If those teachers could learn so much that I had not known about my own family, I reasoned, I should be able to do at least as well, considering that I had spent my entire working life writing and researching all manner of topics and telling hundreds of stories about other people's trials, tribulations and triumphs. Finally, after working on those two memoirs of two absorbing personalities, I knew something about memoir writing. Since that time in late 2016, I have gone online to hundreds of sources, joined Facebook groups, learned about genealogy, read numerous books, articles[2] and more about the Holocaust years, talked to a few distant relatives, other survivors, friends and experts in the field, and worked with professional genealogists, researchers, archivists and Holocaust experts, as well as a variety of translators from around the world. Thanks to some fortuitous connections and a great deal of kindness and generosity of spirit from people I met and communicated with, I have been able to spread my research net far and wide in the US, Germany, Sweden, Poland and Israel.

In the space of five years I have since learned more about my parents – grim dates, deadly facts, empty addresses, archival notations, nameless pictures, actual names, addresses, photos and other records, some of which list the occupations of dozens of murdered relatives – than I had ever learned from my parents themselves or from my own wanderings over the course of a lifetime. Jennifer and I traveled to Sweden, Israel, Poland and Germany. In the process, we even discovered a niece of my father's from his first wife's family. She lived in Israel and, ironically, worked at Yad Vashem in Jerusalem.

Another force impelling me had to do with something our grandson Jacob said to me several years ago. As I write this, he is 13 years old and a superb, exceptional human being. While aware of his youth and innocence, for the past several years I nevertheless have found myself telling Jacob more and more about my parents, his great-grandparents – people he never knew who would have loved him and his younger sister Emma with all their hearts. What happened to them? What was it like living with them? What were their remarkable strengths and their great human weaknesses, and why, if not how, did they survive some of the darkest days and years in modern human history? In 2018 we walked through Yad Vashem together. There I tried to expose him to and also shield him from some of what his great-grandparents and their families experienced.

Throughout this project, Jacob demonstrated great interest, mature patience and extraordinary sensitivity, even though I still wanted to protect him from the most graphic realities of the Holocaust years and what my parents and their families endured.[3] Certainly Emma was not yet ready to learn much of that history. They, along with our son Noah, and daughter-in-law Yanqing and in spirit, our other son Eric, were with us in Israel. There will always be more we can talk about to them someday.

In these past few years, Jacob has come to understand that some people have it in them to get through terrible things that may happen to them and to those they love, even if such things can never be fully overcome. Meanwhile, Sam and Frieda, who endured the unendurable, provide evidence that people come out the other side of such disasters as changed human beings. For Jacob and Emma, and for my sister's children and grandchildren, I have a responsibility to allow those people – my parents – to speak through me to those they left behind.

Then there is the looming question of how my parents' life experiences affected them, and whether or how any genetic changes may have affected my parents based on their life experiences and then been passed on to future generations. One day three or four years ago, such considerations came through even more clearly when Jennifer and I found ourselves talking to Jacob about theories around the notion that experiences in our own lives can sometimes affect our genetic code during our own lifetimes, and may sometimes do so in ways that can be transmitted to our children and perhaps further down our lineages. Jacob took that idea to heart.

"You know what?" he began, during one of our regular FaceTime conversations. "I know it was terrible what happened to your parents during the war. But they *were* survivors, right?" he asked. "Isn't that a good thing? Because maybe now your genes became survivor genes and that means my daddy's genes were survivor genes and that means that some of my genes are survivor genes too. So I think something good came out of them becoming survivors after all. Is that right?"

I told him that I supposed he was right. As always, he had expressed a critical idea in a stunning and simple way, much in line with some of the questions I was seeking to answer here.

Of course, I have no definitive answers for the questions he asked. What I hope the reader will gain from this exploration of Sam and Frieda is a greater ability to reflect on how every one of us survives difficult or even tragic experiences. How do we do it, and how does it affect our humanity and the humanity of others? I hope that in retelling or sometimes reimagining their stories, Sam and Frieda will not only take on dimensions and identities well beyond survivorship, but also provide hints of how we can effectively adapt to, if not overcome, transformative experiences in our own lifetimes.

Before the war, Poland was home to 3.3–3.5 million Jews, that is, more Jews than any place on earth other than Russia and the US. But by the war's end, when the occupants of the prison camps and death camps that held them were liberated, only a tiny proportion of them, perhaps 110,000-120,000 Polish Jews, remained alive to be transferred to displaced persons (DP) camps for resettlement and recuperation. After the German invasion, several hundred thousand more ended up in the Soviet Union, where thousands of them perished. That meant that more than three million Polish Jews were murdered between 1939 and 1945. I was never very good at math, but clearly, the odds of survival during that period were stacked against every Polish Jew.

Many Polish family members who didn't make it are mentioned in these pages. Only for a scant few can I relate what I know or guess happened to them. For some, the trail simply vanished. For some others, it never existed. Several of my mother's brothers and her sister will be discussed, as will her parents. Their disappearance from the story indicates that there was nothing more to tell. I even have less information about my father's mother and sisters and can only guess what happened to my father's first family, though with a somewhat greater degree of certainty. Nearly all of them are gone. Perhaps they disappeared in the way my parents experienced their own departures: suddenly, without any warning. My parents never had certainty about what happened to most of the dozens or even hundreds of family members who were lost to them, and they rarely mentioned their names, even to their own children.

Perhaps Sam and Frieda's lives were largely defined by the existential nature of *not knowing*, by the uncertainty in their lives and their inability to have agency to banish uncertainty or gain control over it. That possibility was brought home to me even more forcefully by the powerful, frightening uncertainty created by the Covid-19 pandemic. The lack of control over one's immediate day-to-day existence was a defining force in Sam and Frieda's lives as well, and to a much greater degree. The pandemic has certainly been a wrenching experience in our own lives, but at least we are still okay. Consider what it must have been like for my parents, not only during the Nazi years but before them as well. Frieda became a refugee at age four. Sam suddenly became fatherless when he was not yet four years old, and by age 12 or 13 he was his family's sole provider. What would it have been like when loved ones simply vanished from the face of the earth without a trace, no record, nothing at all? Adversity is said to make you stronger, and it did for Sam and Frieda, at some level. But it also leaves deep scars that don't heal.

I can now imagine better than ever the terrifying uncertainty of not knowing, especially when not knowing becomes a matter of life and death and means wondering, not just about one's own life, but about whether those they loved ever made it. Not knowing comes to be about others and how they died, when they died, if they died. Add to that the uncertainty of every aspect of my parents' existence, from their childhoods through the years that led them to the US. In retrospect, it seems they teetered on the brink all throughout their lives, trying to keep their balance on a tightrope of uncertainty that too often was out of their control.

How do you survive?

You try to gain control of the people or things you can control. My mother sought to control others, to create a make-believe world or assert herself in other, sometimes inappropriate ways. You declare, as she did as loudly as she could, "Here I am! Hear me!" As for my father, he just gave up on ever being certain. "Fine," he would say to me, "do what you think is best." Or he would simply hide out, go to sleep or run out of the house to escape the voices of his past. He accepted uncertainty and in some way may therefore have found answers through his abiding faith in other things: his religion, Israel, his children.

In many European countries it was forbidden to assume Hebrew names as family names. By selecting names like Friedman, a perfectly good German name, Jews could still preserve a meaning about their past that they might hold dear. Friedman, for example, would translate as "happy" in Yiddish. It was an irony of ironies that my family name would have that meaning, since my mother and father seemed only rarely to be happy at all. Indeed, my mother seems to have suffered from anhedonia, the inability to experience happiness.

As for Frydman, my father's Polish surname, it was German, Swiss and French in origin, and Ashkenazi Jews had adopted it since the 17th century. It derives from the pre-eighth-century words *fried*, meaning peace, and *man*, a man of peace, a servant of God, a friend or a follower, or in German, a man who was happy. Yiddish, used by Polish Jews for generations, is a language in its own right. Its basic grammar is Germanic, and its Germanic vocabulary has mingled with additional contributions of Hebrew, Aramaic and Slavic words and most recently, even some English.

Surnames were not something that came naturally to Jews in Eastern Europe. They did not take surnames until they were compelled to do so, initially in Austro-Hungary in 1787 but as late as 1844 in Czarist Russia. Authorities wanted Jews to take last names so they could be taxed, conscripted and educated, in that order. No wonder so many Jews were reluctant to report and register births and marriages: many were impoverished or close to it and feared that additional taxation would add to their worries. That dynamic will also play out in this story.

Holocaust stories are undoubtedly numerous, and memoirs of those years and the horrors they inflicted are many. But although these stories share many characteristics and even details, each individual story is different. When that story reflects people's lives and their impact on others, it takes on a different series of perspectives. I will do my best to present this story as a remembrance and a memorial that honors two difficult lives, along with the value and dimensions they were still able to share with others.

Today, as immigrant and refugee calamities continue to arise, we need to better appreciate and understand that each of these nameless, stateless people and their children, who become mere statistics to most of us, represent individual journeys that are worth sharing and center on lives that demand dignity and respect. At the very least we should honor them with the kindness every human being deserves. The world community failed to do so for the millions of Jews and others who perished in the Holocaust. Even now we are unable or unwilling to put names to millions of terrified faces that stare into the abyss of the existential threats they must contend with. Sam and Frieda have their own story to tell, and I am hoping that this time they will be heard, and that the lessons offered by their existence and their survival will once again touch lives and hearts. Only then will we better appreciate the stories we carry within us, which too often are buried with us.

Sometimes we know how the story ends before we learn how it began. That's where I would say we are when it comes to the story of my parents, Sam and Frieda Friedman.

PART II

THE PREWAR YEARS: SZLAMA FRYDMAN

ŻARNOWIEC AND BĘDZIN

When I was young, every night before I went to sleep on my convertible couch in the small living room that I shared with my parents whose own convertible couch nearly touched mine (Rachel had our one bedroom), I would mumble the Hebrew prayer Sh'ma (*Shema*) to myself and for God to hear. Sh'ma Yisrael (literally, Hear O Israel) is recited during daily Jewish prayers and sometimes at moments of great danger, concern or uncertainty as Jews for centuries would proclaim their belief in one God and sometimes seek a powerful ally – unquestioning faith. The Sh'ma also served to unite the Jewish diaspora through a shared belief in something greater than themselves, a belief that would give them comfort and provide a link to an ancient past and an eternal future. This pledge, uttered by Jews for generations, sought to recognize a single Almighty God, their faith in shared beliefs and what they represented as a way of life. In return for this proclamation of faith, they would be blessed for all time.

The first two words, Sh'ma Yisrael, are also found in a section of the Torah, the scroll that contains the five Books of Moses, the Hebrew Bible. The Sh'ma is meant to be repeated each morning and evening during prayers, and its words serve as reminders to all Jews of the bargain struck between God and his people: Keep faith in me, and I will provide for you. It never really said anything about protection.

Again and again, my father promised me that if I recited those words and were then to die in my sleep, all my sins would be forgiven (what kind of sins can a six- or seven-year-old possibly accrue anyway?) and my soul would exist in some fashion in a heaven that most Jews spend little time considering. I guess he just thought of it as finding yet another way of protecting me from a world he had long recognized as dangerous for all, but especially for us Jews. Instead, his admonition and that nightly habit left me terrified – the very state in which he (and my mother) found themselves for too much of their lives.

Maybe in the back of his mind he also used the Sh'ma as a protective cloak that would envelop any son bearing his father's name. He had heard many others recite it, sing it and scream it again and again in the slave labor and concentration camps he endured for nearly six years during the Holocaust. Many uttered the Sh'ma as they were marched to their deaths in the camps and ghettos where my parents and their loved ones once lived, and where so many perished. Perhaps at some point in one of his nightmares, he imagined his first wife reciting it to calm their two daughters as they went to their deaths. He hadn't been there to save them or share their fate, and the Sh'ma hadn't saved them either. Years later, he clung to it anyway.

The nightly recitation of the Sh'ma was not for the sake of one lonely, scared seven-year-old voice in a dark room in a sad part of Brooklyn. My father understood it as a call to arms, a blast of the *Shofar*, the reverberation of a chorus of lost souls affirming their lives and beliefs. It shouted to the universe that they still mattered. Ultimately, it was a way to express a belief in something greater than ourselves: shared hopes, shared histories and even a shared, if unknown, future.

My father was brought up to believe in God and keep faith in an afterlife by focusing on God and thanking Him for everything he had, both the good and the bad. It helped him hold on to some measure of his humanity, even as others (my mother amongst them) lost their faith and therefore, he believed, any possibility of happiness. In the worst of times, he held tight to that faith, and also, as I will describe later, to a lovely pink sweater clutched in his hand or held only in his heart and memory. If you believe, there is no question. If you don't believe, there is no answer. To survive his torments, he required answers, real or imagined.

He was a lovely man. Sweet, kind, both stubborn and understanding, he was very religious yet open to flexibility when his difficult, complicated life required it. His faith in his God, his survival against all odds and his need to protect and provide were attributes that gave him strength, if not hope.

My father was born Israel Szlama Frydman in Żarnowiec[1] in the Kielce province of south central Poland on October 3, 1911.[2] Żarnowiec was a small farming community and shtetl located about 50 kilometers (31 miles) north of Kraków and about 70 kilometers (44 miles) northeast of Będzin.[3] He already had three older sisters: the twins, Fajgla Blima and Estera Dwojra, born in 1907, and Blima Jochweta, born in 1909,[4] and two older brothers: Kalma, born in 1900, and Chaim, born in December 1910.

Though he generally volunteered very little if at all about his past, I did once ask him where exactly in Poland he was born, and he answered: "Bendin." For some time I couldn't find that town on any map. Only when I started researching this book did I realize that while he may have pronounced the city as Bendin (its name in Yiddish), it was actually named Będzin. Meanwhile, he never mentioned Żarnowiec at all, which was perhaps unsurprising because from age three on he lived most of his young life in Będzin, where most of his extended family came from and lived.

Żarnowiec was in a part of Czarist Russia called Congress Poland or Russian Poland, a region created by the Congress of Vienna in 1815 (hence the name Congress Poland). The village traced its roots back to the 11th century and was formally established in its current location in the early 1300s, when it developed into a market town that was well-located on the banks of the Pilica River along a trade route that ran through central Poland and to Poland's ancient capital of Kraków. Żarnowiec was destroyed by the Swedes in the mid-17th century and then, after it was rebuilt, destroyed again by a great fire in 1697.[5]

The village had changed hands numerous times over the centuries. For instance, in 1795 it was annexed by the Habsburg Empire for a brief period. At that point the town's population began to grow, mostly due to an increase in Jewish settlers from other parts of the Austrian Empire. By the 1850s, Jews made up more than 50 percent of the town's population, a ratio that held steady till the outbreak of the Second World War. By 1867, the area was officially part of the Russian Empire. Only after World War I was this region incorporated into and recognized by the international community as part of the modern 20th-century Polish Republic.

When my father and his family lived there, the population was only 2,000. Half were Jews, and the other half were Polish-speaking peasants who grew cabbage and other crops in the surrounding countryside.

On a visit to Żarnowiec in October 2018, we encountered a pleasant old town and market square, a few wooden structures and some older brick buildings from the pre–World War I era surrounding the square. There was little else to see that could trace my father's family to the town. That family had lived and worked as traders or merchants near the market square (the Rynek, in Polish). What exactly were they trading on market days, and with whom? Whether for sale or exchange, Jewish traders supplied local farmers with everything from farm equipment to kitchen utensils and other everyday implements of daily life, from clothing to hardware and housewares, while the farmers sold fruits, vegetables, eggs and chickens, among other items. My father's family didn't own a store, but they may have had a stall in the market. They would sell some of what they had traded in other towns and at larger markets. As peddlers, they might also have traveled from farm to farm and to small towns and villages to trade or sell goods to the local populace.

The Frydmans had been tradesmen or peddlers for generations, for the most part barely eking out a living, as many other Jews in Poland did by becoming shoemakers, clothiers, shopkeepers, bakers or innkeepers. Records show that other Jewish men in the town were bricklayers, coopers, tailors or butchers, along with water carriers and even a few cantors.

My father's paternal grandparents were Jochim (Jochym) Frydman (Fridman), born in 1833, who in an official record was described initially as a day laborer and later as a merchant, and Tauba Szwarcmer (Swarcmer), born in 1835. Jochim had grown up in Będzin, which at the time was a large farming community located in south central Congress Poland. As a merchant, he maintained trading relationships with family members, most of whom had remained in Będzin after he left for Żarnowiec, where he married Tauba in February 1853.[6] She was 18 and Jochim was 20. Jochim had several brothers and sisters who also lived in Będzin, along with their many children.[7]

Jochim and Tauba raised a large family in Żarnowiec, including Mailech, my father's father and my grandfather, after whom I was named. Mailech[8] Fridman (Frydman), born in 1870, became a merchant and trader like his father and, as it would turn out, like his son. In Żarnowiec, Mailech maintained business ties with family members who had remained in Będzin.

In 1895, it was Mailech's turn to marry. He was 25 and his bride, my father's mother and my grandmother, Chana Leia Lajchter,[9] a local girl from a neighboring shtetl, was 26. She was born in 1869, one of eight children of Majer Izrael Lajchter and Perla Frenkel. Two of their children died in infancy. One of them was named Szlama, which suggests that my father's name was given to him to honor that deceased child. Mailech and Chana were married in the synagogue in nearby Włoszczowa,[10] where Mailech's mother was born, on March 12, 1895.[11]

My father's parents lived modestly in a small house on or near Żarnowiec's 14th-century market square. The Town Hall and other official offices were on one side of the square, much as they are today. At the time there was also a small hospital. On the opposite side was a group of less impressive houses. These were often where the Jewish shopkeepers, craftsmen and merchants lived and worked. Off that main square there was also an old wooden synagogue. As in other shtetls of similar size, there was also a smaller prayer house and a mikvah (ritual bathhouse) within walking distance. The Jewish cemetery was outside of town on the road leading to the village of Chliny (Chlina).

The Jewish population in Żarnowiec grew over time, leading to the construction of a second synagogue made of brick. Like many Jews in the area, Mailech and his siblings barely managed to earn a living and generally existed on the edge of poverty. On Mondays, the traditional market day, when hundreds of local farmers crowded the market square, Mailech and his fellow traders would be there to help them sell or trade goods, whether locally or for shipment to neighboring towns and cities, or all the way to family members in Będzin. On Sunday nights, local farmers would sometimes pay Mailech for a space on his dirt floor so that they could sleep there and get a leg up on their competition the next morning.

Prior to World War I, Polish Jews simply wanted to make a living, practice their Orthodox Jewish faith and support their large, ever-growing families. At that time, few Jews engaged in politics (especially in a small town like Żarnowiec). They had precious little political power until Poland became a republic. Jews in shtetls often experienced higher rates of poverty than other residents. Local Jewish charitable organizations customarily helped the needy.

Mailech had an older brother, Mosziek (Moszek), a younger brother, Berek, born two years after Mailech in 1872,[12] and two sisters, the younger, named Idessa, and the elder, Estera.[13] In fact, there may have been many more siblings or other close relatives in Mailech's family. Unfortunately, it is difficult to be certain or accurate.[14]

Here is some information about villages like Żarnowiec from JewishGen, the Jewish genealogical site:

"As in all Polish towns, the economy of the Jewish population was based on trade and on crafts. The Jews bought the agricultural produce from the peasants in the neighborhood and sold them manufactured products and handmade products in their turn. However, relations with the Gentile population were not particularly friendly. Despite the fact that they had close trade relations, with most of the agricultural products being sold to the Jews, while Jewish merchants and craftsmen supplied the peasants with clothing, shoes, kitchen utensils, work implements and tools, and other goods, a mountain of alienation was rising between the two sectors of the population."[15]

Moreover, the Russian government at that time did not take kindly to Jews and generally harassed them, depriving them of rights or worse. Czarist Russia had a long, vicious history of state-sponsored pogroms that encouraged the Russian military, local mobs and others to sweep through small Jewish communities and steal, murder and rape at will. At times, local Poles would join them. These pogroms had driven relatives, including some Frydman cousins, to the United States. These first cousins would eventually help our family resettle years later.

But there were other, more immediate challenges. By 1914, World War I was raging all around Żarnowiec. The region of Upper Silesia had traded hands many times over the centuries, mostly among Austrians, Russians and Germans but especially since the 18th century, in large measure because of its rich reserves of coal and other minerals. Danger was everywhere, with the Germans to the west, the Russians to the east and armies colliding in and around the small towns and cities. People constantly emigrated back and forth through these borderlands, but by the end of World War I, these borders had begun to unravel.

Though only about 70 kilometers to the southwest, Będzin
sometimes seemed like a world away from the shtetl Szlama's
family fled in 1914.

Like so many others, Mailech knew it was time to uproot himself and his young family and seek a safer haven. Fortunately, he had his large extended family and longstanding economic ties back in Będzin. Years earlier, his parents had moved back to Będzin from Żarnowiec (where Tauba, his mother, died in 1907 at the age of 72), and his siblings and their families had lived in Będzin for many years. Economically, times were tough. One record noted that at the start of World War I, about one out of six residents in the area, mostly Jews, required systematic support (help from charities) to survive.

Będzin was a world that was very different from anything my father would have experienced if Mailech had stayed in Żarnowiec. Before the First World War and the Russian Revolution, it was part of the Russian empire and was on its way to becoming a center of Jewish and Polish socialist activity. Although no formal Jewish settlement was established there till the beginning of the 17th century, Poland's Casimir (Kazimierz) the Great granted Jews permission to live in Będzin (and other parts of Poland) at the beginning of the 13th century. He created legal protections for them and helped Jewish communities thrive. Będzin's famous castle was a stone's throw from the Jewish area. In 1583, another Polish king granted the Jews of Będzin the right to own and operate prayer houses and a cemetery, buy and sell real estate and engage in unlimited trade. This was well beyond what most Jews in other parts of Europe could have experienced at that time. A hundred years earlier, all Jews had been expelled from Spain and Portugal, while in Italy they had been forced to live under guard in segregated areas: the first ghettos. By the time my father and his family arrived in 1914, Będzin was a cosmopolitan city of nearly 40,000 people, more than half of them Jewish. They were now with the rest of the Frydman *mishpacha* (family). Chana's extended family, the Lajchters, had also taken up residence in Będzin. They all looked forward to a new beginning.

By 1914, however, Mailech and Chana were concerned. They had traded the lack of rights in Żarnowiec, the threats posed by Czarists and the obvious perils of wartime for a city that was already occupied by invading German soldiers.

Ironically, the German occupation of Będzin that year was actually relatively benevolent, as it was customary in some parts of Germany at that time to endow Jewish merchants and craftsmen with rights to participate in the economy and more freely practice their religion. In neighboring German Silesia, for instance, Jews already enjoyed full equality, including allowing Jews a semblance of self-governance by what would become *kehillot*, Jewish community organizations through which Jewish communities in Poland were governed during the interwar years. In fact, the Germans who were occupying this area granted Jews full civil and political freedoms after 1915, which led to the development of formal organizations in the social lives of Będzin Jews. Jewish political parties and trade unions were legalized, and Jews were also allowed to provide services to the booming industrial enterprises in Upper Silesia, including local coal mines and related businesses.

Mailech and his family moved into an apartment at Modrzejowska 28, a street not far from the Great Synagogue of Będzin. The area was home to many other Jewish families, including other members of the Lajchter family.[16] The streets where my father and his family lived were filled with residential apartments stacked above storefronts in three- and four-story brick structures.

Within a few months of the arrival of Mailech and Chana's brood in Będzin, Mailech's father Jochim, the family patriarch, died at age 81. At least the Frydmans could look forward to Chana's seventh child, born a few months later in 1914. He was named Jochim in honor of his recently deceased grandfather.

But shortly afterward, the family experienced an unexpected tragedy. At age 45, Mailech suddenly collapsed and died at five in the morning on January 17, 1915, in the kitchen of their apartment. My father Szlama was just three and a half years old at the time.[17]

Here's my mother's version of what happened:

Frieda would begin by pointing to the edge of the metal table where we ate our meals in the tiny kitchen of our Coney Island apartment.

"I'm telling you, so listen," she would intone to Rachel and me (generally her only captive audience) in an excessively loud and sometimes deeper voice than her small frame would imply. "Always be careful! I'll tell you why. One day, Szlameck's father was just standing in the kitchen where they lived in Poland and didn't pay attention to what he was doing. So he fell down hard and hit his side" (pointing to her own hip) "on the edge of the table – just like this!" She raised her voice along with her hand as she slapped the corner of the table. Then the lesson ended: "He dropped down to the floor and just died. No one could help him."

This scene would be repeated many times in my younger years, first about the mortal dangers inherent in sharp table edges, and second, to let us know that our lives were always in mortal peril.

Frieda's voice then grew even louder and more emphatic. Waving her hands menacingly, she warned, "So listen to me! Be careful and watch out for corners on tables. And don't fall down." Not quite fodder for a fortune cookie, it was just another thing for two little kids to worry about in a rundown apartment facing an alley at the back of a shoe store a block from the unending roar of elevated subway trains.

So what really did happen to my grandfather? My guess is that he suffered a massive heart attack or fatal stroke. It was a case of sudden cardiac death in a family that, I subsequently learned, suffered excessively and disproportionately from various forms of heart disease across generations, at least on my father's side. My father had a heart attack when he was 68. All four of his first cousins, who helped us emigrate to the US decades later, succumbed to heart disease, including Hyman Zuckerman, himself a cardiologist. Indeed, I started taking blood pressure medications when I was just 21. It was our hearts we would have to worry about, rather than the scraping against the edges and corners of our lives.

Sadly, both of Szlama's older brothers died not long after their father. Chaim died of an inflammatory disorder on December 2, 1915. A little more than two years later, on January 20, 1918, Szlama's oldest brother, Kalma, died of unknown causes at age 18 in a Będzin hospital on Malachowskiego Street. Thus Szlama, by the time he was just seven, became the oldest surviving son of five children as World War I drew to a close.

What happened next? My father's family had a great support system in Będzin, but as he grew older, it was important that he find a way to do his part and help provide for his family. It was a burden that aged him too quickly.

My father became fatherless very early in his life, so I doubt he could ever carry a memory of his father with him, and until I began this project, I didn't think very much about his father either. There was no attachment, no real knowledge of who he was. When my friends talked about their grandparents, I simply said I didn't have any. I knew their names. Period.

It took this project, but also the fact of becoming a grandfather myself, to realize just how much I had missed without grandparents.

It allowed me to imagine just how much more my father as a child must have missed his father.

As I said, I knew my grandfather only as a name and namesake. His name (and mine) was Elimelech in Hebrew, Mailech for both of us in Yiddish. He could have been Max in English. Jewish tradition suggests that parents name their children after a deceased person in the family in order to honor and perpetuate that memory.

When my father and I prayed together on Saturdays or holidays, we would note my grandfather's passing when reciting the *Kaddish*, the Jewish prayer for the dead. Or my father would use his father's name when he was called to the Torah as he said his own name, Shlomo ben Elimelech (Salomon, the son of Mailech), or when my Hebrew name was announced on other religious occasions. Mailech's life, who he was, what he hoped for his children: none of this would become a firm memory embedded in heart and psyche or, for my father, as a model for actions for the rest of his life. My father never had his father as a role model. For all the pains we would have to endure when we were exposed to our parents' traumas, I was considerably luckier.

Still, as I consider Mailech, I wonder: Was he a kind man? A good father? A successful businessman? A religious man? Was he smart? Was he funny? Would I have liked him? Would he have liked me? I don't know, and neither did my father, in his short-lived relationship with Mailech.

There is no doubt that I ascribe a special meaning to grandfatherhood, thanks to the relationship we have had with our grandchildren. They represent the DNA that we share, a past that we know and a future that we can hope for, if not expect. None of that was in the cards when it came to Mailech. While my father became a grandfather six times and a father four times, he would barely know any more than I did about his own father.

Indeed, that's why in our house, Mailech Frydman was never really spoken about as we grew older. He was just a name without a memory attached. The only other thing I knew about Mailech was that he died somewhat mysteriously and suddenly when my father was still young.

Mailech is the Yiddish name for Elimelech, which in Hebrew can translate into "My God is King," derived from the Hebrew *el*, for God, and *malakh*, to rule. The name I received was in some way already beyond simple convention or tradition. It was another way for my father to express his faith in his God, even as that God could not interfere with the murder of his family. I represented another family altogether. On the other hand, belief in that God provided my father with the unimaginable faith and therefore the strength and will to miraculously survive the very worst years of his life and then start again from scratch with a new family in a new world. What he brought to all that was an abiding belief in his God as king of the universe.

In the Book of Ruth in the Old Testament, Elimelech was the husband of Naomi and the father-in-law of Ruth. In those biblical times, a great famine had turned their homeland in Judah, the land promised them by God, into a virtual wasteland. There was no food, the earth was parched and unproductive and the farm animals had died. Elimelech decided to leave everything he knew behind and ventured with Naomi and their two sons to a foreign land in neighboring Moab to live among a people who did not worship the Israelites' God. It would be a very different life requiring a different kind of faith. The sons each married Moabites (one of whom was Ruth). Then, Elimelech died suddenly, leaving his family bereft and adrift. Next, the sons died, leaving their Moabite widows behind. The women had to cope, build a new life and eventually return to Judah and their God. The Book of Ruth relates how all this turns out well, in part because they find favor in God's eyes and thus renew their faith in the Jewish God. Ruth goes on to be known as the great-grandmother of David, who became the greatest king of Israel.

The striking similarity of aspects of Mailech's story and his namesake's in the Book of Ruth is uncanny. Would my father have known that story of Elimelech, Naomi and Ruth? Certainly. Did that story and knowledge play any role, even subconsciously, in naming me, his son, Elimelech, not only for his father but also to imprint a related biblical story of enforced migration, of faith lost and then found in a foreign land, all amidst tragedy and despair? That, after all, was his father's story, and in some ways, his story as well. Like so much else about my parents, we will never know.

What we do know is that my father also found himself fatherless in a place where his immediate family was foreign and far removed from their ancestral home. He found himself adrift.

As smart as he was about the world, though with only a grade school education, not even the legendary wisdom of King Solomon could have prepared Szlama for what was to come in his life, especially for what he was to experience so early. The most wrenching, difficult parts were unaccompanied by discernible meanings or rational explanations, even at the worst of times: the loss of his father at the tender age of three, followed by the excruciating, unbearable anguish and pain that would begin on September 1, 1939. His search for meaning in his life would accompany him for the rest of his days. It would require much more than the wisdom of his namesake, Solomon, or the love of Solomon's songs for him to endure.

Any reader of Ecclesiastes is quickly and powerfully reminded of both the fragility and the precious nature of the time allotted to each of us. Famously, it advises that there is a time for everything under heaven. But if there is any consciousness affecting justice in the universe, certainly there could never have been a right time for the darkness that befell my father again and again or the countless beatings he endured during his imprisonment, creating memories and scars that remained for all of his allotted time on this earth.

How did my father take on all this responsibility without a role model to guide him? Much research would indicate that a young boy who grows up fatherless suffers psychologically for the rest of his life. Such children, according to some psychologists, become excessively aggressive, suffer from depression, have low self-esteem, do poorly in school and experience other difficulties.

I never saw any of that. Szlama was fortunate to have many male role models all around him, though admittedly that was hardly the same as having a father. And clearly, from his earliest days, my father learned what it took to be a survivor. He thought well of himself and always looked forward, never back. He kept his sense of humor. He wanted to laugh, unless he had no choice but to cry or despair. And he developed a devotion to his family and his God that gave him deep, enduring strength and purpose.

Years later, he started a second family. Through it all, he clearly never stopped pouring his love into his children and his family. It was all he had and all he could hold onto, as long as he was able. And even at times that seemed hopeless, he kept his faith in himself, his family and his God. He loved to sneak candies and other sweets when no one was looking. He wasn't brought up with much formal education, but he excelled in math and loved to learn. He wasn't perfect, but at an early age he realized that he would have to continually invent and reinvent himself, and seek love and give it, even when it sometimes wasn't returned. He remained a kind soul.

His actions came out of a foundation in his faith: people are good, children are great, the past is past and all there is now is today. Much of what he would experience in his life was sad and tragic, but not always, and not forever. Each of us has the capacity to be what we wish, in part by looking ahead and never looking back.

He was blessed with two families, even though his own childhood family had been broken apart. If there is any justice in the world, it seems to be that such a good father had the chance to be a father again, even if his first family existed for only a few years. He became the father he always wanted to be but never really had, and he got to do it twice more. In his mind, he would consider himself to be very lucky. His children certainly were.

He was fatherless from a young age but never clueless about what a father should be and how he should behave. In Hebrew, his name was Shlomo, meaning a wise and peaceful man, a peacemaker. Whether he learned that from a father, from the family that took on his father's role, or from the vicissitudes of life, we'll never know.

Each of us finds our own Moab: a foreign place to which we must escape because of some great terror, trauma or change in our lives, in order to renew ourselves and discover a new path. In the final act in his own life before his untimely death, my father's father found his Moab in their family's flight from war to Będzin. He then passed that sense of possibility on to his son as a lasting legacy and a critical key to survival. My father understood what it meant to journey to a strange land from the familiar, and to navigate through its hardships and possibilities with faith in oneself, with and for the love of others.

In the interim between losing his father and gradually learning more about what fatherhood demanded of him, there was some growing up to do. Very early on, Szlama had begun to learn to abide by Jewish traditions. He got a haircut, possibly for the first time in any formal way since he was born, in a ceremony held by some Orthodox Jews called the *Upsherin* (to shear off). The practice came from a tradition that compares human life to the life of a tree. Therefore the Hebrew Bible commands that no one is allowed to eat fruit from a tree during the first three years after it's planted. At least among some Orthodox Jews, that translated into a practice of cutting a young boy's hair at age three (or thereabouts) to signify his first step toward manhood. At that time Szlama was also given a *kippah* (skullcap) and *tzitzit* (fringes to wear under his clothes).

At nearly four years of age, he would be enrolled in a *cheder* of a local Talmud Torah, which he would attend after his Polish school day and on Sundays once he started first grade[18] to begin learning his *aleph bets*, memorizing the morning, afternoon and evening prayers and being introduced to the Torah and Jewish rituals. These primary-grade religious schools were for poor Jewish boys. He quickly became fluent in the prayers, so much so that I still remember how fast he could run through pages of prayers under his breath on Shabbos and holidays. Speed praying, I called it.

According to some Swedish documents he attended Polish primary school until the age of 12 or 13, so only through sixth grade, though a more recently discovered document added a year of a trade school where he may have learned skills for working a desk job in a commercial enterprise. He learned Polish at school, since by then Poland had begun to require all children (including Jewish children) to learn Polish, which was not taught in Jewish schools.

Once he turned 13 in 1924, Szlama became a *bar mitzvah*, a son of the Commandments and thus – according to Jewish tradition – accountable for his life choices. That brought consequences fairly quickly. Though he was a good, engaged student, he left the Polish school and went to work.[19]

Until World War I ended, the economic situation was certainly tough for everyone in Będzin, and more so in a family without a breadwinner. Many local workshops suspended production, and poverty and hunger were more apparent. Some estimates indicate that poor people made up about 50 percent of Będzin's population, with Jews accounting for more than half that number. In addition to the support and guidance of his uncles, other family members and whatever he could earn on his own, help also came from the robust Jewish community in and around Będzin, which sought to take care of its own and provided aid through a variety of charitable organizations. Occasionally help also was forthcoming from a number of American and British Jewish relief organizations that sent packages of food and clothing to poor Polish Jews. Although the majority of Jews were self-employed during the global Great Depression and thus not at great risk of losing their jobs, they still suffered, for without customers, even independent shopkeepers and craftsmen became impoverished.

Ultimately the Frydmans were blessed with a safety net of uncles, aunts, cousins and more distant relatives to help them through the worst of times. My father at one point claimed to have had 100 cousins in and around Będzin.

During those early years after Mailech's death, it is likely that the family also was directly supported by one of my father's uncles, Mosziek Szuml Fridman (Frydman), Mailech's older brother. Mosziek died in Będzin at age 69 in 1928. Most of my father's family were merchants at Będzin's large marketplaces and wholesale warehouses selling wheat grown by local Polish farmers, so my father started training to become a tradesman in Będzin, possibly apprenticing himself to his Uncle Mosziek.

Two other uncles, who may have married Mailech's sisters or perhaps were otherwise related through the Lajchter family, were a rabbi named Zvi, who ran a yeshiva out of his home, and a sugar merchant named Majer, who was wealthier and may have helped as well, the former stewarding Szlama's religious upbringing and the latter sharpening his business acumen. Szulim Kopel, yet another uncle by marriage, signed Mailech's death certificate, which suggests that the family was everywhere.

On the plus side, Będzin had a great deal to offer a young man like Szlama. Before the outbreak of World War II, the city's population had grown to 60,000, half Jewish. Its landmark Great Synagogue was larger than any shul most Jews had ever seen anywhere. And while Jews were still involved in the trades as merchants and working in shops, they were also beginning to support the new industries that flourished near the Silesian coal fields and fueled ore mining, metallurgy and metal manufacturing businesses. Będzin's Jewish-owned businesses also included paint and chemical factories and garment workshops.

Meanwhile, unlike Żarnowiec, where people simply tried to subsist and weren't much involved in politics, Będzin was a center of political and cultural ferment both before World War I and, increasingly, thereafter. Most importantly, and of considerable interest to young Jews seeking greater opportunity and a larger voice, a strong Zionist presence developed in Będzin, including the Mizrachi, a religious offshoot of Zionism, as well as more secular Zionist groups. Socialist and worker parties like the Bund flourished, representing trade unions. In the 1920s, unions began to focus their efforts on tailors, porters and domestic workers. By the 1930s, prominent Zionists, most notably David Ben Gurion, who later became the first prime minister of the Jewish state, visited Będzin and rallied additional support for their movement. Various religious groups, including those who would be considered modern Orthodox and others that were more Progressive, opened their doors as well as the minds of the young and curious. If you were a dedicated Zionist, which my father became, you could support the Hebrew-speaking socialist and non-religious General Zionists or the Orthodox Mizrachi Zionists. If you were a socialist, you could join the Jewish Bund. If you were ultra-Orthodox, you could join the Agudath movement.

During most of the interwar years, Będzin was also a cultural mecca, a great place to broaden perspectives. Yiddish theater and books abounded. Modern Jewish schools that had developed there in the late 1800s now flourished. The city boasted a vibrant Jewish press, as well as Yiddish, Polish, and Hebrew elementary and high schools. It offered outlets for gathering, learning, exchanging ideas and socializing to Jewish men and women of all stripes. Yiddish and Hebrew competed with Polish and sometimes, given the proximity to Germany, with German. My father became conversant in all four languages, which helped him in business as well as with greater challenges later in his life.

Będzin was a great place for young Jews to grow up – until it wasn't. In the mid-1930s, a wave of rabid antisemitism swept through Poland and engulfed the Jews, who made up 10 percent of the Polish population.

Because Szlama had to work to help support his family, he didn't really have the opportunity to participate in the political ferment as much as he would have liked when he was younger, though he was clearly exposed to the Zionist/Palestine movements and found common cause in what would become a lifelong obsession with supporting a Jewish homeland.

My father's family members were among the many Jews who experienced economic difficulty but took solace and pleasure in their religion and sense of community.

It is hardly surprising that with all the challenges of youth and of taking on responsibility without a father, Szlama grew into a complicated man prone to practicalities and compromises, resilience and adaptation. He was buoyed by faith in God, and the survival of the Jewish people became his passion. He said he believed there was a reason for everything in life, and even if he could not discern it himself, it was God's will. So a part of him was clearly serious and later on even rigid in some cases, seen from a religious perspective.

But my father was also charming. He had a playfulness that he often kept deep inside; however, it would surface in many ways. You could sense it when you saw the sparkle in his eyes.

For instance, during one Passover he talked about how as a young boy no more than 10 or 11 years old, he played pranks, which he called jokes, especially during holidays like Passover, a favorite of his and ours as well. That year we had invited my college roommate, who was a Muslim from Turkey, and my best friend from high school, who for the first eight years of his education attended Our Lady of Solace Catholic School, to experience their first *seder* with us. My father was in a particularly good mood because he loved the idea that I had friends and wanted to teach them a bit about Judaism. However, he ended up teaching them and us more about himself. He rarely spoke about his life in Poland before or during the war, but maybe that second or third cup of wine got to him. Anyway, during the *seder* service, when it came time to open the door and invite Elijah to drink from his special cup of wine and relive the promise of returning to Jerusalem one day, he revealed something from his past.

"When I was young during Passover," he said, "I would sometimes run around with my friends and play tricks on the other families." For example, he and his friends would lurk outside of neighbors' homes, and when they opened their doors to welcome Elijah, he and his friends would have a good laugh by pushing a goat through the door and into that family's home. Other times, they would balance a bucket of water atop a door, so that when the door was opened for Elijah, the bucket would empty onto the unsuspecting *seder* participant.

Perhaps my father was not the ultra-religious Jew he had made himself out to be as a youth. At least he was not the pious boy we assumed he had been, based on his strict observance of Jewish laws and customs in the years when we knew him. If he was such an observant Jew, even as a younger man, what was he doing outside of his own home on Passover instead of participating in his own family's lengthy *seder*? Anyway, his story gave us all a good laugh. And he loved to laugh.

How did his life progress in those earlier years without a father to guide him? And what effect did it have on him psychologically? In some ways, he grew older before his time, as early on he was responsible for taking care of his mother, sisters and younger brother. Family was everything to him. That never changed.

Also, apart from the Passover story, I'm not at all certain just how religious or assimilated his family was, at least, once he left the cheder. A surviving picture here from that period shows him at age 17 or maybe a bit older, sitting with his family, including his three sisters, possibly their spouses or boyfriends, maybe his younger brother, all surrounding their mother, seated in the center. While his mother looks stern and appropriately modest in her dress, the others, including my father, look as though they had just come from a local café, without a hint of Jewish garb. Sleeves on the young women are short, hair is stylish, we see their bare arms and legs, the boys aren't sporting beards, *payot* (side curls), hats or yarmulkas. They are clean-shaven and fashionable.

*My father was somewhere between 17 and 20 years old when this
picture of his family was taken in Będzin. He is to the right of his
mother (in the center dressed in black.) Others pictured probably
included his younger brother Jochim, his three sisters (the twins sit
at their mother's feet) and their spouses or significant others.*

I also gained new insights into my father's religiosity by mulling over
what I learned from my own research, weighing the stories he told us,
looking at that family picture, and considering information gleaned
from the son of one of my father's first cousins, Milton Zuckerman,
who emigrated with his parents and siblings to the US in the 1920s.

That son, Aaron Zuckerman, who today is a rabbi in Lakewood, New
Jersey, told me he accompanied my father to an interview for a
possible job in in the US in 1952, serving as his translator. Aaron was
an ultra-Orthodox Jew and dressed accordingly. While my father was
sitting next to him on the bus, he commented on how similar his
upbringing was to Aaron's.

Aaron reported that my father had told him he was brought up as a
seriously religious and observant Jew in Poland. He added that
Szlama's grandfather was a cantor (perhaps on his mother's side) in a
local synagogue and that one of his uncles was a leading rabbi. Also,
a famous rabbi named Chaim Friedman may have been his great-
grandfather. All that may have been. Meanwhile, we know his other

grandfather, Jochim, was a laborer and then a peddler for most of his adult life. He was sure to keep kosher and pray on the Sabbath, holidays and perhaps even weekdays, but I don't think he spent much of his time studying the Talmud. The more I learned about my father, the more I began to understand that he would sometimes stretch or reimagine the facts of his life in order to fit in and be accepted in a new situation. That was one of the ways he survived in the worst of times, and how he managed to fit in when times were better.

Szlama playing the violin as a young man in Będzin.

Finally, there is the picture of my father as a young man playing a violin. Again, there is nothing here to suggest a religious person, certainly when I compare that picture to the ones of Eastern European shtetl Jews, with their long black kaftans, distinctive hats and other often seen characteristics.

Despite his challenges when he was young, he was loved and cared for, and hoped that he would eventually find someone to love who loved him as well. To tell that story, we move from Będzin to a neighboring, somewhat smaller town just three miles to the east, called Dąbrowa Górnicza.

It is there that we fully learn the meaning of a painful joy, as seen through my father's eyes.

DĄBROWA GÓRNICZA

If there are only two holy books that stand out now as I consider my father's life journey, at least during his formative younger years – they are Ecclesiastes and the Song of Songs.

Why those two? First, both are purported to have been written by King Solomon, his namesake. Second, Ecclesiastes is filled with wisdom, especially when it focuses on the meaning of life and death, of loss, of wandering. And it includes these now famous lines:

Everything has an appointed season,
and there is a time for every matter under the heaven.

A time to give birth and a time to die;
a time to plant and a time to uproot that which is planted.

A time to kill and a time to heal;
a time to break and a time to build.

A time to weep and a time to laugh;
a time of wailing and a time of dancing.

A time to cast stones and a time to gather stones;
a time to embrace and a time to refrain from embracing.

A time to seek and a time to lose;
a time to keep and a time to cast away.

A time to rend and a time to sew;
a time to be silent and a time to speak.

A time to love and a time to hate;
a time for war and a time for peace.

Indeed, in life, timing is everything.

The Book of Ecclesiastes, one of the 24 books of the Old Testament, got its name from a Greek translation of the Hebrew word *Kohelet*, which is a pseudonym used by King Solomon. It is attributed to him because of its many insightful ruminations on and guides to wisdom, including its multi-faceted exploration of the meaning of life, particularly while each of us faces the inevitability of death.

Though modern scholars disagree about its actual author (or authors), Ecclesiastes has always held a prominent place in Jewish liturgy and tradition and beyond. Its teachings and stories are read each year during the week of Sukkot, a holiday that generally falls during the week of my father's birthday in October. By chance or not, my father was also named Salomon: Szlama in Polish and Shlomo in Yiddish, perhaps because of that very connection to the wisdom of a key figure in the Jewish tradition.

Sukkot also marks the 40 years that the Jewish people were forced to wander in the desert as punishment for forsaking their God. They had turned to idols while Moses was receiving the Ten Commandments on Mount Sinai. It was only the next generation of Jews who could enter the Promised Land to rediscover their faith and therefore a newfound hope for their future.

Despite the tragedies in his life, my father always seemed to be the wise and steady one in our family. Yet he also took on the mantle of a wanderer, seeking hope and faith in the darkest of his days, never quite fitting in, whether in Poland, the camps, Sweden or the US. In many ways he was rootless, especially as he was determined to hide, perhaps deny, or even sometimes reimagine some of his past. That had an effect on my sister, mother and me, as we found ourselves with no concrete past or traditions to hold onto and only a few family members to help us feel secure. Instead, in our early years we lived in a present that seemed like a hand-to-mouth existence. On the positive side, wandering in our own kind of desert forced us to value what we had. That was certainly true of my father, Rachel and myself, but perhaps less so of my mother. In the process, it helped us discover positive attributes like perseverance, resilience, faith and love.

The second book is the Song of Songs, about marriage, love and the bonds that tie two people together even if they come from different backgrounds and must work hard for their love to endure under all sorts of circumstances. Again, the Song of Songs was traditionally attributed to King Solomon, though it was written centuries after his reign. However, it is not a religious document, and if taken literally it is more about lovers, or even a celebration of physical love. It has also been interpreted as an allegory about God's love for Israel. Beyond its authorship, the link to Solomon is that it is read on the Sabbath during Passover, which commemorates the Exodus from Egypt. And for me, it is a direct cultural or religious connection to the love that my father discovered when he met Chaja and then married for the first time.

What do these two books have in common? They focus on a time for love, even as time runs out.

My father would soon learn how events beyond his control could alter the path of his life forever, along with his intention to discover love in his life.

In his youth and then as a young man, Szlama was full of promise, yet found himself tested again and again by challenges to his resilience, his faith and what remained of his positive personality. That earlier part of his life, which we know so little about, formed who he became, that is, the person I knew.

My father's timing and the circumstances in which he found himself never seemed quite good enough to him. For example, although his timing upon becoming a husband and then a father for the first time started as a perfect dream and a new beginning, it eventually turned into just about the worst of all possible nightmares.

The dream of what might have been began when Szlama was about 24 years old. He had first encountered his beautiful Chaja in one of her uncle's stores, which she managed and where my father was working as a clerk. Although Chaja came from a wealthy family, she followed in her mother's footsteps and worked in the family business.

Chaja Kotlicki was four years older than my father. Born in 1907 in Dąbrowa Górnicza, she was one of 10 children of Jakob Kotlicki[1] and his wife, Maria Szandla Parasol. Members of her family[2] lived in a large compound that had been passed down by the Parasol side of the family over several generations. It was located at Konopicka 4.[3] The structures included a large inner courtyard, quarters for a nanny, a cook and a maid, and its own *Bet HaMidrash* (house of study and prayer) or synagogue. There was also a white dog named Lily. Chaja's mother worked all day in the family's building materials business, while her grandfather, who was very religious, studied *Gemorah* (rabbinical analysis and commentary on the Mishnah, the original written version of what were previously orally transmitted laws of Judaism.) When we visited Dąbrowa, we learned the compound had been demolished and replaced first by a factory and later, by a large Soviet-era Palace of Culture.

Chaja Kotlicki Frydman, my father's first wife.

As you can see on this photo, Chaja deserved her reputation as a beauty. I pictured my father at the time as someone who couldn't believe his good fortune. His life and future course would have changed forever – and for the better – if their world hadn't exploded. Both Chaja and my father seemed well assimilated into the mainstream of life in their small town, a couple who could fit in and be quite successful as partners in business and more importantly, in life. But that dream would not last. The war changed everything.

The Parasols were among the landed gentry (if any Jews could be described in such a context in that part of Poland) in terms of their social, financial and even religious positions in Dąbrowa. The first Parasol, a trader named Szlomo, came to the region in 1869. He was also one of the first Jews to own a home of his own in an area called Ksawery. Furthermore, he was among the first to open a cheder for young Jewish boys and later, as described here, installed a prayer house in his home. The Kotlickis were relative newcomers, having arrived sometime between 1890 and 1900. Over the years the Kotlickis and Parasols would own and operate a number of family-owned enterprises in Dąbrowa and Będzin. The Kotlickis were suppliers of building materials, including wood and iron, to local industry.

Dąbrowa Górnicza began as a small village founded sometime between 1700 and 1800 on the outskirts of what became the thriving city of Będzin. In those early years, Dąbrowa was home to just a single Jewish family. The area began to grow in importance and population when layers of coal were discovered in the late 18th century. Although Jews were not allowed to work in the mines that would develop as a result of that discovery, by the first half of the 19th century they were attracted to the area by the growing need for suppliers to meet the needs of the mines and their workers. Dąbrowa Górnicza was under the control of the Russian Czar until the outbreak of World War I.

By the time my father arrived, Dąbrowa was no longer a beautiful place because of its industrialization. Residents complained about the environment, saying the sky was always covered in a layer of smoke and the flames from the smelters were reflected in the sky, making it difficult to differentiate between night and day. Just about everything was covered in soot: the walls, the houses, the footpaths. A miner in his sooty clothing with a carbide torch in hand was an integral feature of the town's landscape. Still, it was also a place where making a living and settling down to a decent life was possible, even for Jews.

Despite antisemitism, poverty and other longstanding challenges, the economics of Polish industry and the role that Jews would play in it evolved continuously over time. For example, by the time textile industries were established in Łódź, Piotrków and Zabirz, Jewish commerce extended beyond Poland's borders. With the introduction of French, Italian and Belgian capital for the development of industry in Dąbrowa, Jewish merchants followed. By the 1930s, more than 5,000 Jews were living there, making up about 14 percent of the town's population.

Most of the family businesses were operated out of the main shopping street, Sobieskiego Street, in the Old Town of Dąbrowa, which today retains only a hint of the flavor and appearance of those years. Some of the older stores still survive, but they now face a large retail shopping mall and the nearby railroad station.

In that world of the early and mid-1930s, Chaja and my father may have crossed paths in her uncle Jakob Parasol's *galanteria*, or fancy goods store, which sold items such as women's underwear and hosiery, at Sobieskiego 4. The store also sold small pieces of fabric, silk, wool and cotton for decorating apparel, as well as buttons, scarves, gloves and hats. They may have also met in nearby Będzin, where Szlama lived, at the store of another of Chaja's uncles, Izaak Parasol, who had a store and home at Kosciuszko 2.

Back in Dąbrowa at Sobieskiego 3, Jakob Parasol also ran a stationery supply store and owned a second stationery shop at Jadwiga 13 or Jadwiga 16. Chaja's father and his wife operated their own iron works and building supply business out of Sobieskiego 3. Other family-owned stores in the Old Town included a leather store at Okrzei 16 in a house where Juda Parasol, one of Chaja's aunts, lived with her six brothers and sisters. Yet another store was owned by Dawid Parasol, at Narutowicza 35. As was common at the time, the courtyard of Juda's house also boasted a food and imported goods store, an iron articles and paint shop and a place where large wagons drove in to load and unload goods. Dąbrowa's first mechanized carpentry workshop, owned and operated by another Jewish family, was next door.

Precisely because the Russians forbade Jews to own or even work in the surrounding mines, Jewish merchants instead supplied the mines and offered items on credit, which allowed the Polish mine workers to operate successfully in towns like Dąbrowa. Indeed, over time, Jews were actually allowed to own and operate some of these mines, until the German invasion. With the expansion of bus and railroad routes, Jewish shops were now even more accessible to the area's residents, so shopkeepers no longer needed to rely exclusively on neighboring Będzin wholesalers (some of whom may have been relatives of my father) or on products bought and sold in the open-air markets that operated twice a week. For the most part, the trading was conducted on credit provided from the beginning of one month to the beginning of the next.

Regarding the anxieties of Jews' existence in Dąbrowa, it was once noted that even when economic conditions were favorable:

> "The Jew worried that there would be a stoppage in the continuity of work in the factories. When he woke up in the morning, he would look out at the smoke-spewing chimneys, a confirmed sign that the factory was "breathing" and the laborer buying in his shop by credit would pay his debt. More than once the Jewish merchant was destitute because of a strike, dismissals or a stoppage of work in the factory. Trade by credit forced the Jewish merchants in the city to find sources of finance and credit that would allow him to carry out continuous trade. To this end, Jewish banks were founded, also providing loan funds for the tradesmen for buying raw materials."[4]

In this dynamic environment, what did Chaja and Szlama have in common?

They were both young, enjoyed being merchants and traders and were very good with both numbers and people, finding ways to attract and retain customers from all backgrounds in order to make their businesses successful. Szlama didn't own any businesses, of course, but my guess is that he hoped to someday. He was a fast learner and had a good head for numbers. All this considered, being a merchant was practically in his genetic code.

They were certainly a handsome couple. My father, though barely 5'4", was athletic, muscular, slim, clean-shaven, and always well dressed in a white shirt and tie. Chaja, as that one picture demonstrates, was quite lovely.

Chaja and Szlama also shared a passionate involvement with the various Zionist movements of the time, especially because Chaja's oldest uncle, Pinchas, had resettled in Palestine as an early kibbutz pioneer in 1920. They may even have shared a yearning of one day also emigrating to Palestine.

My father retained that yearning his entire life. Like so many other young Jews at that time, he and Chaja would both have attended meetings of the Youth Mizrachi, a religious Zionist movement that was an offshoot of the religious Agudath Yisrael party. Another popular group that attracted young men and women was Hashomer Hadati, a religious Zionist organization that focused on Jewish education and Jewish identity. At weekly meetings they would dance the hora and sing "Hatikvah," which would eventually become the national anthem of the Jewish State. They may have even learned about the less religious Zionist organizations.

For a time, religious Jews and their political movements in Poland shunned Zionism because it had evolved within a secular tradition that had its own summer camps where young Jews were able to practice life on kibbutzim and that expressed more liberal social mores and philosophies about the roles of men and women. Unlike many religious Jews in Poland, many Zionists made a point of learning Hebrew, sometimes even rejecting Yiddish, the primary language of Polish Jews. Zionist socialists were most active in organizing the pioneering Zionist movements for younger Polish Jews, including those in Dąbrowa.

Even though moving to Palestine was a goal of many who joined, in truth less than five percent of Polish Jewry (139,756 people) emigrated to Palestine between 1918 and 1942.[5] Often that was simply because of the strict quotas and controls the British had placed on Jewish emigration to Palestine, or because the cost of emigrating was often too high for many poor Jews. Still, they may have practiced for eventual migration to Palestine, that is, making *Aliyah*, one of the core tenets of Zionism. Aliyah literally means the "act of going up" (in this case to Jerusalem), and is likewise used at Sabbath services where members of the congregation are given an Aliyah to go up and stand at the reading of the Torah.

Chaja already seemed liberated: she enjoyed working in the family businesses and would have taken charge if things had gone differently. She had gained a high school education in one of the Agudath's Beit Yaakov schools for girls in Dąbrowa. The curricula incorporated lessons on the Torah (something Chaja's mother would never have been formally taught) as well as practical subjects. This school network began in 1917 and expanded across Poland. By 1938 there were 250 branches across the country. Chaja may also have been attracted to a Tarbut school, in which young people could learn Hebrew. These schools aimed to transform Hebrew into a living language. Chaja actually would have been one of a relatively small handful of Jewish girls who went beyond the compulsory six or seven years of schooling to attend a gymnasium, which encompassed the middle and high school years.

However, antisemitism had been a constant undercurrent throughout life in Poland for hundreds of years. It has been said that Jews were Poland's Blacks. Other rules applied to them. They often lived segregated from the rest of the population, whether by choice or by law. They developed their own culture, kept their language and often attended their own schools. They faced continuous discrimination regarding where they could work, the schools they could attend and the economic, political and social opportunities available to them.

Still, the years between 1926 and 1935 saw progress for Jews under the rule of Polish World War I war hero General Jozef Pilsudski. He served as the Chief of State and First Marshal of Poland after the end of World War I and was then considered the *de facto* leader of the Second Polish Republic when he led a coup d'état in 1926 and became Poland's strongman. Unlike his chief political opponents, who were nationalists and sought to promote a Roman Catholic identity, he believed in a multi-ethnic Poland that encompassed and welcomed religious minorities, including Jews.

Unfortunately, with the onset of the global Great Depression and then the rise of the right-wing National Democratic Party (Endecja) after Pilsudski's death in 1935, the lot of Polish Jews took a drastic turn for the worse. The Endeks (the name given to the party's supporters) launched a relentless campaign to promote antisemitism and periodic economic boycotts of Jewish stores across Poland with the ultimate aim of creating an ethnically pure country that would largely exclude Jews. Indeed, Jews suffered greatly from these boycotts, a nonviolent form of economic warfare that played the main role in the impoverishment of Polish Jews at the time.[6]

During the same period, the government felt pressured to adopt a variety of other anti-Jewish measures. These led to a revival of pogroms and violent physical attacks on Jewish people. Ethno-nationalistic stances gained popularity, and by the late 1930s there was a visible increase in discriminatory laws targeting Jews in ways that were meant to motivate their emigration.

For instance, the Endecja party introduced the term "Christian shop" in the late 1930s as it sought a national boycott of Jewish businesses and advocated for their confiscation. A national movement was also organized to prevent Jews from carrying out the core Jewish belief and tradition of kosher slaughter of animals, with animal rights as the stated motivation. Violence was frequently aimed at Jewish stores, many of which were also looted and their windows broken. Jews were sometimes attacked. Jewish shopkeepers suddenly lost most of their non-Jewish customers. The economic impact was devastating.

Deteriorating economic conditions overall also had a severe effect on agricultural countries like Poland, reducing the living standards of Poles and Polish Jews alike. By the end of the 1930s, a substantial portion of Polish Jews lived in poverty. And though the Jewish community in Poland was large and vibrant internally, it was also, with the exception of a relatively small number of professionals, substantially poorer and less integrated than the Jews in most of Western Europe. Aid both from the American Jewish Joint Distribution Committee and other Jewish charities in Europe and the US poured in to help poor and lower middle-class Jews.

Still worse news lay ahead. In January 1937, Polish Foreign Minister Józef Beck declared that Poland could house only 500,000 Jews.

Almost 3.5 million Jews lived there at the time. Therefore Beck and his party hoped that 80,000–100,000 Jews would leave Poland each year. Toward that end, Poland actually supported the creation of a Jewish state in Palestine, hoping gradual emigration there would reduce the Jewish population in Poland to the target number.[7] To speed up that process, Poland also cooperated with Ze'ev Jabotinsky, the leader of Revisionist Zionism, who hoped Poland would inherit the mandate of Palestine from Great Britain. His "Evacuation Plan" called for settling 1.5 million Jews, including 750,000 Polish Jews, in Palestine within 10 years. This idea was warmly received by the Polish government, which was pursuing a policy of mass emigration for its Jewish population and looking for locations in which to resettle them.

Ironically, one result was that the antisemitic Polish government did its best to circumvent British official policy related to Palestine. For example, in the 1930s Poland actively supported the Irgun, a military arm of Revisionist Zionism, and trained its members in the Tatra Mountains. According to Irgun activists, the Polish state supplied the organization with 25,000 rifles, additional materiel and weapons, and by the summer of 1939, Irgun's Warsaw warehouses held 5,000 rifles and 1,000 machine guns. Training and support from Poland allowed the organization to mobilize 30,000–40,000 men in Palestine.[8] As early as 1937, Poland issued passports to facilitate illegal immigration to Palestine and also supplied the Haganah, the military arm of Zionism, with weapons.

At the same time, the Polish government was trying to resettle Polish Jews beyond Palestine. One major initiative that ended nowhere was to ship the Jews en masse to the island of Madagascar, off the southeast African coast. Poland's Nazi neighbors in Germany actually welcomed the "Madagaskar-Projekt," intended to deport up to four million Jews from Austria, Germany and eventually other areas of Europe. In 1936, Léon Blum became the first Jewish prime minister of France, setting the stage for cooperative efforts to resettle Polish Jewry in the French colony. At the instigation of the Polish Foreign Ministry, and with the agreement of the French authorities, a three-man delegation set out on a fact-finding mission to Madagascar in May 1937. Their arduous journey included a long sea voyage followed by what was surely a bone-rattling car ride on potholed roads and finally an overland march of several days to tour possible sites of settlement. The commission's report ultimately expressed muted optimism for the venture. Two of the members felt that settling Madagascar would be nearly impossible due to the inhospitable climate and widespread malarial swamps. One warned that it would be "especially difficult to convince the shtetl Jews... to settle on the soil."[9]

Thus, although it is the fourth largest island in the world, Madagascar, with its jungles and mountains, was ill suited for a generally urbanized Polish Jewish population. The most generous estimates indicated that no settlement would number more than several thousand. Kraków's Jewish population alone (a quarter of the city total) was 60,000. It was not to be.

Instead, anti-Jewish sentiment grew. Jewish students in high schools and colleges were forced to stand during classes, and eventually their numbers were reduced by official and unofficial edicts and quotas. Store owners were attacked, and violent acts against Jews increased markedly, surpassing the latent antisemitism that remained a constant undercurrent through much of Polish history. In the Polish state schools that both Szlama and Chaja would have attended in the early grades, Jews had to sit separately from Polish Christians. Dąbrowa did not escape this fresh wave of antisemitism. By the late 1930s, hate crimes against Jews were commonplace in Dąbrowa, including instances of Jews being thrown off electric trains and street cars, according to one account.[10]

Meanwhile, the politics of the day had its effect on the couple and their future plans. They no doubt experienced the daily effects of the powerful waves of antisemitism and discrimination pervading Poland, even as the growing influence of Nazi Germany next door spilled over its borders to its neighbor to the east. In the 1939 municipal elections in Dąbrowa, many of the town's Jews voted for the Socialist Polish party, hoping to curb the power of the right-wing antisemitic parties.[11]

It was then that their love and their shared desire to start a family suddenly took on a new level of urgency. Chaja and Szlama married on December 28, 1937 at 11 a.m. in Dąbrowa, with Rabbi Gael (Gecel/Giesl) Dychtwald (Dichtwald) officiating.[12] Rabbi Dychtwald was murdered in Auschwitz a few years later. Chaja was 30 and my father had just turned 26. Izaac Parasol was one of the witnesses. My father also officially registered his new wife at his mother's address in Będzin.

This marriage was preceded by three readings of the banns issued in the Dąbrowa synagogue on 11, 18 and 25 December 1937. The readings of the banns represented a long established custom and were meant to announce the groom's intentions to marry and then allow anyone in the congregation to voice an objection or concern.

Marriage customs, especially the wedding ceremony, remained largely unchanged, even as the traditional reliance on matchmaking was transformed during the interwar years in Poland. Prenuptial agreements included the *nadn* or dowry and the *kest*, the obligation of the bride or groom's parents to support the new couple for a specified period. Szlama was to receive the generous dowry of partial ownership of the large, sprawling Kotlicki/Parasol family house and grounds. Later in Sweden, he would try to claim that dowry as he sought desperately to support what would become his second family.

As it turned out, my father was already living in the Kotlicki household before his marriage, perhaps as a boarder so he wouldn't have to commute from Będzin, where most of his Frydman family relatives lived and worked. The married couple stayed in Dąbrowa for the most part, though they did briefly rent a small apartment in Będzin near Szlama's mother and sister.

Still, there may have been another reason for my father moving into the family compound well before the marriage. I experienced an epiphany about my father and Chaja when the official record, the registration of their marriage by Rabbi Dychtwald, revealed the date of their marriage and the official registration of the birthdate of the couple's first child.

According to the official records, the marriage of Szlama and Chaja took place only a couple of months before the birth of their first child, a girl named Ada. I was surprised, if not somewhat shocked, that two young people brought up in the Jewish Orthodox tradition[13] that Chaja would have experienced in her household would conceive a child outside of marriage, especially back then. The evidence suggests Chaja would have been some six or seven months pregnant at the time of the wedding. Yet despite this seeming reality, they were not disowned, thrown out of their Orthodox households or written out of the family's significant fortune. Indeed, the situation seemed just the opposite.

As was often the case during the later stages of this research, I had to rely on Matan Shefi, a wise professional researcher and guide who helped arrange our 2018 visit to Poland to research this book, to remind me of the reality of their lives and the complicated world they lived in.

When I asked what he thought of what I had concluded from the records, he said, "I don't think that was either shocking or outrageous. Those things happened." He continued, "First, I would not state with high certainty that the date we have for the civic registry is the one for the ceremony. We need to understand that in many cases, the civic marriage and the religious one are not happening together, or even in proximity. So there is the possibility that the actual religious marriage happened a year or so earlier (1936?) and all they say in the civil registry is made up.

"Also, even if they married when she was seven months pregnant, if he married her eventually it would not be a major scandal at the time, just a minor one, as it was resolved. You can find such cases in books, novels or other stories, so I guess it's not that drastic."

I started to hunt through what might have been the "religious" perspective and concluded that although their situation was certainly unorthodox, especially for that time, it was not necessarily the *shanda* (disgrace, in Yiddish) one might have imagined. After all, we know that Chaja's family did not shun her or banish her from the family's very comfortable compound in Dąbrowa around the time of their wedding. In fact, my father lived in that compound under the same roof as his future in-laws for at least six months before the wedding ceremony took place under the traditional *chupah*. He was also promised a generous dowry, which might have been further complicated by the circumstances of the wedding. He nevertheless was welcomed into the family, at least outwardly. After all, even though these two young people were clearly from different economic classes, circumstances and backgrounds, they had worked together in a family business and found that they shared a vision of the future, even in those most perilous times for Jews across Poland. If their families accepted them, who was I to be shocked?

Matan acknowledged that this was a difficult situation. The letters my father wrote from Sweden to a lawyer in Poland pointed to complications in recording the ownership of the property promised to him as part of his dowry. He intended to sell his share of the property after the war to help fund the new life he sought in America. It was then that he discovered that despite the promise of the dowry, the property was never formally recorded in his name. Moreover, he reported that Chaja didn't trust her parents because on the eve of the marriage they had tried to temporarily put the property into the name of one of her sisters, for what they said were practical considerations. At some point after that it was to be transferred from the family to Szlama, but there was no record of that happening and therefore no way to prove his claim.

Some other explanations about premarital relations and Judaism make sense. According to one source: "The Torah does not outlaw premarital sex, as it does many other types of sexual relationships, and the child of such a union is not considered illegitimate."[14] In addition, according to a rabbi who was queried: "Jewish law would say that when a couple is living together, that in effect is a consummation of marriage and it becomes like a common-law marriage whether the couple realizes it or not."[15]

The other point to be made, since I assume both Szlama and Chaja shared an intense devotion to the tenets of Zionism, is that they both respected the rights and privileges of a modern independent Zionist woman, along with the changing cultural norms and independence that stance might have implied.

I apologize for this digression, even if I thought it is worth noting. I believe, as Matan counseled, that these two people had been in love for some time. When they married was incidental to that love. No matter what others thought, Szlama and Chaja were pleased to begin their life together, in every sense.

The Kotlickis cannot add their perspective, and I have no wish to criticize or cast aspersions on my father, Chaja or any other members of her family. Suffice it to say, theirs was a love story from the start till the end. In a world turned upside down and a search amidst memories clouded by years of concentration camp deprivations, the records may have been wrong or missing, as my father later discovered concerning the dowry. Often, nothing is as it seems, especially more than 80 years later.

Whatever the backstory accompanying the wedding, the outcome was perfect, and having their first child was clearly the sweet icing on the cake. On February 14, 1938, they celebrated the birth of Ada, born at home at 11 a.m. with the help of Chaja's oldest sister, Leah, who was a professional midwife. I suspect that the day she was born was the happiest day of my father's life up till then. They had a second child nearly three years later, though under more trying circumstances.

PART III

THE WAR YEARS: SZLAMA

FINALLY, A FATHER'S TALE

Late in August 1970 when I was a senior in college, I found myself worrying about the possibility that I would be drafted to fight in the Vietnam War. I had drawn a low number in a draft lottery, so being a student would not protect me from conscription. However, I had recently learned that I might be able to avoid wartime service by way of something called an emotional draft deferment, for which I might qualify if I could prove that someone close to me was emotionally dependent on my availability and safety. Both my parents clearly fit in that category, as they continued to suffer from the emotional trauma of losing nearly every member of their families during the Holocaust. It was therefore truthful to state that if I left the US to put myself in harm's way, the trauma of anticipating another loss would be too much for them to bear. I needed statements from both my parents, which I drafted on their behalf. Although my mother had talked about some of her wartime losses, I knew virtually nothing about my father's first family.

A few days before I was to appear before the draft board to make my case, I sat down with my father to hear his story for the first time in both my life and his. It had been nearly 30 years since he lost his wife and his two young daughters. He spoke to me in Yiddish, softly and sadly, yet methodically. He didn't look at me. Instead he stared ahead at the waves crashing on the beach where we sat while he recalled or perhaps relived the details of the last time he saw his first family alive.

"It was August 1942, and the German soldiers were rounding up Jews where we lived," he said. "They told us to bring one suitcase each and to assemble in the town square. We were afraid and worried of being sent into the unknown, so we decided to hide from the soldiers in an attic near where we lived. That night, I went out to organize some food. We had two little girls; one was still a baby. But when I returned, they were all gone. I knew they had been discovered. The Germans arrested me the next day. The only thing they left on the floor of that attic was my wife's pink sweater. I took that with me and kept it with me in the concentration camp. But I didn't know for certain what had happened to them. I was so worried, but what could I do?"

In telling this story, my father never mentioned their names or their ages, what town they were in or which concentration camp he went to. I thought I had pried enough and didn't want to upset him further, so I didn't ask. The last thing he told me was that toward the end of the war, as the Russian soldiers were approaching, the Germans had evacuated his concentration camp and marched the prisoners to another camp. That camp was Bergen-Belsen.

"I remember spending a night at a farm," he added, "where I met someone I knew from my hometown but had never seen in the camp. He told me he had seen my wife and children on the ramp where the train let them off at Auschwitz. He said that they took the children from my wife but she wouldn't let go of them. So she went with them and the other children and old people to the gas chambers. That's how I found out that they were killed in Auschwitz."

My father finally faced me. He sighed deeply, and his voice cracked. "So I took that pink sweater that I had been carrying for years and left it on a stack of hay in the barn."

A day or two later I appeared before my draft board in Coney Island. After reading my father's statement and my mother's, in which she enumerated the loss of her husband, brothers and parents, no one on the board asked any questions. All the chairman said was: "Deferment granted. God bless your parents."

As I said, that was the first time my father ever spoke about his first family. I was 20 years old and he was 60. It was also the last time we ever spoke about what happened to him and his family during the war. It was only upon writing this book that I learned anything more about the probable details of the night when they were taken, or about the camps, his wife and his little girls. I still remember the day I learned the names of these two girls, just a few years ago. I sobbed. I didn't know what they looked like, but when I discovered their names for the first time I saw them as real people, as innocents murdered. We shared our DNA with them, but they were not members of my family. Still, I thought now I knew them, if only just a little bit. I took a moment to imagine, if it was possible, the terror that these little girls felt. It was then and still is horrible. The effect it had on my father is also unknowable and, I realize, fully unimaginable.

I had no reason to doubt what my father had said. I knew him to be a religious man who didn't lie. He may not have been particularly forthcoming, but if he spoke, I knew him to be honest. And even today, as I have come to a better understanding of what might actually have happened, I can appreciate how he could have believed his own story. Maybe it's because he had to.

Here's what his journey was like during those years.

BĘDZIN

On September 4, 1939, the German army entered the city of Będzin, where most of my father's remaining family lived. Five days later they burned down the Great Synagogue in the Old City. By then my father was married and living a few kilometers away in Dąbrowa with his wife and daughter. Their second child wasn't born yet.

In Będzin, meanwhile, the Holocaust was about to descend in earnest.[1] About 50 houses surrounding the Great Synagogue and inhabited exclusively by Jews were also burned. Sixty Jews died in the fires in both the houses and the synagogue. Soldiers shot some as they fled. Others weren't allowed to escape the flames. But even after the initial and continuing terror in Będzin in 1940 and 1941, the situation in Będzin was considered preferable to the outlook in many other parts of occupied Poland. Będzin and its neighbor Sosnowiec were, for some time at least, the only large cities in Poland with no ghettos. For this reason, thousands of Jews fled central Poland to seek refuge in Będzin. Furthermore, several thousand Jews from the district were expelled from their own towns and forced to reside in Będzin. Among them were some Jews from the town of Oświęcim[2] who arrived in Będzin prior to the construction of the Auschwitz concentration camp.

Conditions continued to deteriorate. Acts of terror by the Nazis became commonplace in and around Będzin, though the first deportations of Jews to concentration or extermination camps didn't take place until May 1942, when several thousand people from Będzin were sent to their deaths or forced labor in Auschwitz. On August 1, 1942 there was a second deportation in which some 5,000 Jews were sent to Auschwitz and a small number were shot on the spot.

Left: Szlama's sister Estera (1930). Right: Estera 10 years later, in a picture taken for an ID card in the Będzin Ghetto.

Also in May 1942, the Będzin Ghetto was formally established in East Upper Silesia. At that point, more than 20,000 Jews from Będzin and approximately 10,000 Jews from other areas who had been resettled in Będzin were moved into the ghetto. It is clear that Szlama's entire family was swept up in the deportations. A few records indicate that several of them, including his mother Chana, his sister Blima and Blima's family, with whom she lived at Modrzejowska 47, were in the Będzin Ghetto, having been moved to Potockiego 5. Estera Dwojra Frydman was moved to Jasna 4. We found a picture of her taken there, in which she seemed to have aged dramatically compared to another picture we found of her from 1930. I assume all these people were subsequently sent to Auschwitz or Belzec and murdered there. My father tried to locate his sisters after the war, obviously without success. I never did find out what became of my father's younger brother Jochim.

THE SLAVE LABOR CAMPS

Despite having an address in Będzin in 1939, Szlama was living in Dąbrowa with his new family, practically next door to Będzin and about to share the same fate as his mother, sisters, brother and so many others in their family. Within a day or two after war broke out, the Germans entered Dąbrowa and began rounding up the 5,000–6,000 resident Jews, "kidnapping" able-bodied young men, my father among them, eventually to work as slave laborers in other parts of Poland or Germany. The Nazis were eager to make use of the mines and foundries in the area. However, they did not want the Jews. Within a month, all Jews were compelled to wear the Star of David. They were forbidden to engage in trade or leave their houses after 7 p.m. and were also subjected to other restrictions. Jews, especially those wearing beards, were harassed mercilessly. German soldiers cut off their beards with knives. Jewish men caught on the street without permission were forced to dig their own graves and then shot. In April 1940, the Jews in the town were moved into the Dąbrowa Ghetto.

Izzy Randel, then a teenager growing up in Dąbrowa, recalls the day the Germans came. "We first heard the roar of the motorcycles, five hundred of them. These were followed by goose-stepping soldiers...

The people of Dąbrowa shivered with fear, we were that scared."[1] It turned out their fears were not unfounded, to say the least. Randel recalls that "every day we saw many killings. If someone was waiting in a line for food and had a beard, he could be shot, and often was. If a person forgot to bend his head to a passing German, he could be shot."

Within a month of the establishment of the ghetto, my father became one of the slave laborers who were sent away. His first experience came at *Arbeitslager* Grädiz.[2] The prisoners there cut and carried wood and did other heavy work, including road construction. Not until very recently, in some newfound documents, did I learn just how sudden my father's disappearance into the slave labor camp system had been. He recalled this in testimony related to a reparations claim. He said, "Each day we were supposed to report to the courtyard in front of the city's municipal administration to get work assignments. One day, it was in May 1940, as we gathered in the courtyard, suddenly we were surrounded by members of the Gestapo with weapons. They started hitting and beating people and screaming at us. We were all arrested and from there we were put on trains and taken to a transit camp in nearby Sosnowiec, and then to Grädiz, about 500 kilometers to the northwest." He wasn't even given the opportunity say goodbye to his wife and young child. He stayed in the Grädiz camp till about December 1940.

Grädiz was deep in Germany, 45 miles northwest of Dresden and about 12 hours by train from Dąbrowa. A survivor of that camp who was interviewed by a US Holocaust Memorial Museum representative reported that the conditions there were "horrible, with people dying right and left," and added that "with no water, no soap, people could not wash or clean. We were so filthy so everybody had lice."[3] Inmates were only ever seen as temporary, and from the Nazis' standpoint they could always be replaced with others; hence the complete disregard for the prisoners' health. They were subject to shortages of food, medicine and clothing while working long hours with little or no time for rest or breaks. As a result of these conditions, death rates in labor camps were extremely high. One prisoner described receiving her scant portion of food: "You swallowed so fast that you don't even know you're eating. But if you make a ceremony out of it and prepare, you simply know you have eaten."[4]

In Grädiz, Szlama worked for the Mittelstahl Company, which was located there as part of the much larger Flick industrial enterprise. It produced the steel used in armor plating for German submarines, ships, tanks and other fighting vehicles. The camp workers also made 250 and 500 pound bombs. At the Nuremberg trials after the war, Flick's founder, Friedrich, was found guilty of using approximately 48,000 forced laborers during the war, including my father. Szlama, as it would turn out, was one of the "lucky ones," given that about 80 percent of these workers died because of the way they were treated during their slave labor at Grädiz. Although Flick was found guilty of war crimes in 1947, he was pardoned after three years in prison and then resumed control of his conglomerate, for a time becoming the richest person in what had become West Germany.

After that first stint, my father was transferred to the Laurahütte labor camp in Siemianowice near Katowice – about 12 kilometers from Dąbrowa – for some eight months until July or August 1941. This camp would later be transformed into a subcamp of Auschwitz. Laurahütte was primarily known for its huge iron works. Initially he was assigned to heavy labor and construction work, including building structures, roads and bridges for a company called Holzbau. He was worked so hard that he later admitted, "My strength failed and for a time I had to be brought to the camp hospital." He was probably involved in the construction of another related forced labor camp called Faulbrück. Among other tasks, his labor also may have been connected to war-related armaments and chemical production, some of which was being developed to support the German industrial conglomerate I.G. Farben. He either loaded and unloaded gravel or moved heavy cement blocks on trolleys. At other times he might have been making iron ropes used by concrete workers. The camp was located in a town that also housed the Laura foundry, where cannons were produced for the German navy.

Szlama might have spent some time being shuttled around other, smaller labor camps in the first few years of the war. They remain unrecorded, but it is known that all these camps initially were part of what became known as the Organisation Schmelt, an SS organization run by Albrecht Schmelt, the police chief in Breslau. The Organisation Schmelt became a forced labor camp system supporting the German armaments and construction industries in the region. As the war progressed, these slave labor camps were eventually transformed into sub-camps of larger concentration camps and camp systems controlled and guarded by the SS. Then conditions worsened as the Germans' aim metamorphosed from forced slave labor to the complete extermination and annihilation of all Jews.

Jews who were assigned to other camps or living in ghettos in the region were further integrated into an evolving Nazi labor strategy that required slaves to enable and support the Nazi war machine. That was one reason these ghettos were not liquidated as quickly as they might have been in other parts of Poland. Silesia boasted rich coal reserves on both the Polish and the German sides of the border and was therefore a perfect location for steel and quarry works. In the first two years or so after the German invasion, existing labor camps were modified and expanded. In the autumn of 1941, more than a year and a half after my father had entered the slave labor system, the Germans began to conscript more people from Dąbrowa and the surrounding region for forced labor.

By early 1943, the Schmelt system extended to 160 labor camps and held more than 50,000 Jewish forced laborers, including my father. Schmelt, a pragmatic businessman, focused on deriving maximum profit from his laborers. By 1945, more than 14 million people had been exploited in a network of hundreds of forced labor camps stretching across the whole of Nazi-occupied Europe.

The concept of slave labor was stated quite simply by Nazi Minister of Justice Otto Thierack, who declared, "Killing Jews through work is best." And although tension existed between the Nazi priority of exterminating all Jews on the one hand and the immediate need for labor to produce armaments and other wartime supplies on the other, there was never any question or disagreement about the ultimate aim. Here Schmelt found common cause with Heinrich Himmler, the main organizer of the extermination plan for Jews: "To delay their immediate removal and replace it with work to the death."

Nevertheless, Schmelt allowed mail to flow until July 1943, considering it a good propaganda tool that boosted productivity and controlled the anxiety of those left at home. Sadly, no letters exchanged between Szlama and Chaja or with other members of his family still exist. Also, in winter and on some holidays laborers were sometimes sent back to their ghettos to be with their families, at least in areas like Dąbrowa. Of course, this was only in the first few years. Later, the Organisation Schmelt would be replaced by the concentration camp system, with its own labor and its killing components.

During this period, my father likely managed to return to Dąbrowa several times in late 1940 and 1941. He would have had the proper documentation to travel the rails, and with his family as hostages and the German Army monitoring his movements and activities in Dąbrowa, he would have been compelled to return to his camp after any visit. His second child might have been conceived on one of these rare and precious visits during this terrifying period in late 1940. He joined Chaja and Ada and may also have had some contact with his mother and sisters in neighboring Będzin.

The good news first: Szlama and Chaja welcomed their second child, a girl they named Feigla – Yiddish for little bird. She was born at 4 p.m. on June 15, 1941, in the same house where they once had lived as a family. However, it was now part of the Dąbrowa Ghetto and therefore was crowded with many neighbors as well as strangers, with perhaps as many as six or seven people living in the same room. Chaja's eldest sister Leah was again at her side as midwife.

After that, the facts get fuzzier. According to Szlama's 1945 DP interview, a few months after Feigla's birth he was transferred to a third camp, this time in Bunzlau (Bolesławiec in Polish), located more than 300 kilometers (200 miles) to the northwest near the village of Gross Rosen, close to what once was the border between Poland and Germany. At Laurahütte, it had been a short distance to his family, but now it was unclear how often he would be able to visit, if visiting was allowed at all anymore.

Indeed it may have been that after Laurahütte in August 1941, he hadn't yet gone to Bunzlau, but instead was allowed to work for the local government as a slave laborer on construction projects, staying in Dąbrowa for some eight or nine months and thus able to enjoy his wife and family for what would be the last time. It is possible that he didn't have to go to Bunzlau until May 1942, when more Jewish forced laborers were conscripted and sent to labor camps in the Breslau region. It was then that he may have joined a group of 300 young Jewish men from Dąbrowa at Bunzlau.[5]

During this same period, on May 2, 1942 the Germans initiated the first of the larger and more significant organized deportation *Aktions* in Dąbrowa. The *Judenrat* (the Jewish council administering German orders) was required to prepare a list of 650–700 residents of the ghetto who would be permitted to bring 10 kilograms (just 22 pounds) of personal luggage as well as food. They presented themselves in the square facing the Jewish council building and were then deported to Auschwitz.

A niece of Chaja's survived the war and recalled some of what took place.

Ada Lewenberg[6] was the daughter of Chaja's eldest sister, Leah. Born in 1900 in Dąbrowa, Leah had married Mauric (Mendel Moritz) Lewenberg and had two daughters: Frida, born in 1917, and Ada, born on May 19, 1926. Leah and Mauric were murdered in Auschwitz, but both daughters survived. Ada was first consigned to slave labor in a munitions factory and then sent to the Ravensbrück concentration camp in Germany. She became one of the fortunate Ravensbrück inmates who in 1945 were traded for a large payment in gold as part of a deal struck earlier that year between Swedish Red Cross vice president Count Folke Bernadotte and Heinrich Himmler, which resulted in the release of 14,000 female prisoners, 2,000 of them Jewish. She was eventually transported to Denmark and then to Sweden in what became known as the White Busses. From there she emigrated to Melbourne, Australia, where she gave testimony about her family for Steven Spielberg's USC/Shoah project in 1997, a few years before she passed away.

Ada's father had his own jewelry shop on Dąbrowa's main shopping street. Nearby was her uncle's fancy goods shop, which probably was where my father met his wife Chaja. The Kotlicki grandparents lived in the family compound as well. Ada recalled the difficult days of the antisemitic Jewish economic boycotts throughout Poland in the late 1930s. "When antisemites came and used to block people from coming into our shop, giving papers to people passing by not to buy from us, my father grabbed the papers from the person distributing them. When I saw that, I was frightened that they may come back to kill him." She also talked about life after the war broke out, when the shortages began. Her grandmother's family, the Parasols, also had a big store in Będzin where they sold food wholesale, so in those early days lack of food wasn't yet a major issue, though it would become one very soon. Rather than staying in the Dąbrowa Ghetto, as many others in her extended family did, she and her family were moved to the nearby Kamionka Ghetto, a ghetto for Będzin and neighboring areas that was established in the Kamionka neighborhood of Będzin and bordered on the Sosnowiec Ghetto. When those ghettos were liquidated, she and her family were sent to Auschwitz-Birkenau. The selection that took place there was the last time she saw her parents.

Ada could never leave behind what happened to her and her family. She recalled her lasting memory of Auschwitz-Birkenau. "When we went inside to the barracks, we would smell the bones of children from the ovens. When they were burning, you could see the redness in the sky and smell the human bones when some were burned alive... I still wake up sometimes when I dream the Germans are after me. In the dream I would run, full of sweat, into a ditch. I was so upset after the war that I used to take antidepressants for a very long time."

Back in the Dąbrowa Ghetto things were more or less predictable: random shootings, humiliations, punishments, privation. For the several thousand Jews who were native to Dąbrowa, the terror was everywhere. People were selected for various infractions, from deliberately lying or trying to hide something or someone, to buying bread on the private market: anything and everything.

During the spring and summer of 1942, selections and transports of Jews to be killed or imprisoned and worked to death continued intermittently. Chaja and the girls survived the earlier selections, as Szlama was serving in Bunzlau, until only 3,000 Jews remained in Dąbrowa. At the same time, the ghetto itself was expanded by the resettlement of thousands of additional Jews from neighboring towns. By August 1942, more than 30,000 people, mostly children, women and older people, had been sent to Auschwitz and killed there immediately, without registration.

The *Aktion* of August 12, 1942 became known as "The Great Turning Point." This day would signal the end of Szlama's family. On one day, at the same hour, some 60,000 Jews were rounded up from the entire district. At 7 a.m., Jews were ordered to assembly points throughout Zagłębie, the industrial district that included Dąbrowa, Będzin, Sosnowiec and Katowice. In Dąbrowa, the Jews were ordered to present themselves at 8 a.m. in front of the community building for registration and selection. They complied with these orders, most of them dressed in their best clothes. The selection process began at 10 a.m. on the order of Friedrich Kochinsky of the Organisation Schmelt. Kochinsky represented SS Officer Dreier, who was in charge of all the deportations from Zagłębie that day.[7] In fact, a parallel *Aktion* was taking place in Będzin, where all remaining Jews were ordered to assemble at the city's main soccer field. They were divided into four groups: those employed in factories, those to be transferred to slave labor camps in Germany, those who were to be deported for extermination in Auschwitz and some whose fate was yet to be determined. No records were kept of those taken directly from the trains to the gas chambers.

Back in Dąbrowa, the head of the German killing squads, known as *Sonderkommandos*, arrived and began to segregate the people. Jews were divided into three groups: people with work permits, families in which one or more member had a work permit, and adults or families with children. Each person was then sent to one of three areas. The three distinctions translated into a first group used for work details, a second group awaiting further examinations and a third group destined for deportation, i.e., extermination. People in the second area were later merged with those in the third area. All were deported.

Of the 3,000 Jews present at the selection that morning, 1,500 were sent home. The rest were marked for deportation. They stayed in the square under guard all night. A torrential rainstorm gave some an opportunity to flee the square and go into hiding. The following morning, those remaining were transported to the Będzin Ghetto, where they stayed before being transported to Auschwitz along with Jews from Będzin and Sosnowiec. The Jews in the labor groups left in Dąbrowa were concentrated in the ghetto, which had been sealed following the *Aktion*. A *Volksdeutsche*, defined as a Polish citizen of German origin, was put in charge of the ghetto residents. The overcrowding in the ghetto was extreme.

By August 17, just five days later, most had been sent to Auschwitz for extermination. From what I could piece together, Chaja, a young, strong woman, had a choice to make upon her arrival in Auschwitz: leave her children to their fate, which was death, and become a laborer, or stay with them.[8] She chose to stay with them, whether or not she realized what her fate would be. She was murdered alongside her children shortly after they got off the train on the ramp at Auschwitz. Her daughter Ada was four and a half years old. Ada's little sister Feigla was a little over a year old and had just started to walk.

What about the story my father told about his last days in hiding with his family in Dąbrowa? It is of course possible that everything he said happened the way he described it. Perhaps he was in Dąbrowa on leave from his slave labor and thus was with his family during that fateful August 1942 *Aktion*. Maybe he was on leave from Bunzlau, which was still a slave labor camp in the Organisation Schmelt system that had not yet been transformed into a concentration camp. Perhaps during the downpour they were dismissed for the night and he hid with his wife and two daughters, with no intention of returning.

My doubts have mainly to do with the fact that Bunzlau was quite a distance from Dąbrowa, and he had fairly recently arrived at a place that was already being transformed into a concentration camp, a prison with no possible escape or return to Dąbrowa. There were no passes issued from concentration camps. Even if it was possible to leave at the tail end of a slave labor stint, why would the Germans have given him leave to go home, knowing what they had planned for Dąbrowa and the mass deportations? Also, if we assume that he had arrived in Bunzlau only a few months earlier (or even a year earlier), why would the Germans allow him to take a home leave at that point, given that the entire system was transitioning toward concentration and extermination camps for all Jews?

Finally, if Chaja did indeed hide out, whether with Szlama or by herself with the children, why would the Germans have arrested my father that second night and then sent him to Auschwitz, only to then have him leave Auschwitz right away for Bunzlau? He would have had to go on a transport, but I couldn't find any record of it. Or, if it was a home leave, after hiding from the Gestapo, why would the Germans trust Szlama to go back to Bunzlau on his own? They had already disappeared the hostages who would have ensured his compliance. They would more likely simply have killed him on the spot or made him a slave laborer in Auschwitz, which had similar facilities.

An interview conducted with Szlama after he was resettled in Halmstad, Sweden, once indicated that he said he had arrived with his family in Auschwitz on August 12, 1942. I doubt that, given that other interviews he gave at the DP camp after his liberation made no mention of him ever being in Auschwitz. He may have misunderstood the question, or the person transcribing his answers may have misunderstood what he said. In fact, in a letter he wrote in relation to his dowry claim in August 1947, he noted that his entire family was deported to Auschwitz that day in August 1942, though this time he added, "I was in Germany at work in that time." So he was in Bunzlau as I suspected.

I have come to believe that my father reimagined parts of his story, including the sweater he talked about at the beginning of this chapter. It may have been an article of clothing his wife liked, or one he liked, so he may have held onto it symbolically in his heart, rather than physically. Perhaps he sincerely wished to be with his family at that time to try to protect them or to join them in their fate, but was instead at work at the time, breaking rocks in a German quarry. Like so many other survivors, he likely suffered from a heavy load of survivor guilt or shame. He needed to believe that he had done his best and stayed by his family until they were captured; that he had tried to protect them. They may have hidden, but I just can't see how he could have been there with them in those final days. Then again, there is so much we don't know and never will.

Some of that survivor guilt or shame derived from his initial forced recruitment into the slave labor system. Perhaps he decided in retrospect that he should have gone into hiding with them much earlier. Maybe he could instead have refused to leave his family when he was assigned to a slave labor camp, or returned and then hid with them during his home leave visit. He obviously didn't do any of those things. Of course, if he had refused to go to Gräditz or Laurahütte, the odds are he would have been executed on the spot. Perhaps some part of him thought he should have done just that: taken his chances, fought back with his bare hands and died an honorable death with the Sh'ma on his lips and his family by his side.

What would I, or anyone reading this, have done? There are no good answers, only more questions. I could never judge him. Surviving is not a crime, and he did not sacrifice his family for his own sake. Indeed, for many, hiding did not seem necessary (though generally not possible) until it became more widely understood that the Jews who were moved to camps were actually being exterminated. Of course, it would have been especially difficult to really hide. Jews may have spoken Polish, but a Jewish accent would give them away. Moreover, anyone hiding Jews would also have had to feed them at a time when food was exceedingly scarce and being rationed, and anyone found hiding Jews would have also been killed. And to hide with two little children – for years?

What's more, at least in those years up to the summer of 1942, being a slave laborer – even in a horrible camp –meant that his family was protected and provided with food for a time. The family units of slave laborers were considered productive and therefore would have been treated a bit better than others. In effect, my father was helping to feed and protect his family even as he labored far from their home, at least at first. It all suddenly became illusory when the Nazis invaded the Soviet Union in mid- to late-1941 and realized they could quickly murder many thousands of Jews through the use of special mobile killing squads, which made the option of using mass murder a reality. The only questions were how that effort could be made more productive and how the murderers could distance themselves from their victims. In response, gas chambers were developed and incorporated into the concentration camp system.

I can certainly imagine how, during those long years of solitude in the concentration camps, Szlama might have found himself reliving those doubts and decisions again and again. Hence the story he told me, and his long reluctance to share it or, even after doing so, to share anything else about the war ever again. It is also reasonable to understand how his brain could have reintegrated facts and memories to give him some peace of mind or to cope with the disorientation of the concentration camp experience. Creating a story he could believe in and live with itself became a mechanism of survival.

I saw him answer questions about where he was during the war and noticed that he provided a wide range of answers at different times and places. Who would know what time of day or day of the week or what year it was, amidst so much trauma, and in a world so unreal and beyond any control?

He probably also somewhat reimagined the nature of his religiosity before the war, believing he was more devout than he might actually have been. I doubt any of these reconstructed memories were necessarily conscious decisions at first; rather, they were more instinctual. What was true? I think that at some point, he just didn't know. I don't know either. All I can do is guess and eventually accept the story that makes the most sense or that seemed to give him the greatest peace.

Back to the story of Dąbrowa. After my father's family was gone, it was relatively quiet in the ghetto until new selections began on June 6, 1943, causing 6,000 Jews to be taken from Będzin and 2,000 from Sosnowiec. That day, however, there was no *Aktion* in Dąbrowa. Another selection was carried out on June 22, 1943, again in Będzin and Sosnowiec. This time, many elderly people and children were hidden away in bunkers. Because of this the Germans had to meet their quotas by seizing 8,000 otherwise healthy people who had hitherto been spared for work locally.

The last Jews of Dąbrowa, some 1,000 people, were deported to the Środula Ghetto in Sosnowiec in July 1943. Most of them were then taken to Auschwitz with the Jews of Sosnowiec. A few were sent to labor camps.

At the war's end, approximately 300 of Dąbrowa's Jews had survived, almost all of them in various camps. In the year that followed, almost all of them left Dąbrowa and moved westward to DP camps in the regions controlled by the Allied forces in western Germany.[9] As for Będzin, in June 1945, 1,034 Jews had survived and returned to Będzin.

By July 1946, the number had fallen to 249. In 2004, only three people in Będzin declared that they had Jewish origins.

When it came to my father's family in Będzin, I found no record of even one of them surviving the war. My father held out a glimmer of hope in Sweden when he asked officials at the World Jewish Congress in Stockholm to help him find his wife and two children, as well as his sisters Estera and Blima, but he seemed to have lost hope or already knew what had doubtless happened to his other sister Feigla, as well as to his mother.

When Jennifer and I visited Auschwitz in 2018, we were told that the crematoria had produced so much ash from burnt bodies that there was no longer anywhere to dispose of the ash, so they simply buried the ashes in the ground. As we walked through the camp, we were walking on the remains of these three souls: Chaja, Ada and Feigla – and so many other members of our family. It is a memory I can never accept, comprehend or forget.

BUNZLAU

The first prisoners had arrived in the area around Bunzlau and the village of Gross-Rosen in August 1940, and by May 1941 Gross-Rosen became an independent camp. Bunzlau would become part of that system of camps. The population of these camps and subcamps grew from 1,500 inmates at the end of 1941 to 80,000 or more when they were evacuated in early 1945. At least 125,000 inmates are estimated to have passed through Gross-Rosen and its sub-camps.

After the ghetto at Dąbrowa was largely liquidated, my father remained in Bunzlau until February 1945, initially as a slave laborer and then, starting in 1944, under the even harsher conditions of a concentration camp.

Szlama found the conditions at Bunzlau inhumane. In addition to hunger, disease and severe winters, the physical labor was unrelenting, even though the prisoners were malnourished and starving. Prisoners were given soup once a day and a little bread every three days. There were frequent haircuts, including shaving the heads of inmates so they would be immediately recognizable if they escaped. Moreover, there were two or three selections at Bunzlau every month when prisoners, especially those who were sick, were sent to Auschwitz to be murdered.

My father's life got more difficult and surviving became still more challenging when the Organisation Schmelt was eliminated in 1943 and an SS-owned company established a concentration camp to exploit the nearby marble and granite quarries at Gross-Rosen, an area near Breslau long known for its ceramics and pottery.

That meant, for example, returning every day to the excruciating labor of excavating granite quarries at Gross-Rosen under the most horrific conditions. No wonder these camps had extremely high mortality rates. Hardships in the daily battle for survival included everything from lice and wretched food to beatings, executions and near-starvation conditions. Bartering and helping other prisoners became important strategies for survival.

Consider being placed in what effectively is a cold, dark room with no escape possible, a great unknown that promises only torture, beatings, starvation and backbreaking work ending in death. Your past doesn't exist. Your future is unlikely. That is the nature of the Nazi camp system. Only the present exists, and tenuously at that.

When prisoners arrived at the concentration camp, their heads were shaved and their clothes were taken from them. They were given striped uniforms and wooden or leather clogs. They were also given numbers, which were sewn onto the left front of their shirts. Their names and the lives their names represented were gone. Now, they were only numbers. Jews also had yellow triangles sewn onto their shirts to form the Star of David.

The routine, though unimaginable, became your only reality.

Every morning your day began at about 4 or 4:30 a.m. You had 30 to 45 minutes to relieve yourself, wash, and eat breakfast in crowded facilities with very little space, and in worse conditions than you had ever experienced before. The water was dirty, and there was no soap or toilet paper. Your first meal of the day was usually a piece of stale bread or some rancid porridge, as well as something barely drinkable.

Then it was time for the roll call, the *Appell*. It took place in the *Appellplatz*, an area outside the barracks where everyone stood, sometimes for hours, to be counted and usually recounted. If anyone was missing, the count would start all over again. Sometimes those who had died during the night were brought there. If you moved out of line, talked, didn't appear promptly or wavered in the line, you were beaten or worse. You stood in the cold, the snow, the rain, the heat. Then you would be marched to your work, out to the stone quarries to begin your daily labor. Sometimes the work assignment was close by. Other times it might be several kilometers away.

You would return for lunch, if you could call it that. Sometimes, to get more work out of you, lunch would be brought to you. Again, it was a little soup and maybe a piece of bread. Work ended at 5 or 6 p.m. Then there would be another *Appell*, another count that could last for hours. Dinner was soup and again maybe a piece of bread. Lights out was at 9 p.m. You would sleep on stacks of wooden shelves, three or four bodies huddled together on each section for warmth or simply because there was no other space.

The caloric intake of prisoners in these camps was initially about 1,300 calories a day. That compares to the general daily requirement of 2,500 calories for men; and 2,000 calories for women. By 1944, with the war going badly, the increasing scarcity of supplies and the pressure to liquidate more Jews even faster, the food allotment could become as little as 700 calories a day, literally a deliberate starvation diet.

In any free time you had you would be organizing food, digging root vegetables up from the ground or trading buttons and any other valuables you might have come across, found or hidden, for food. Food was everything. Sometimes you would steal. If you were caught doing any of these things you were punished. You received no food, stood for hours in small enclosed spaces and could be beaten or killed. Survival each day was all there ever was or would be. Every day you were reminded that this could be your last day on earth –

bodies all around you, dead bodies lying next to you in the morning, bodies of those taken to be shot, sick or broken bodies forced to work, never to return.

Soldiers from the SS or *Schutzstaffel*[1] formed by Hitler as his personal bodyguard in 1925, together with the self-described political soldiers of the Nazi party led by the racist and fanatic Heinrich Himmler, would guard you much as they had in the slave labor camps. These soldiers had grown into an elite corps that administered the concentration camps. They were called the *Totenkopfverbände*, the Death's Head Battalions. Trained in racial hatred, they were the most fanatical of the Nazis and the most feared. They were with you, in charge of your life – and death, every day.

And then there were the Kapos. Sometimes they were fellow prisoners who were given extra rations to keep you in line and whip you if necessary. Sometimes these duties were assigned to ordinary criminals. You had to find a way to exist with them if you were to exist at all. Through these days and nights, you lost track of time, maybe also of who you were or what your life used to be. Like most of the prisoners, you would have to get used to being hit and beaten. My mother thought the beatings ultimately caused my father's dementia as he aged. I don't doubt it.

And while Szlama admitted in interviews after the war that he was "exposed to persecution" throughout the war years, it was in Bunzlau that the "mistreatments," as he called them, were constant for three long years. In sworn testimony he recalled, "I wasn't just beaten once, but many times." The harsh winters invited additional suffering. "I wore wooden shoes, without any socks and just a pair of trousers and a thin shirt. They were just rags. So to protect against the cold some of us would wear empty cement sacks under our shirts. If you were caught – as I was once – you were beaten." Eyewitnesses testified that at one of these beatings, during the morning roll call, a "camp elder," actually a convicted German criminal who my father called Rossi and who was given responsibility for work details, "beat Szlama horribly on the head with a club to the point that he collapsed, lost consciousness as well as losing a number of his teeth."

The result was that after the war, in Sweden and in the US, my father was diagnosed with cerebral concussions, chronic depression, nervousness and anxiety, and muscle damage in his arms and legs. Horrible headaches would last throughout his lifetime, along with bouts of vertigo that would be so bad that he couldn't see and would have to lie down. The result were periods in his life when he wasn't able to work for weeks at a time. The man who beat him then and again and again, was likely Oskar Wecks (nicknamed "Ossi"). He was known to be particularly notorious and brutal in treating prisoners.[2] Wecks was investigated by the West German police in 1980 for his wartime actions. However, by then he had disappeared.

At some point, my father may have been given kitchen duties at Bunzlau.[3] He could be charming and collegial, so perhaps a Kapo or a senior camp officer favored him for a brief period. While working in the kitchen, my father saved the life of a fellow Polish Jewish inmate named Isaac (Itzchak) Urbach.[4] I never discovered exactly what my father did for him. In recent correspondence, Urbach's daughter Raquel, who wrote that her father always spoke highly of Szlama, said, however, her father never spoke very much about the specifics of the war. My best guess is that Szlama smuggled food out of the kitchen at the risk of being discovered and killed. Then again, perhaps Urbach was weaker than my father and Szlama also helped him move around, since the Germans killed anyone who couldn't keep up or follow orders.

In any case, they became lifelong friends. Like Szlama, Urbach was resettled in Sweden for a brief time, after which he emigrated to Caracas, Venezuela. When I was young he came to visit several times, once with his wife and daughter. I recall how – when he came to Brooklyn – he repeatedly declared that my father had saved his life many times and had earned his eternal gratitude. After each declaration, he would give my father a big hug. While Urbach only arrived in Bunzlau and met Szlama in July 1944, they were in the same barracks and so Urbach witnessed some of the harsh beatings my father endured. In a sworn affidavit Urbach wrote: "These mistreatments were often repeated and because of the beatings, over time his (Szlama's) strength just seeped away."

THE DEATH MARCH AND BERGEN-BELSEN

As the war came to an end in the autumn of 1944, German forces began evacuating many of the concentration camps and sending inmates under guard to march farther away from the advancing enemy's front lines. These so-called death marches, which continued until the Germans surrendered, resulted in the deaths of some 250,000 to 375,000 people. Professor Yehuda Bauer claimed that when it came to the death marches, the "Nazis were driven by their ambition to complete their annihilation of the Jews at all costs."[1]

Organized by the SS, the forced evacuation of concentration camp inmates toward the interior of the Reich was an effort to keep large numbers of survivors from falling into Allied hands. The Germans had at least three purposes. They wanted to eliminate witnesses to Nazi terror in order to keep the Allied troops from hearing the prisoners' stories. They thought prisoners could still be used in other camps to continue arms production for the Nazi war effort. And SS leaders, including Heinrich Himmler, believed they could use Jewish prisoners as hostages to bargain for a separate peace in the West (with the Western Allies, not the Soviets) and thereby guarantee the survival of the Nazi regime. At first these evacuations were carried out by train or by sea, but as winter approached in 1945, the Allies had already reached the German borders and taken control of the skies. The subsequent marches were thus conducted by foot.

My father and his friend Urbach were in a group of Polish prisoners sent from Bunzlau to Mittelbau-Dora, not far from where he first had been a slave laborer in 1940. They were evacuated by foot during that brutal winter of early 1945. The SS guards had strict orders to kill prisoners who could no longer walk or travel.

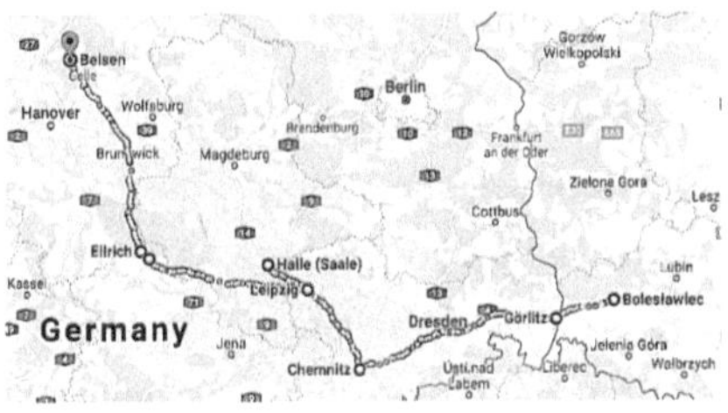

The route taken by my father and the other Bunzlau prisoners, walking for six weeks on a death march that ultimately ended in Bergen-Belsen.

On February 8, 1945, it was announced that all the prisoners were being moved out of Bunzlau. The evacuation began with a column of 541 prisoners and their SS guards. Some of the prisoner groups began their marches on February 10. Others started two days later. Before their departure, the prisoners were given wooden shoes. It was nearly impossible to walk in them that winter, which would turn out to be one of the coldest in Europe's history. Snow stuck to the wood, making walking difficult. Feet froze, which for many meant death. One survivor recalled that in the first three days of marching, the SS guards shot several of the inmates dead and wounded others. More such violence would follow, as anyone who couldn't keep up was killed on the spot. The prisoners walked via Görlitz, Chemnitz, Halle and Leipzig to the Mittelbau-Dora concentration camp. The march covered around almost 500 kilometers (310 miles) and lasted until March 25th. In those harsh winter months, my father and his fellow prisoners walked for six weeks to reach the camp, which turned out to have no room for the surviving prisoners. A group of around 70, including my father and Urbach, continued their march to a subcamp called Ellrich. By then Szlama had lost nearly all hope. A few weeks later they were put on a train pulling cattle cars to Bergen-Belsen, where they arrived in April 1945.

One man recalled what happened to his brother from Bunzlau:

> "Stephen and the other prisoners were forced on a death march through February and March, with the sound of Russian gunfire always just behind them. Prisoners who fell behind or tried to hide were immediately shot, and everyone became physically and mentally drained. He was marching right outside of Dresden on February 25th and witnessed the famous Dresden air raid that night. On March 25th he arrived at Dora, where he stayed for ten days until the American forces bombed the German barracks there and all of the prisoners were moved to the camp at Bergen-Belsen. He recalled that only about half the prisoners survived the march."

Late in the march – as other inmates wandered aimlessly till they dropped dead from hunger or beatings by their guards – my father somehow learned that upon arriving in Auschwitz his wife had refused to leave their children. As he admitted in that story he told me on the beach, he had met someone from his hometown who reported seeing Chaja and the children being led away to the gas chambers. However, there was never any official word that they were then murdered, and later, in Sweden, he said in a letter that he was still looking for his wife and children but was certain by then that women with children were automatically gassed in Auschwitz. Most of those who were taken directly to the gas chambers from the train ramps at Auschwitz were never registered, so their names were never recorded. Indeed, one source estimated that only around 10–15 percent of those arriving on each transport were kept alive. The rest "went into the gas straight away."[2] Hence his inability to learn of their fate with any certainty. In 1946, when he was already in Sweden but had not yet married my mother, he queried the World Jewish Congress (WJC) in Stockholm for any news of his wife and children. The WJC found no definitive reports, and to this day I have not found anything either. But clearly, no one in his immediate family (or hers) ever contacted him after the war. Only silence.

After marching those six weeks in the cold and snow and then being loaded on wagons and cattle cars, pressed together like "herrings in a barrel,"[3] as one survivor recalled, they traveled several more days until my father, Urbach and the others arrived at Bergen-Belsen. They had survived one circle of Hell, only to arrive at another that seemed even worse. At Bergen-Belsen bodies were stacked everywhere. Thousands of prisoners who had come from various concentration camps were crowded into small, cramped spaces. There was virtually no food. Diseases of all kinds were rampant. When they arrived, they each received a small bowl of watery soup. Thousands of inmates already there were dying of hunger every day or suffering from dysentery or typhus. My mother already had been at Bergen-Belsen for a number of months.

The good news, though they didn't know it at the time, was that a few weeks after they arrived, Bergen-Belsen would be liberated by the British, with the first English tanks arriving on April 15, 1945.

What was it like toward the end for so many of these concentration camp survivors, once they were soon to be liberated? In his classic book *Survival in Auschwitz*, the Italian Jewish author Primo Levi described his own state of mind, as well as that of his fellow inmates in Auschwitz the day before Soviet troops arrived at that camp in January 1945: "We lay in a world of death and phantoms. The last trace of civilization had vanished around and inside us. The work of bestial degradation, begun by the victorious Germans, had been carried to conclusion by the Germans in defeat."[4]

The prisoners, both Jews and Christians from many countries, were separated into different blocks. Records indicate that my father and Urbach left Bergen-Belsen a few weeks after the liberation and were brought by the British to Celle, Germany, where a displaced persons and transit camp had been set up nearby. Both Urbach and my father were mentioned in the *She'rit Hapleta* (Jewish Survivors in Celle) list compiled by Rabbi Eli Munk.

Szlama and Frieda (whose wartime story follows) had survived. The war was over. But inside them, other battles had just begun. Where would they go now? To do what? And with whom? Who was left, if anyone? And what part of humanity was left inside them? And what part of who they once were was gone forever?

In 2017, while trying to learn more about my father's childhood and first family, I discovered his niece, the daughter of one of Chaja's brothers.

Having just begun to seriously research this book, I had posted a query about my father's first family in Dąbrowa on a Facebook group page of descendants of Jewish families who had been incarcerated in the ghettos of Upper Silesia, including Będzin, Sosnowiec and Dąbrowa.

A response came from someone who thought she knew someone living in Israel who was related to one of those families. That woman turned out to be Chaja's niece, Yona Kotlicki (married name Kobo). Yona's father, Herszel[5] Kotlicki, was the youngest of Chaja's siblings, one of three members of her nuclear family to have survived the war.[6]

Yona currently works at Yad Vashem as an Online Exhibitions Coordinator in its Internet Department/Media Division. We met at the memorial site in 2018 and exchanged our stories, hugs and tears. Later she recalled in a note: "Only when I was 35 he [her father] told me his secret – [about] his first wife and daughter. I was so overwhelmed that I didn't ask for their names, which I found only two years ago. My father passed away in 1988, a few months after he told me. My mother died in 2004. I understand now that talking about his family and the atrocities he had been through were too painful for him. Telling about them was reliving the trauma."

I recall much the same experience and emotions after my father revealed his "secret" family and when, just a few years ago, I discovered his children's names for the first time. Suddenly they were real, as was the sadness and pain of understanding his loss. As for my father's Chaja, Yona remembered that whenever her name would come up at family gatherings, everyone would say how beautiful she was.

What about Chaja's pink sweater? Probably it was long since lost during the endless months in the camps and then on that death march. Or maybe it was never in his hands, and only in his memories. Either way, it stayed inside my father's heart, till even that memory was erased by yet another harsh reality that would assault him much later: Alzheimer's disease.

PART IV

THE PREWAR YEARS: FRIMET ENTENBERG

SIENIAWA

My mother had a particularly vibrant imagination. When Rachel and I were growing up, she told us all kinds of stories about herself. They were not children's stories or fairy tales. Unfortunately, our bedtime stories were mostly about the horrors of her time in the concentration camps. Back then we would quite frankly have been happy not to know about any of that. She also offered flashes of memories from her life as a young girl. It is likely that some of those stories were products of her imagination, or more appropriately, her reimaginations.

She would change dates and places when she talked about how old she was or where she came from. It was never clear whether that was by mistake, which would certainly have been understandable, or intentional. Either way, I have tried to convey some of what I have discovered and put her early life into context to understand her behaviors, actions and reactions as she grew older.

My mother was born Frimet Entenberg on December 14, 1910 in Sieniawa, Poland.[1] By the time World War II began, she had settled on calling herself Frieda or Frida.[2] When asked, she would list her maiden name as Singer, which in fact was not her maiden name but the surname of her grandmother Estera. Her mother, Ruchela

(Rachela) Entenberg, was born in 1876 in the small neighboring town of Wiązownica. Frimet's father, Jakub Goldman, was born in Sieniawa in 1872. However, his name was not listed in her birth records or most other related official records,[3] which forced Frimet to take her mother's maiden name, Entenberg.

There was a reason for that. At the time, Jewish births often were not officially recorded when they occurred but registered with civil authorities later, if at all. Instead, they most often were initially registered only with the local synagogues. The same held for marriages. If and when marriages finally were registered, however, the civil authorities often regarded any births that preceded those registrations as illegitimate. Children therefore took their mother's known surname, leaving the father's surname out or, if it was known, making it secondary. I have a feeling my mother was either confused by that or actively declined to use her mother's surname, which would have implied illegitimacy. However, all her siblings adopted the Entenberg name as their own.[4]

Her birthdate also complicated record searches of her early life. My mother said more than once, when we were still too young to wonder why, that one of her rules of the road was "A woman needs to be younger than her husband, but not too much younger, because who wants an old man for a husband? It wouldn't look good." True to form, on the certificate of my mother's marriage to her first husband, who we will get to later, he was at least five years her senior, and she gave her birthdate as December 14, 1910. That birthdate was also recorded by the civil authorities in her hometown of Sieniawa. In Sweden after the war, when she married her second husband, my father, her birthdate became December 15, 1912, making her a year younger than him. Another document made her younger still, asserting that she was born in December 1917 sometime between December 12 and December 15 or, on yet another record, December 25. Adding to the confusion, a record in the Kraków City Archives lists her birthdate as November 6, 1911. By the time she entered the concentration camp system in Poland, Frimet had settled on

December 15, 1912 as her official birthdate, which she later used when she came to the US.

A graphic rendering of the central area (literally, according to the picture's description, the 'Downtown') of Sieniawa in the early 1900s, near where the Goldman/Entenberg family lived.

Frimet's mother, Ruchela, taken from a German ID card in 1940 when she was 64 years old.

In 1910, Sieniawa – Frimet's birthplace – was part of the Austro-Hungarian Empire in a region known as Galicia. Jews had settled in the region since the 12th century, and by the eve of the Holocaust their population was close to one million, even though many Galician Jews had emigrated at the beginning of the 20th century to escape the poor conditions in the region. These "Eastern" communities were usually Yiddish-speaking Orthodox Jews. My father would often say, half joking, that "Galicianers" were known to have been born without a sense of humor. Indeed, my mother rarely cracked a smile. She lacked a sense of humor and was unable to take or understand a joke, an assessment that became an understatement as she grew older.

Sieniawa is about 200 kilometers east of Kraków. One of many small Polish shtetls, it comprised about 2,000 people and was located fairly close to what is now the border between Poland and Ukraine. Historically, it was roughly half Jewish and half Catholic. In the town, Jews worked as merchants or semi-skilled craftsmen, trading goods with the local peasant population or working as tailors, hatters, shoemakers, grocers, butchers or blacksmiths. The Jews of Sieniawa worked and lived in and near the market square, while their Polish Catholic neighbors worked as farmers, living mostly on the outskirts of town.

This 1919 map of Sieniawa pinpoints #82, the birthplace of Frimet and her brother Abraham (second house circled from top), one street away from the main square.

Nearly all Jews in this region at the time came from Orthodox Jewish families. The union of Jakub and Ruchela was an arranged marriage with a dowry supplied by the bride's family. A dowry often took the form of a small house or part of one. By the early 1920s, the majority of Jews, including my mother's family, had started leaving the shtetls to live in larger urban centers where there was greater opportunity to make a living and indeed, to seize new opportunities of all kinds. In the 1920s, Jews made up between 25 and 50 percent of the population of Poland's larger cities, including the regional hub of Kraków. Interestingly, Jakub and Ruchela, like most poor, uneducated Jews, only knew how to write in Yiddish. Unlike their children, poorer Jews of their generation had no opportunity to attend Polish schools and were brought up with Yiddish as their sole written language. Frimet's parents were thus unable to sign their names in Polish. Other Jews tended to have mercantile livelihoods, but Jakub was a tailor, so perhaps he didn't need to write in Polish to make a living. The point is that my mother's family were not secularly educated Jews. In 1940, when they applied for German ID cards, neither Jakub nor Ruchela was able to sign their forms. Instead, three literate witnesses watched them sign their names in three squares, confirming who they were and where they lived. Their children, on the other hand, all eventually attended Polish primary schools.

Naturally, Jews spoke Polish and interacted with Poles on the streets and in markets, despite a sense of "otherness" between them. They mixed when they had to but strictly observed their own religious and cultural traditions. They dressed differently, they prayed differently and in doing so they lived together and apart at the same time. Beginning in the 18th century, relationships became even more complicated as wars and diplomacy led to many Jews living under Russian rule. Because of their religion they suffered persecution, including violent attacks, repression and a general lack of both freedom and economic and social opportunity.

When my mother was a little girl, Galicia was still part of the Austro-Hungarian Empire, possibly the most hands-off and benevolent (especially for Jews) of the countries that had carved out Polish territories: Prussia, Russia and the Austro-Hungarian Empire. Most Jews were poor and eked out a precarious living to support their often outsized families. In the meantime, challenges to Frimet's identity and various dislocations in her early life were already forming who she was and would become.

The size and fragility of Frimet's family was a fact of life she would face starting in childhood. Based on existing records and some suppositions it is reasonable to conclude that Ruchela and Jakub had as many as 13 children, too many of whom didn't survive infancy. Ruchela surely had her hands full and was likely exhausted and stressed most of the time. She was busy having babies from age 19, if you believe one record, or from age 24 if you trust another. One record indicates that she gave birth to her last child at the age of 41. The babies came virtually every year at the beginning, starting with a little girl named Miriam, born in 1900. Her sister Chaja was born the next year, and so it went. Their last child was born in 1917. As for Jakub, he was challenged trying to make ends meet as a shtetl tailor.

Frimet was one of the younger children. She had four older sisters, but only one survived to adulthood. Four older brothers also died very young. All were likely children of Jakub Goldman, but only one child was recorded with Jakub officially listed as the father.[5]

With nearly every birth there came a move to a different house. Except for the first one, these dwellings were located on the main market square in Sieniawa. "House" may be too grand a word for what was initially a two-room cottage constructed of stucco, wood and brick, with a bare floor and possibly a chicken coop somewhere in the front or back.[6]

Years later, my mother would recall how she walked along the dirt roads of her shtetl with her grandmother, Estera, and how they would sometimes gather eggs from the few chickens her family owned. "We were very poor," she would remind us, "and had almost nothing. Sometimes we didn't have anything to eat. But still we were happy." Life was tough, and she and her family would face even more difficult times ahead. The family had moved at least six times by the time my mother was born, and six of her siblings had died or would soon.[7]

Frimet worshiped her mother: "My mother was a holy woman. She was very religious. She could do nothing wrong. And she loved me more than anyone else." Not surprisingly in such a large household, even if only seven children remained, Frimet felt she had to compete for that love. It's hard to say how religious the rest of her family was.

Surviving pictures of Jakub and of Frimet's brothers Naftali and Abraham suggest they were fairly assimilated in terms of their dress and the length and style of their hair. And knowing my mother, she likely had little room for religious law in her life, apart from keeping kosher, lighting candles on the Sabbath and observing the holidays. My mother never mentioned her father by name, except to say he was a tailor.

Her competitive spirit would come to her aid to help her survive the war years, but it would later also hinder her ability to establish and maintain relationships with others, including her relationship with Genia, her one surviving sibling. Their relationship was strained at best and disastrous at worst. That spirit also affected my mother's relationship with her own daughter, my sister Rachel. "Our mother would seem to compete with me for our father's love and attention," Rachel recalled just recently. "She would try to put me down in front of him, and raise herself up instead."

REFUGEES FROM WAR

The times also created uncertainty and turmoil in Frimet's youth. She lived in tenuous economic circumstances and her family, as Jews, faced challenges created by an inequitable economic and political system and overt antisemitism. On top of that came a massive dislocation in her early years. In 1914, World War I broke out when she was just four years old, engulfing Galicia and other parts of what later became the Republic of Poland. She and her family consequently became refugees at a time of massive displacement of local populations that affected millions, including hundreds of thousands of Jews.

The period from 1914 to 1919 was the first of four distinct periods in which Frimet would find herself emotionally and physically unmoored, stateless and/or a refugee. Her first encounter with homelessness as a young child was doubtless particularly jarring to her sense of identity and security as she and her family escaped the onslaught of fighting. The second period was rife with the horrors of the Holocaust. She then became stateless when she was resettled in Sweden. Finally, she became a refugee/immigrant in the US. Each period came with a copious share of stresses and traumas, some obviously worse than others. Naturally, she tried to adapt.

It was these unsettled times that sparked her continuing flights into fantasies of a world she wanted, as opposed to the one in which she lived. These daydreams buttressed her tough view of life and her need to survive in what she saw as a particularly competitive environment, given her many dislocations. Indeed the feeling of being a stranger even came in her twilight years, when at the age of 80 and for reasons of health, she and my father left Brooklyn, their home for more than 35 years, for another culture and way of life to live near my sister and her family in Mobile, Alabama. In each of these periods, she seemed again to have no choice but to live as a stranger in yet another strange land. In many respects, that would be true for my father as well.

World War I was Frimet's first challenge. Though Sieniawa was in a region of Galicia governed by the Austro-Hungarian Empire, it was quickly captured by Tsarist forces during World War I, then by Germans and then again by Russians. Sieniawa was a small town, but it occupied an important strategic spot on the San River and was located on the main road to Kraków and beyond. The town very quickly found itself amidst a battlefield overrun by Russian soldiers, with shelling occurring on its outskirts.

English newspaper reports of May 31, 1915 led with headlines and dispatches from Sieniawa such as "Stubborn Battle Raging on the San," and "Sieniawa Carried by Assault." An earlier May 29 report began: "On Thursday night, the Russians inflicted heavy losses north and east of Sieniawa. Six thousand Germans and Austrians were taken prisoner." There was even a report of Turkish (possibly Bosnian) troops allied with the Germans in the area and clad in Austrian uniforms and "Turkish" fezzes.

The Russian invasion generated a massive flight of Jews from areas that seemed liable to fall into Tsarist hands. At least 200,000 Jews, and by some estimates as many as 450,000, more than half of Galicia's Jewish population, were uprooted by Russian conquest or its threat. By autumn 1915, some 75,000 Jews had taken refuge in Bohemia during the months of the Russian advance. Bohemia, then part of the

Austro-Hungarian Empire, an area itself rooted in both German culture and Slavic traditions and language, later became part of Czechoslovakia.

The Goldman/Entenberg family sought refuge from World War I. Even today, it would probably take many changes of trains and other transportation modes to get to Prague from Sieniawa (top right marker).

Not surprisingly, the Goldman/Entenberg family fled their hometown sometime in 1914 or 1915. It must have been quite an expedition to organize, for a mother and father with at least six children and all their belongings. They probably went from Sieniawa by horse cart for several hours to nearby Przeworsk and then took several trains for 15 or more hours, as much as a full day, to Prague, some 750 kilometers to the west. The train would have taken them through Kraków, but that city was also under attack, so the family had to keep moving. Once they arrived in Prague, they stayed for the duration of the war. While there and at the age of 41, Ruchela bore their last child, Jozef, in April 1917.

My mother never mentioned it, but Jozef was born deaf and always seemed sickly as he grew older, according to his father Jakub. Health facilities were seldom available for these refugees, and the newborn may have suffered from the combination of his mother's advanced age and a dearth of adequate facilities for newborns and their mothers amidst what was clearly a refugee crisis in Prague. Food was scarce and starvation was increasingly an issue during their time there.

Why did they choose Prague? A natural guess is that Jakub or Ruchela had some family there who might have escaped the fighting in Galicia, which had been under Austrian control. However, this supposition is not confirmed by records. Another guess is that both Bohemia and Sieniawa (as part of Galicia), being part of the Austro-Hungarian Empire, welcomed or at least tolerated their own refugee populations. The choice would have been between Vienna and Prague, and though Vienna was closer, Prague, as a Slavic city, might have been a bit more comfortable from a cultural and linguistic perspective. They would have been able to communicate in Polish, Yiddish, Czech or German. Bohemia was also a region where Jews enjoyed more freedom and rights than in areas that came under Russian control. Finally, and quite simply, the whole family had just been swept up in a human tide of neighbors and friends migrating from Galicia to seek safety.

At least 30,000 Jews from that region in Poland are estimated to have flooded into the city within just a few months of the start of major hostilities. That number was equal to or greater than the total number of Jews already living in Prague. More arrived in subsequent years. Most of these newer arrivals were considered exotic "Eastern" Jews, meaning mostly destitute Orthodox or Hasidic Jews who, with their beards, black hats, side curls and long kaftans, looked and behaved quite differently from the generally assimilated Jewish populations that had long resided in Prague. Some assimilated Jews saw these strictly observant religious men as symbols of the ghetto, but others considered them a source of authentic Jewish national culture that "Western" Jews seemed to have lost in the process of assimilation. "For the assimilationist group the presence of Jews who differed so clearly presented a problem because it undermined their ideology of being Czechs or Germans, differing only by their religion," according to one report.[1]

Encounters by these "Eastern" Jews with local inhabitants stimulated a discussion about Jewish identity but also stoked prejudices against their alleged backwardness. Like other refugee groups, Jewish refugees were targeted in vicious press campaigns, portrayed as "uneducated criminals, dirty, involved in all kinds of shady dealings and so on. [These reports] drifted from some kind of assistance and understanding at the beginning towards hatred, especially as the living conditions in the monarchy were getting worse."[2]

During those war years, food and shelter were immediate challenges. These refugees had arrived from another part of the Austro-Hungarian Empire, so the monarchy actually acknowledged some responsibility for helping them, at least during the first months of the war, since these people were citizens of the state. However, it is likely that when they first arrived, they had to live in hastily and poorly constructed housing or on the streets of the city. Then Austrian soldiers constructed barracks and refugee camps to house many who had previously camped out in the streets. The barracks were built to accommodate groups according to their ethnic and national identities. Various local Zionist youth groups also helped with refugee relief, soup kitchens and housing.

Small groups of Jewish refugees were also dispersed in villages and accommodated in dormitories or apartments where they shared space and necessities with the local people, resulting in frequent conflicts. In any case, living conditions were very poor and epidemics were rampant. Many died from lack of proper hygiene or medical support.

All told, by the end of 1915, up to 200,000 refugees, two-thirds of them Jewish, had fled the fighting. Schools were eventually organized for family groups like the Entenbergs.[3] The famed writer Franz Kafka, a Jew and a native of Prague who took an early interest in cultural Zionism and lived in the city at the time, participated in the relief efforts, offering lectures at these refugee schools.

Orthodox Jewish refugees from Galicia also sought safety in Vienna during World War I.

Hatred of "Eastern" Jews originally helped to spread Czech nationalism but also played an important role in the development of Czech antisemitism. Demand grew for these Jews to return home, particularly after Czechoslovakia was founded at the war's end. With the end of World War I, the Goldman/Entenbergs joined the thousands of others who returned to Poland. But they would not return to their shtetl. Instead their destination was a grand cosmopolitan metropolis that offered all of them new opportunities.

SETTLING IN KRAKÓW

By the time their train arrived in Kraków on November 10, 1919, they were no longer under the rule and protection of the Austro-Hungarian Empire. Galicia had now become part of Poland, a newly formed independent republic. The family had struggled to survive for nearly five years under very difficult conditions. Meanwhile, my mother was still just a young girl, but also had grown and experienced more than many of her contemporaries. She was nine.

Considering Frimet's still fragile state and impressionable age, and her family's difficult life in Prague, it is unsurprising that she had learned a life lesson during their time as refugees: to do everything she could to fit into any of the foreign situations in which she found herself. Certainly she would have tried to learn German, one of the two languages spoken in Prague, and to rely less on her native Yiddish. What she learned about fitting in during this first of her refugee experiences would serve her well later on.

From a young child's perspective, Kraków was something of a foreign land, but Frimet would learn to love it. The city was Poland's second largest, a beautiful and historic metropolis. It had been the capital of Poland when it was still ruled by kings and boasted an impressive

Royal Castle, a vast Old City Market Square and imposing city walls. From the outset, her family settled in Kazimierz, an enclave inhabited mostly by poor or lower middle-class Jews just south of the Old Town in Kraków. They took an apartment in Jozefa 12, flat #23. Sadly, upon their return they learned that Jakub's father, Meilech Goldman, had died that same year in Sieniawa at age 66.[1] That may have been what precipitated the move to Kraków instead of a return to Sieniawa. It seems Meilech hadn't made the trek with the rest of the family, perhaps because he wasn't well.

Since the 14th century, Kazimierz[2] had been what amounted to a separate Jewish city within Kraków. In 1495, due to growing opposition to the Jews by the local population, King Jan Olbracht expelled Jews from the Old Town of Kraków and sent them to Kazimierz. They soon converted the quarter into a relatively prosperous, viable destination with synagogues and markets. Subsequently, what had been an autonomous governing authority in the interwar years in Poland gave way to civil governance as the intelligentsia and more assimilated, middle-class Jews moved out of Kazimierz, leaving the area to poorer Jews and those generally less assimilated. In that same time, the Jewish population in Kraków had grown, coming to represent about 25 percent of the city. Kazimierz was where most of Kraków's 68,000 Jews lived and worked. Kazimierz itself became a focal point for the religious life of Kraków's Jews, with its six major Orthodox synagogues and its wide range of political, educational and cultural organizations. It even boasted a Progressive synagogue.

Having arrived in Kraków, Frimet was soon enrolled in a local Polish primary school, and although she was older than others in her class because of her five years in Prague, she stayed in school through the sixth grade. Her formal schooling ended at age 14 or 15, around 1926. Her brothers and her sister also attended Polish schools and after-school Jewish education programs.[3]

When I was older, my mother claimed that she had actually also gone to a gymnasium, which would have been at the middle school level.

That is unlikely, as her parents couldn't afford to pay for school and she never reported that additional level of education when applying for jobs in Sweden. She was probably more truthful about her memories of having friends. Certainly she always seemed to need people and have others pay attention to her, so she sought an active social life. Fortunately, her father was a tailor and could make the party clothes she so cherished. Years later, she described those days: "I would have beautiful dresses made of organza. I was very thin and put my hair up just so. I would look like a princess and all the boys and girls loved me." She would motion to her hair and then trace her body with those expressive hands of hers, smiling coquettishly as she transported herself back to those happier days.

Again, who knows what her boundaries were between truth and imagination, reality and wishful thinking? She never made any pretense of adhering to those distinctions. They all blended together as the moment required and as her imagination recalled. Given her Orthodox upbringing, for example, it was unlikely that she went to many dances with boys. It definitely took some time for her family to arrange for a husband for her.

The building where Frimet lived, Jozefa 12, also became home to a number of the Entenberg children, and several others lived on adjoining streets. For at least some period of time, the occupants of apartment #23 included my mother, her parents, possibly her grandmother Estera, her brothers Jozef and Naftali, a tailor's assistant, her older brother Abraham, who was a hatter and tailor, and his wife, Ann Vogler. Jakub and several of his sons ran their own small tailoring and hat making business from apartment #23. After my mother married, she moved into apartment #7 with her husband.

Two of Frimet's brothers, Abraham (left) and Naftali, early 1930s.

Frimet's youngest brother Jozef also lived for a time at nearby Jakuba 17 with his brother Leib, wife Chana and their son Chaim, born in 1940.[4]

My mother's sister Genia lived around the corner at Meiselsa 22 with her husband Sussel Beitscher,[5] an airplane worker, and their daughter Frymeta, born on December 3, 1935.[6] Brother Leon, a merchant, lived with his wife Sabina (Goldberger) and their son Josef, born in 1940 in Nowy Korczyn, a small town about 75 kilometers northeast of Kraków on the road to their birthplace in Sieniawa.

The Goldman/Entenbergs remained in Kraków, living mostly on or near Jozefa 12, until the Nazi invasion. Whatever the ups and downs of their lives had been before they arrived, the move from Prague back to Poland afforded Frimet a level of stability, security and identity that hadn't existed during the first nine years of her life. The privations of the World War I years and the economic challenges her family had faced before then must have had an effect on her emotionally. It is no wonder that Frimet would always fantasize about another life, be it the one she found in Kazimierz or the one she had dreamt could be.

Frimet's dream life started with how she wanted to perceive herself and how she thought others might see her. At some level, she envisioned her persona as a beautiful, popular, vivacious young woman full of style and grace. What did she want to do with that person? She didn't want to change the world or herself. Instead she wanted to use her skills and talents to help others to dream as well. She wanted to do something very different from what seemed possible by operating her own dance studio. True, the war changed everything, but for a year or two, she insisted years later, she and her first husband had made that dream come true.

Frimet married Abe Friedmann[7] on April 10, 1938.[8] The ceremony took place at what was known as the Alte Synagogue, the oldest in Kazimierz, and their wedding was officiated by Rabbi Samuel Kornitzer, who was either the Under Rabbi or the Chief Rabbi of Kraków, like his father before him. Their marriage certificate noted that their witnesses were mostly scholars and teachers. Two years later, in March 1940, Rabbi Kornitzer sought to prevent the Nazis' expulsion of Jews from Kraków. He was arrested by the Gestapo and taken to Auschwitz, where he was murdered.

Abe, the son of Izak Bader and Perel Friedmann, was born in Kraków on June 3, 1905. Before he met his wife he lived at Starowiślna 77 on a large thoroughfare at the eastern boundary of Kazimierz.[9]

At the time of their marriage, Abe was nearly 33 years old and Frimet was nearly 28. For her, that was a good thing, given her belief that a man should be older than his wife. It is true that by the time she applied for a German identity card with her husband on February 18, 1941, she had advanced her birth year from 1910, as noted on her wedding certificate, to December 15, 1912, so by then she had decided to be younger still.

Frimet's parents were pleased with the match, having finally arrived at the important milestone of marrying off their youngest daughter. They had probably given the newlyweds a relatively generous dowry, mostly to cover the costs of furnishing their modest apartment at Jozefa 12, #7, a two-room corner flat on the second floor facing the street. The apartment was considered a good one because of its relatively prestigious location in the building. However, the couple needed much more if they were to live the way my mother dreamed of doing. In the US, my mother would claim that she had a five-room apartment, a maid and a thriving dance studio business before the war. I believe her reality was quite different and much more modest.

Abe worked full time at a luggage shop. By the time the war began he was making about 90 złotys a month, an extremely modest amount in terms of purchasing power.[10] With no particular skills, she would later claim to have been a seamstress during that time. Frimet instead became a part-time washerwoman, taking in other people's laundry, putting their clothes into the apartment's small bathtub and scrubbing the dirt away using the metal and wood washboard she shared with the rest of her family. She earned less than half her husband's wages every month. Later, in Sweden, she listed that job as "laundry mender," though she admitted once that when she was a young woman she could not sew at all.

How did that dance studio memory arise? There was room in Kazimierz for a diversity of ways to spend free time. After all, not all Kazimierz residents were ultra-religious. While most residents were Orthodox Jews, they ran the gamut of religious observance, from the ultra-Orthodox to Hasidim to Progressives. There was also a wide range of Jewish youth groups to join, and popular culture attractions of all kinds, like dance crazes popularized on the radio, including the rage of the day, the Polish tango. Modeled on the passionate Argentinian tango, it was adapted to the more conservative Central European mentality to make it more subdued, proper and polite. Vibrant Yiddish theater and Yiddish-language newspapers were also plentiful, so a dance studio to serve this population, operated by fellows Jews in Kazimierz, didn't seem all that far-fetched. Still, the mid- and late-1930s were difficult years for Jews, because of widespread antisemitism, especially the economic boycott of Jewish shops. They probably didn't have a lot of extra cash or disposable income to spare for dance lessons.

Still, for many years Frieda told us that she had achieved that goal and hidden the large sums of money they earned from these dance lessons in a big, dark walnut wardrobe that was part of the dowry

Abe received. But when the Nazis forced them to leave their apartment for the Kraków Ghetto, my mother claimed, the soldiers found their stash of cash and her dreams came to an end. I think she came to believe all that had happened, but from what I could gather, it hadn't. Sadly, I have come to believe that none of it was real.

FRIMET'S KRAKÓW HOME: JOZEFA 12

Built in 1802 as an inn with two stories and an inner courtyard, Jozefa 12 itself is interesting for several reasons beyond being my mother's family home for 20 years. Its exterior was a central setting for the Steven Spielberg film *Schindler's List*, representing a building housing Jewish families in the Kraków Ghetto. It is actually outside of the real ghetto, which was across the Vistula River in a district called Podgórze.[1]

Located in the heart of Kazimierz, the neighborhood declined after the war, especially since only a handful of Jews remained in Kraków. At first it was poor Poles who lived there, but by the early 1990s Jewish tourists had begun to visit the area as a stopping-off point on tours of Polish death camps. Eventually Kazimierz was hit by a wave of gentrification and became a fashionable area in which to live. It subsequently became an even more important stop for Holocaust tour groups. A Progressive Jewish center began to operate there and still does, amidst storefronts that sport signs in Yiddish, seeking to recreate a semblance of a way of life that had been extinguished.

The inner courtyard of Jozefa 12, an apartment building in Kazimierz where my mother and her family lived for 20 years. Their apartment was on the second floor, seen here above the archway.

Though full of memories and "what-if" moments, what remains is more a memorial than an attraction. Sadly, some of the souvenir stalls still sell images of coin-counting Jews sporting long noses and other stereotypical, macabre signs of the lingering effects of a history of antisemitism. From what we came to understand during our visit, elements of Polish society still had not fully come to grips with what was, how it happened and the role Polish citizens played during those years, sometimes heroically and sometimes otherwise.

As for my mother's former home, today it is sometimes used as a place where Polish couples have their pictures taken. The apartments in the building have been upgraded and renovated for young professionals who have moved in.

What kind of life did craftsmen like Jakub Goldman and his sons have, working out of homes like Jozefa 12 in Kazimierz? Not a bad one, really. For instance, a hatter like Frimet's brother Abraham would certainly have known how to create a *shtreimel* (fur hat worn by many Hasidic Jews, mainly on the Shabbath and other festive occasions.) Usually a bride's father would purchase the shtreimel for the groom for their wedding day. The grandest of the hats were made with several furs. They generally consisted of a large circular piece of black velvet surrounded by fur. Sometimes Polish Jews would wear a high shtreimel pointed upward, called a *spodick*. The hat could actually be made with up to 42 tails taken from Russian sable or related animals. Other popular hats included *tshikapes*, caps with visors, warm winter hats made out of various animal skins and square peasant hats called *konfederatke*. There were also ordinary round cloth hats for weekday wear and satin hats worn only on the Sabbath.

Jakub's profession, tailoring, originally starting among residents of the shtetls, had developed into a primary means of making a living for many thousands. From there, the profession of making and altering clothing moved into the larger towns and cities. In 1931, about a half million Jews were actively involved in making clothing. Indeed, they made up about 44 percent of all clothing workers, evenly divided between those working in their homes and those in factories.[2] About half were independent tailors and hatmakers, like Jakub and his sons. However, from 1935 to 1937, Jewish tailors, hatmakers and shopkeepers were imperiled by the right-wing National Democratic Party's nationalistic antisemitic movement and its calls for a national economic boycott of these craftsmen and small business owners. Over the years, the economic effects of that boycott became even more pronounced. A poster proclaimed: "Remember: Don't buy from Jews. Buy from Christians. Remember that the Jews are the major cause of the current impoverishment of Polish society." Nothing could have been further from the truth. Life had always been difficult, but such boycotts paved the way for the nightmare still ahead.

PART V

THE WAR YEARS: FRIMET FRIEDMANN

SCHINDLER'S LIST OPENS MY EYES

My sister and I spent our youth finding ways to make sure our parents never watched any documentaries, movies or TV shows depicting the Holocaust. We knew precious little about their lives before we emigrated to the US, except that they had lost their families in the Holocaust and been imprisoned in concentration camps. What we did know was that they relived those nightmares too often at night. The terrible dreams that made them scream in their sleep never did go away.

When the movie *Schindler's List* came out in 1994, I was frankly hesitant to see it, but eventually if reluctantly, I joined my family and went to the movie theater. After all, it represented a piece of my heritage, and I had read that it covered events that took place in places my mother had mentioned to us. She was still alive. Sharing in some of those memories was the least I could do.

In fact, *Schindler's List* opened my eyes and my mind in ways I hadn't imagined. Suddenly I saw at least a version of my mother's world when she was a young woman, and as she might have experienced it. I saw more realistically than ever before what she had faced in trying to survive. She was not a Schindler Jew saved from extermination by

Oskar Schindler, but just about everything else I saw in the film aligned with her experiences in the war.

On the screen, I saw the Kraków Ghetto as she might have: its establishment, its liquidation and the monstrous commandant Amos Göth of the Płaszów concentration camp, where she and members of her family were imprisoned. I saw the train ramp at Auschwitz, where the Angel of Death selected some who would live and some who would die. I saw that angel deciding the fate of my mother and aunt, who survived, and the fate of most of the rest of her family and my father's family, who were all murdered. I didn't know then that a quarter century later, I would be sitting on the steps of Jozefa 12 in Kazimierz, where my mother grew up, with a laptop computer provided by our Israeli guide Matan Shefi, watching *Schindler's List* where it was actually filmed. It was there that my mother and her family cooked, cleaned and lived. And it was from there that they were deported to their prisons or sent to their deaths. Life is strange, very strange. Here is my mother's story of those war years.

DEPORTATIONS

The Germans had elaborated their plan for Kraków prior to their invasion. It was quickly implemented. Persecution of the Jewish population began immediately after the German troops entered the city on September 6, 1939, when Jews were ordered to report for forced labor. An order announced in November mandated that all Jews within the General Government[1] were to be identified as Jewish by wearing an armband with the Star of David sewn on it. Kraków's synagogues were shut down, and all their valuables and religious items were confiscated.

Later it was announced that Kraków would become the capital of the German zone, but in May 1940 the German occupation authority decided that it also would be "unseemly" to allow Jews to remain in the new Polish capital. Instead, Kraków would become a showplace, the "racially cleanest" city in the General Government. Implementing this would require a massive deportation of Jews from the city. Of the more than 68,000 Jews in Kraków, only 15,000 Jewish workers and their families were permitted to remain, at least for some period, until additional steps leading toward their complete eradication were implemented. All other Jews were ordered out of the city to be resettled in the surrounding rural areas.

From May to mid-August 1940, a voluntary expulsion program was implemented. Jews who chose to leave were allowed to take all of their belongings and relocate elsewhere. After that date, Jews were told to report to specific locations for transport. Their expulsions were now mandatory, and all belongings they brought could not weigh a total of more than 62 pounds (the amount held by one very large suitcase). By early December 1940, 43,000 Jews had been removed voluntarily and involuntarily. Jews still residing in Kraków at that time were deemed "...economically useful... They had to obtain a residence permit that ... had to be renewed each month."[2]

Abe Friedmann qualified as an essential worker in this latter group, so he and Frimet were allowed to stay. And while my mother's imagination had him co-directing her dance studio in Kazimierz, in fact he had been a skilled luggage maker for the previous 15 years. His boss, David Lipshitz, whose suitcase shop was at Krakówska 12, attested to the German authorities that Abe was reliable and expert at what he did. Unlike other Jewish shops, this shop had not yet been seized by an Aryan administrator and thus was still under Jewish ownership for some time after the Germans arrived. Abe applied for and was given papers for himself and Frimet, allowing them to stay in Kraków and enabling Abe to work (at least for a while) outside of what in 1942 would become the Kraków Ghetto, where the remaining Jews of Kraków would eventually be resettled. At the time he was unaware that the Germans needed workers like himself to make luggage to hold the belongings of Jews who soon would either depart to slave labor camps, enter concentration or extermination camps or stay in and around Kraków, only to meet a similar fate at some future time.

*Frimet and her husband Abe Friedmann in February 1941 in photos
from their German ID cards.*

From 1940 until March 1942, my mother worked, first in forced labor making bricks, and then later mending and washing uniforms for the Germans. For a short while, she was paid a small sum, earning enough weekly pay to buy a few loaves of bread on the black market. She told us that she survived in part by always saying yes to whatever the Germans asked her to do, even if she had no idea how to do it. Though she was the daughter of a tailor and several of her brothers were also tailors, she told us she hadn't a clue about how to sew. But when the Germans asked if she could sew in order to work in a factory, she answered, "Of course." Then she told us she had basically learned on the job. Even with the permissions they had received, for some reason Abe and Frimet left Jozefa 12 later in 1940 and moved to Berka Joselewicza 18. This was before they were forced to leave once more upon the creation of the Kraków Ghetto.

Generally, the Germans moved Jews out of the city on specific transports. These were special trains sent to nearby villages and towns where they were held until extermination camps were completed for the passengers' eventual murder or, for a "lucky few," the opportunity to first have slave labor extracted from them. I found evidence that several members of my mother's family were initially given permission to stay, but most were sent out of Kraków relatively quickly. They included Frimet's brothers: Leib Entenberg with his wife Chana and son Chaim,[3] Leon Entenberg with his wife Sabina and their young son Josef,[4] and Jozef Entenberg. Leib's family was sent to the Lubicz slave labor camp in northern Poland in February or November 1941. We have no record of what happened to them after they arrived.

On March 20, 1941, Leon's family left Kraków on the day when the city's remaining Jews were moved into the newly established Kraków Ghetto. They went on a transport bound for Międzyrzec Podlaski, a town linked to a transfer ghetto near Lublin that ultimately held 20,000 Jews. Jozef was in that same transport. Most of those who arrived in Międzyrzec Podlaski were destined to be murdered after the transfer ghetto where they were held was liquidated, sometime between 1942 and 1943. They were sent either to Treblinka or Majdanek, two of six massive extermination camps that had been constructed.[5] They were either gassed to death or forced to work under starvation conditions until they died. Anyone in that transport who was murdered in Treblinka died in August 1942.

Jakub Goldman had petitioned the Board of the Jewish Community in Kraków to allow Jozef to stay with his parents, since the Board had accepted Jozef's application for a *Kennkarte*, a German ID, the previous month. He pleaded, explaining that Jozef was "deaf, very weak, stays in bed and should stay with his family." He asked them to reissue Jozef's ID and attach a special note stipulating that Jozef was not to be transported to any place outside Kraków. Jakub said they had previously attached such a note to his own ID (not that it ended up saving Jakub either). Not surprisingly, his pleas were rejected and his youngest child was sent away. Since Jakub appeared to be unable to write in Polish or German, both notes to the Jewish Community leaders were evidently written and signed by Jozef on Jakub's behalf.

Additional records that I uncovered from that terrible period concerned Abraham and Naftali Entenberg, Frimet's husband Abe Friedmann, my mother and her sister Genia, Genia's husband Sussel Beitscher and their daughter Frymeta, and of course, Jakub Goldman. Each of them would face longer journeys after the Kraków Ghetto and their time in the Płaszów concentration camp, but except for Frimet and Genia, they all met the same tragic end. Beyond knowing that Ruchela Entenberg made it into the ghetto, I could find no records for what happened to her. I believe she was killed, probably gunned down in the streets of the ghetto during its liquidation.

133

THE KRAKÓW GHETTO

The Kraków Ghetto was formally established on March 20, 1941 in the Podgórze district just across Kraków's Vistula River and not, as is often believed, in the historic Jewish district of Kazimierz. Displaced Polish families from Podgórze took up residence in the formerly Jewish dwellings outside the newly established ghetto.

This ghetto was one of the major metropolitan ghettos the Nazis created in the new General Government territory. It was established for the continued exploitation, terror and persecution of the Jews who were allowed to remain in the city, and was later used as a staging area for separating the "able workers" from those who were to be deported to extermination camps as part of Operation Reinhardt, a specific plan developed to exterminate the Polish Jews in the General Government region.

Meanwhile, about 16,000 Jews were crammed into an area previously inhabited by 3,500 people who used to live in a district consisting of 30 streets, 320 residential buildings and 3,167 rooms. One apartment was allocated to every four Jewish families. Many who were even less fortunate lived on the street. To accommodate the density, apartments within the ghetto were divided on a per person basis or a standard of three people to one window. The remaining members of

Jakub Goldman's family were moved into a building on Janowa Wola 2/6. Jews relocating to the ghetto were allowed to bring belongings weighing no more than a total of 55 pounds. The rest of their possessions were taken away.

In April 1941, the ghetto was enclosed by a wall made of barbed wire and stones that looked like tombstones. The wall was constructed using Jewish forced labor. Small sections of it still remain. One part features a memorial plaque that reads: "Here they lived, suffered and perished at the hands of Hitler's executioners. From here they began their final journey to the death camps."

Any Jew found outside the ghetto was killed. Over time, living conditions in the ghetto worsened as Jews from nearby villages were moved in. Deportations of Jews from the ghetto to the Belzec extermination camp began later that year and accelerated during 1942.

As part of Operation Reinhardt, the ghetto was liquidated between May 1942 and March 1943, and most of its inhabitants were deported to the Belzec extermination camp, the Płaszów slave labor camp right outside of Kraków or the Auschwitz concentration camp just 60 kilometers (37 miles) away by train.

During these systematic deportations, the Jews were first assembled on the large Zgody Square, not far from the train tracks but still inside the ghetto walls, and then escorted to the nearby railway station. The first transport consisted of 7,000 people, and the second held an additional 4,000 Jews. They were deported to the Belzec death camp in June 1942. The final liquidation of the ghetto had been carried out under the command of Amon Göth, who then took charge of the nearby Płaszów labor camp, with 2,000 Jews deemed fit to work among the first to be moved there. Eventually they included my mother, her husband Abe, her sister Genia, Genia's husband and daughter, my grandfather Jakub and possibly Frimet's brothers Abraham and Naftali. Those deemed unfit for work, who comprised another 2,000 Jews, my grandmother Ruchela among them, were killed in the streets of the ghetto. Those still standing were sent to their deaths in Auschwitz.

In a memoir, ghetto survivor and movie director Roman Polanski revisited his childhood thoughts about the mass deportations in Kraków. "My own feeling," Polanski wrote, "was that if only one could explain to them that we had done nothing wrong, the Germans would realize that it all was a gigantic misunderstanding."[1]

PŁASZÓW AND AUSCHWITZ

In October 1942, my mother was selected for slave labor at the Płaszów concentration camp. It had been established within the city limits but was on the other side of the river, a few kilometers inland. She joined the other members of her family who were also imprisoned there, at least for a time.

My mother recalled her time with vivid and frightening memories. She described Amon Göth, the infamously cruel SS camp commander at the time, again and again. She remembered him sitting with a rifle at the bedroom window of his villa, which overlooked the camp, randomly shooting prisoners with the aim of striking terror into their daily lives, including her own. She was standing near some of those women as they were shot dead, a scene that was later depicted in Spielberg's movie.

Płaszów was constructed on the grounds of two former Jewish cemeteries and populated with additional prisoners during the final liquidation of the Kraków Ghetto. The camp was originally an *Arbeitslager* (labor camp) that supplied forced labor to several local armament factories and a stone quarry. In 1943, Płaszów was expanded and integrated into the Nazi concentration camp system.

Most of the prisoners were Polish Jews. Compared to other camps, it had high numbers of women and children.

The camp was divided into multiple sections. There were separate areas for camp personnel, work facilities, male prisoners and female prisoners, and a further subdivision between Jews and non-Jews imprisoned as slave laborers. Men and women were separated, but they still managed to have some contact with one another. Forced labor was the camp's primary function, but it was also a site of the mass murder of both inmates and prisoners brought in from the outside. The main targets were the elderly and the sick. There were no gas chambers or crematoria, so the mass murders were carried out by shootings. The Płaszów camp became particularly infamous for both the individual and mass shootings carried out at Hujowa Górka, a large hill close to the camp that was commonly used for executions. As a result, the death rate in the camp was very high. Many prisoners also died of typhus and starvation.

The camp also was notorious for its other terrors, particularly Göth's sadistic treatment and killing of prisoners. It was believed that he never started his breakfast without shooting at least one person,[1] and he would sic his Great Danes on prisoners if he didn't like their expressions. Göth would also step outside to hunt humans, wearing his Tyrolean hat to mark his intention. For seasoned prisoners, it was a signal to try to hide.

The female guards treated prisoners as brutally as the males did. "When we were loaded on the train in Płaszów, an SS woman hit me on the head," one prisoner recalled. "They were so vicious, brutal and sadistic, more than men. I think because some of them were women and you expect kindness, it was shocking."[2] One of the senior female commanders was known for whipping women inmates in the eyes.

Someone who knew Frimet before the war in Kraków and then again after the war's end, recalled her horrible treatment. "In Płaszów, Frimet was beaten, very often in the worst possible way. Once she was beaten so badly by an SS officer that she broke down and was taken, covered in blood, to a hospital in Płaszów." Beatings to the head and the face also resulted in her losing many of her teeth and repeated bouts with severe headaches for years afterward.

Göth and the other camp personnel punished inmates for a variety of actions. Any perceived act of sabotage, such as smuggling items into the camp, disobeying orders or carrying an extra piece of food in one's clothes was an offense punishable by death. As for methods for killing, death by hanging was one of Göth's favorites.

Although food was scarce, inmates who possessed any number of złotys could buy extra food. A food-for-food trading system also developed; for example, two portions of soup were equal to half a loaf of bread.

Despite the horror of it all, Frimet was lucky in at least one regard. Until about August 1944, she spent some of her time there sewing German Army uniforms. It is likely that work assignment helped her survive. She was fortunate to work at a factory in the camp called Madritsch Płaszów. Julius Madritsch was an Austrian who made clothes, including German uniforms. Despite the terrifying conditions all around the camp, Madritsch made a point of trying to protect his Jewish workers, including my mother. In fact, Madritsch was a friend of Oskar Schindler's and Schindler had added some of Madritsch's Jews (though not my mother) to his list of protected workers.

On September 13, 1944, Göth was relieved of his position and charged by the SS with theft of Jewish property, which according to Nazi legislation belonged to the State. He was also charged with failure to provide adequate food to the prisoners under his charge, violation of concentration camp regulations regarding the treatment and punishment of prisoners and giving prisoners and noncommissioned officers unauthorized access to camp personnel records. Göth was tried in Poland in 1946, sentenced to death for "personally killing, maiming and torturing a substantial, albeit unidentified number of people" and hanged 10 days later.

Here are some journal notes from my visit to Płaszów and a chance meeting with the daughter of another Płaszów prisoner.

October 13, 2018

We visit Kazimierz again, and the Old City (castle, squares, churches.) Lunch in a café. A walk to see a remaining wall of the Kraków Ghetto (that looked like gravestones writ large). Then a short drive to Płaszów – a powerful place, it would turn out to be, even though it is today mostly a park and grassy field.

As we walk we encounter an 80-year-old woman named Janina Polanska and her husband, who come every day, even twice a day, because they live nearby but also because this woman's father (she said his name was Roman Weigling) was imprisoned in Płaszów. She seems to come to look at visitors and try to connect with others who have some palpable connection to this place of the dead and dying. She tries to comfort them. She approaches us and tells our guide Matan in Polish a bit of her story. She was about five in 1943-4, when her mother, who was Catholic, came here to visit a prisoner, her husband, a Jew. She remembers this place then, including a quarry (the Liban Quarry) that she urges us to see (she comes with us) where she says members of the Gestapo used to come to laugh at the prisoners toiling away, doing their backbreaking work in the quarry, smashing the rocks and loading them onto carts and railcars. They saw it as a great amusement. The guard towers remain as well as pictures and descriptions throughout. We hug this woman, take pictures with her, and Matan promises to try to discover something more about this woman's Jewish grandfather and what became of him. She was fortunate that her mother was able to bribe guards and rescue her father, who survived the war. But the memory even for her family, remained forever.

This was a place where I could see my mother working to 'organize' a potato at the risk of losing her life. I could see my grandfather's face again, for the first time. One document seems to say that he was involved in the camp bakery. I hope so. But what became of him after that? At nearly 70 years of age, our guess was that when Płaszów was liquidated as the Soviets approached at the end of 1944, so was he, in Auschwitz, where my mother also went for several terrifying months, before it too was liquidated. Because we found him on several lists in Płaszów, it was clear that he was among the last prisoners to actually leave. He appeared in a December 10, 1944 list as one of the qualified (educated) workers. He had been working since September 1944 demolishing the barracks. If he was among the last to leave on January 14, 1945, he was among a group of 600 prisoners who were led in the direction of Auschwitz, taking three days on that death march. The Red Army arrived shortly afterward on January 20, 1945.

While at first we heard that the Soviet memorial was another grand gesture by the Soviets who enjoyed building on a monumental scale, when we came closer to it, set on the highest point in the area, I found it moving. It portrayed a few faces, each worn and weary, with arms at their sides, some fists clenched, others open, still others limp. They carried their burdens wearily, but also with a strength that seemed to be ebbing away. The Jewish Community of Kraków created a much more modest memorial, in Hebrew and Polish. It said in part: 'This monument is erected to honor the victims of bestiality and unimagined cruelty where hundreds of thousands died – call them Jews. Why? Call it Hitlerism.'

As I think about my mother's imagination, one begins to think about one's own. The fields are grassy and still all around us is this killing field. As in Auschwitz, the visions we create of what happened here remain in our imaginations, in our heads. In Auschwitz though, the tangible evidence lies everywhere around us. The wreckage of the crematoria and showers, the bunkers, the ashes at our feet. Here all that remains is grass and the memories and visions we bring to this place – to remember, to honor and to mourn.

It is here that it becomes clear to me how much this trip has meant to me. And as difficult as it has been and will likely continue to be – on this journey, and in writing this story – I'm glad I have and am doing it. And as that Polish woman who visited here at age five and insisted on a picture with Jenny said, she "wanted to hug the woman who is here to support me in all this. She is also a brave soul."

In July and August 1944, several transports of prisoners left Płaszów for Auschwitz, Stutthof, Flossenbürg, Mauthausen and other camps.

My mother and Genia may have been sent to Auschwitz during that period or possibly in the fall, when the liquidation of the camp was beginning as the Soviet Army steadily approached Kraków. And what of the other members of her family who were here?

On August 10, 1944, Abraham Entenberg was sent from Płaszów to the Mauthausen concentration camp in Austria. He was first assigned to something called the *Bergkristall* (Rock Crystal), where prisoners of Mauthausen's Gusen sub-camp were building a series of underground galleries to accommodate the production of Messerschmitt pursuit fighter planes. Supervised by the SS, thousands of prisoners lost their lives in the course of the project. He was transferred back to Mauthausen on March 1, 1945 and then, presumably because he was sick, moved to the infirmary, where mortality was extremely high. He was then sent to what was called the *Sanitätslager*, which was "little more than a place to pass away."[3] Hardly any prisoner survived being sent there. I believe Abraham was killed there by the administration of a lethal injection into his heart. He died on May 1, 1945. The US 11th Armored Division liberated the camp four days later. Abraham's younger brother Naftali Entenberg was also sent from Płaszów to Mauthausen, where he died on January 17, 1945. The cause of death was listed as heart muscle weakness and colitis.

My Aunt Genny (Genia) and her family made it to the Kraków Ghetto and then to Płaszów. Upon arriving at Płaszów, the two sisters were separated from their husbands, as well as from Genia's daughter Frymeta and my mother's father. Like Abraham and Naftali, Genia's husband, Sussel (Zysl) Beitscher died at the Mauthausen/Gusen concentration camp in Austria, on October 13, 1944. He had arrived there from the Melk subcamp of Mauthausen, where he was listed as a laborer on August 10, 1944.

Their daughter Frymeta also was murdered in Mauthausen sometime in 1943, according to an eyewitness who registered her death with Yad Vashem in the 1950s. However, my mother and aunt had other stories. My mother once said that she had seen both her mother Ruchela and one of her brothers hanged in the early months of the war, adding that my aunt's daughter might have been hiding out with her grandmother around that time. If so, she may have met a similar fate. On another occasion I recall my mother telling us that Genia blamed herself for her daughter's death because she had allowed Frymeta to stay with her grandmother, rather than accompany her mother to Płaszów. Perhaps my mother got it wrong and my aunt was upset for allowing her daughter to go with her father. Sadly, no matter what happened or when, a little girl eight or ten years old was murdered. If she had stayed with her mother, she would have died in Auschwitz. Yet the self-doubts, self-recriminations and terrors attached to the "what if's" haunted my aunt for the rest of her life.

What about my mother's husband, Abe Friedmann? My mother told an interviewer after her liberation that she had somehow learned in Auschwitz or later in Bergen-Belsen that Abe had been seen alive in Buchenwald in late 1944.

Buchenwald was an important source of forced labor. Workers were needed in armaments factories, stone quarries and construction projects. But what happened to him before Buchenwald? As discussed earlier, Abe and Frimet were given permission to stay in Kraków, and later in the Kraków Ghetto, in part because of Abe's work as a luggage maker. However, on November 29, 1940, even after getting the German *Kennkarte* ID and permission to continue working in Kraków, records indicate that Abe was put on a transport to Dębica, a town east of Kraków toward the Ukrainian border. At that time the Germans were building a massive SS-staffed military base on the outskirts of Dębica for weapons testing and training and therefore were importing slave laborers for the project.

Other records from February 1941 show that Abe was cleared to work in Kraków. Perhaps, like my father, he was sent out on a slave labor assignment and then returned to Kraków. We know he had been in the Kraków Ghetto and then sent to Płaszów around the time of the ghetto's liquidation. Records indicate he was arrested by the SS police in Kraków and arrived in Płaszów on March 17, 1943. Since March 17 was at the tail end of the ghetto's liquidation, my guess is the arrest was a formality recorded for the German bureaucracy, as fit workers were moved to Płaszów.

Then, as Płaszów was being liquidated, Abe was transferred to the Gross-Rosen concentration camp on October 16, 1944 and then to Buchenwald, where he became prisoner number 56898 on November 4, 1944. A card in the International Tracing Service archives includes a sick bay card for Abe, meaning he was already in poor health when he arrived at Buchenwald. A few weeks later, on November 17, he and 150 other inmates from Buchenwald were sent to Sonneberg-West. These inmates often worked alongside German workers who, according to reports, would sometimes beat them. Beatings by the SS guards were also common. Abe, his fellow slave laborers and the Germans all worked for a subsidiary of a German firm, G.E. Reinhardt, which paid the German government four Reichsmarks per inmate per day to build an underground factory to support the German war effort. Sonneberg was a slave labor, punishment and concentration camp that the Germans had used since 1933. Eventually it became a sub-camp of Buchenwald where prisoners made aircraft and tank parts as well as parts for the V-series rockets that were used in the Blitz attacks on England. Sonneberg therefore became a key target of numerous Allied bombing raids. I assume Abe was killed in the final days of chaos, either during an Allied attack or in the course of his imprisonment.

My grandfather, Jakub Goldman, is the final person to be accounted for in my mother's family. In January 1945, the last of the remaining inmates and camp staff left Płaszów on a death march to Auschwitz. Many of those who survived the march were killed upon arrival. We have a record showing that Jakub Goldman was in Płaszów in February 1944 and then again on December 10, 1944. He was therefore among the last prisoners to leave Płaszów for Auschwitz, where he was murdered. The Russians liberated Płaszów just a few weeks later, in January 1945. For my mother and aunt, however, while they were still alive, the suffering was to continue.

Auschwitz

When we were children, another bedtime story our mother seemed compelled to relate concerned her arrival from Płaszów at the train ramp in Auschwitz-Birkenau in 1944. Upon their arrival, prisoners were to line up for a quick examination by a Nazi officer who would signal whether you would go in one direction or the other, that is, to be either killed directly or saved for the time being as a slave laborer. It was called the selection: you were being selected for life or death. Our mother claimed that when she and her sister arrived, the examining Nazi was the infamous Dr. Josef Mengele, who not only enjoyed conducting these selections but also performed horrible medical experiments on some of those selected to live, if only briefly. As she watched what was happening around her, she quickly determined that the group she was pointed toward looked younger and stronger, while her older sister Genia had been sent to the other side to join another group composed of older and clearly weaker women, men and children. At that moment she realized Genia was going to be killed, so she ran through what was clearly a somewhat chaotic and crowded area to her sister's group, braving the German Shepherd guard dogs that were set upon her as she grabbed her sister and pulled her to the other side. It worked, and it probably actually happened, according to an expert I consulted who has written extensively about Auschwitz.

*Frimet probably slept with hundreds of others on these slats of
wood in Barracks 22B in Auschwitz-Birkenau.*

When exactly my mother and her sister arrived at Auschwitz is
unknown. The Płaszów concentration camp was being liquidated as
the Soviets moved to liberate Kraków and neighboring regions. The
Russian attack began in northern areas of Poland in August 1944 and
continued southward, closer to Kraków, through December and into
the new year. My mother and aunt could have arrived at any time
during those months. It could have been as early as August 6, 1944,
when several thousand Polish Jewish women arrived from Płaszów,
more than half of whom were sent directly to the gas chambers. A
number of other transports were carried out from October to
December 1944, first to Auschwitz and from there to Bergen-Belsen.
And indeed, on October 21 or 22, 1944, a transport arrived at
Auschwitz from Płaszów, where the selection of Jews was known to
have been carried out by Dr. Mengele. Regardless of whether she
arrived in August or in the September–October period of transports,
it was not until November that Frimet was registered as Auschwitz
prisoner serial number a-27359.[4] By then the Germans had destroyed
the gas chambers to eliminate evidence of their heinous crimes. In
one sense, because Frimet worked at Madritsch Płaszów, her arrival
in Auschwitz was delayed and thus she was spared at least some of
the horrors that prisoners would endure there.

A book kept by a female prisoner lists Frimet Frydman being placed in Block 22B in the women's camp in Birkenau with a different prisoner number. On May 16, 1945, the book itself was given to the District Commission to Investigate Nazi Crimes in Kraków. The barracks consisted of 15 brick buildings in three rows. Later, several former inmates described the barracks for the Auschwitz-Birkenau memorial museum. "There were battered straw mattresses in the bunks ... dirty and torn paper sacks filled with old, pulverized straw," Anna Tytoniak recalled. "We were dirty and louse-infected ... what we found in these barracks went far beyond any understanding of dirt and insects. Huge, hungry lice wandered across the mattresses, like ants in a dug-up anthill. Rats large like cats strolled on the barracks' dirt floor and on the ceiling beams... This was an indescribable den of dirt and misery. Here the strongest body and the most invincible character would give up." Another inmate, Seweryna Szmaglewska, added: "The living conditions are health-destroying, leading to physical and mental debasement. They kill."

Luggage taken from inmates arriving in Auschwitz. (Photo Credit, United States Holocaust Memorial Museum, courtesy of National Archives and Records Administration, College Park.)

During our fall 2018 visit to Auschwitz, the largest of the Nazi concentration camps, we saw a great pile of luggage of all sizes like the one in the picture here, which shows suitcases of myriad shapes and colors bearing scribbles left by their owners. It was displayed in one of the old barracks that had been converted into a museum. Other rooms in that converted barracks contained towering mounds of shorn hair, even more imposing piles of toys and dolls taken from young children before they were gassed to death and thousands of pairs of worn shoes and broken eyeglasses that had been removed before their owners entered the "showers."

These possessions were taken from Jews as they arrived from places like Będzin, Dąbrowa and Kraków, even before most of them joined the lines to the gas chambers, that is, before their bodies were consumed by the fires of the crematoria nearby. As noted earlier in discussing the murder of my father's first family, so many ashes were generated from the countless burned bodies that there was no place to dispose of them. Instead camp inmates strewed them on the ground. Today, visitors to the memorial walk across them, grinding them under their feet. Those ashes of my parents' families and friends, of lives and memories lost, are all that remain as Frimet's fanciful dreams were transformed into vivid, ever present nightmares when she became a prisoner among the dead and dying.

As for the luggage, those waiting their turns were told to place the single bags they had been allowed to bring for their "resettlement" on the ground, promised that their luggage would be returned after showers that would cleanse them from their cattle car journey. The bags represented at least one reason why the Nazis temporarily spared my mother and her husband Abe. She would survive; he would perish.

Auschwitz, with its four gas chambers and crematoria, was the single largest scene of the Nazi genocide and the largest of the German concentration camps. At least 960,000 Jews were murdered there, representing some 90 percent of all those who perished in Auschwitz. Other victims of the Nazi terror whose lives ended there included some 75,000 ethnic Poles, 21,000 Roma (Gypsies) and 15,000 Soviet prisoners of war.

The Auschwitz memorial site lists 1.1 million people, including 200,000 young children, who were killed immediately or soon after arrival. Only one out of five people getting off the trains was kept alive to perform slave labor, mostly constructing new parts of the camp or working for German companies involved in the war effort. Sometimes they were sent to subcamps nearby or in other parts of Upper Silesia.

Many of the barracks housing slave laborers still stand at the site. They feature large wooden shelves for beds, with five or six prisoners packed onto each shelf. Each barracks held around 500 prisoners. The original barracks were designed as military stables to hold 52 horses each. One survivor recalled about this sleeping arrangement: "If we wanted to turn over, we all had to."[5] Prisoners were starved and beaten, battled lice and dysentery and were subjected to every other manner of inhumane indignity. Insufficient nutrition and hard labor contributed to the destruction of their bodies, causing emaciation and starvation sickness. Those suffering in this way were called *Muselmänner*. It was said that when they gave up on life, they looked like Muslims at prayer, with their bodies bent forward and heads touching the ground. They could no longer work, so they were often selected for the gas chambers.

Before the early months of 1942, the Nazis deported only a small number of Jews to Auschwitz, but by mid-1942, Jews made up the majority of the camp population. My father's family in Będzin and Dąbrowa, who arrived a month or so after the regular selections began, were among the early victims of the gas chambers. My mother and aunt arrived more than two years later.

We visited Auschwitz with a terrific researcher and academic historian, the German-born Giles Bennett. The son of a British father and an Austrian mother, Giles lives and works in Munich at the Center for Holocaust Studies. He is a wonderful, generous, gifted scholar who provided an extraordinary abundance of help and contacts during our years of research. He came to Kraków to take us through Auschwitz. We spent about eight hours there, visiting what must have been a version of Hell, if not worse.

Here is what I wrote in my journal when we visited, including what we said and did the day and night before we went to Auschwitz.

October 8, 2018

We arrived in Kraków after our flight from Tel Aviv and thought we could spend the afternoon at Schindler's factory – but when we got there, the ticket allotment for the day had been exhausted. We did go to the Galicia Jewish Museum instead. In it was a great photo exhibit about the Jews in and around the area of Galicia (where my mother was from.) I told the attendant at the museum that my mother was born near there and we were visiting for that reason. She seemed a bit astounded, impressed or something. It's not something that I would normally do – opening up like that to a stranger, unsolicited. Interestingly, when they were alive, I was oddly ashamed of my parents so too often I was actively avoiding any association with them. I'm sorry to say that now. Anonymous was good for me. But this trip was about them (and by association, quite a bit about me and my sister as well) after way too long. Maybe better to have come after they had died – this was about them, of course, but it was to be just as much if not more about those who they left behind – those who had been murdered – and also for the family we now have – so that they could learn their story – of sacrifice and survival, yes, but also just of living for the day – not as Jews necessarily, but as human beings. There's the rub. They fell into a category from which there was no escape for them – at least not in time – nor for those they loved.

At this exhibit, as well, we saw a picture for the first time – a picture that became famous – from Spielberg's 'Schindler's List' – of Jozefa 12 – where my mother and her family lived in Kazimierz – the old Jewish Quarter of Kraków. Here we saw a photo of the building, associated with 'Schindler's List' and not with my mother. But we were to visit that address that day and pretty much every day we were in Kraków (as well as the area around it, where others in my mother's family also lived.)

And while Yad Vashem (which we visited a few days before) brought an onslaught of emotions, so did this one picture – and our subsequent visits and explorations of their neighborhood. Before meeting Giles, the son of a Capetown high school classmate of a friend and former colleague Colin

Baigel, at a restaurant called Starka (next door to Jozefa 12), we visited my mother's apartment building and courtyard.

Giles knows many languages and so much about the Holocaust and Kraków. At dinner, we talked about victimhood and survivorhood, about families. He has spoken to dozens of survivors. Picturing my mother and brothers and parents at Jozefa 12 cut deeply into me. As always I also spoke of her quirks, her imagination and her frequent mentions of Dr. Mengele to anyone who would or wouldn't listen.

October 9, 2018

Auschwitz. We spent eight hours there. I broke down a number of times (as did Giles and Jennifer). We toured it as well as Auschwitz-Birkenau, which is more likely where my mother went through her selection (as did my aunt) at the ramp where the trains pulled up and disgorged their human cargo (both my mother's and father's families had been there). All the detritus of this enterprise, from shorn hair, to shoes, to luggage, to cups and basins – were gathered to be seen. Also, the national exhibits had their own take on the events that took place there (Soviets and Poles emphasized the national tragedies as much or more than the Jewish tragedies). Auschwitz after all at first housed Poles and was where Poles and dissidents, as well as resistance fighters, were killed. Soviet war prisoners built Birkenau, before they were killed there.

Being there meant picturing individual family members – especially the children – getting out of the cattle cars and then entering the gas chambers for a shower, and seeing the machinery created to torture, to starve, to use up, and then to kill the ones who weren't immediately murdered. As we were told, there were so many corpses that the ashes were simply spread on the ground everywhere. We were walking on those ashes, every step of the way.

What continued to go through our heads was one of many questions: Why make these people suffer? They were already terrified, why did the Germans need to add to their terror on a minute by minute basis? I can't get over that aspect of all this. Giles said that some of the Nazi hierarchy truly believed or came to believe that the Jews needed to be eradicated at all costs.

They believed or led others to believe that the Jews were responsible for the loss by Germany of World War I and the privations that followed. So, I thought, why not just shoot them in the head? Why this dramatic deadly charade, using resources that could have been used more productively to fight enemy soldiers? Giles said that they believed they had to do this as well. As importantly perhaps. The idea went beyond subjugating and terrorizing the Poles to eliminate any opposition. It was also to destroy a race of people. Jews. Once and for all.

We saw starvation cells. The disagreements among the Nazis came about whether to exploit these prisoners before killing them or just to eliminate them as soon as possible. Two camps of Nazis had differences on this score. Naturally when you enter, there is the famous and chilling wrought iron letters which in English unashamedly proclaim: Work Makes You Free. So does the death that accompanies it.

Today, Auschwitz attracts a million visitors a year. I would encourage everyone above the teen years to visit. You will find, as we did, that there are ghosts here, everywhere you walk, ghosts that will haunt visitors forever. Rightly so.

BERGEN-BELSEN

A harrowing and seemingly endless train ride awaited Frimet and
Genia when they left Auschwitz in cattle cars for Bergen-Belsen.

I believe that my mother and her sister arrived in Bergen-Belsen concentration camp on December 10, 1944, via a transport from Auschwitz, which was being liquidated as the Soviet armies approached.[1]

It is also possible that my mother and Genia arrived as early as the autumn of 1944 on another transport from Auschwitz. At that time, ever more workers needed for heavy labor were being shipped to Germany from Poland and other parts of Europe. In September and October 1944, transports of 3,000 women from Auschwitz arrived at

Bergen-Belsen. They were housed in new barracks set up for them in the Star Camp (Star for the Jewish stars they wore). The barracks (sometimes they were just tents) had no water, no beds and no other facilities of any kind. Anne Frank and her sister Margot were among the prisoners who came from Auschwitz around that time.

Bergen-Belsen, first established in 1943 on the site of a POW camp in northern Germany, was originally meant to be a detention camp for Jews who were to be exchanged for Germans held in Allied territories. In March 1944 it was transformed into a regular concentration camp for prisoners considered too sick to work at other camps. They were housed in a new section of the camp where living conditions were awful, so bad that in 1944, most of the arrivals died soon after getting off the trains. The year progressed into late 1944 and then 1945, and conditions only got worse in the months before liberation.

My mother was initially housed in a tent camp where most of the women evacuated from Auschwitz had lived. After a storm she was moved to a smaller women's camp, which happened to be the camp where Anne Frank and her sister Margot died of typhus sometime in February 1945, just weeks before liberation. Their mother Edith had died in Auschwitz in January 1945.[2]

The conditions under which the prisoners lived continued to deteriorate, especially in early 1945, when tens of thousands of prisoners arrived after death marches from camps that had been evacuated. Bergen-Belsen was originally designed for 10,000 prisoners, and the arrival of Jewish prisoners forcibly evacuated from Auschwitz and other camps to the east, including my mother and also my father, who arrived after a death march in early April 1945, made conditions unbearable. Sanitation was astonishingly inadequate, with only a few latrines and water faucets for tens of thousands of people. Overcrowding, poor sanitary conditions, and the lack of adequate food, water and shelter led to outbreaks of diseases such as typhus, tuberculosis, typhoid fever and dysentery, causing deaths in ever increasing numbers.

More prisoners arrived, and the camp population soared to more than 60,000. I spoke to Judy Altmann, a former prisoner in Bergen-Belsen, when she was 93. She was a Czech survivor of Auschwitz and Bergen-Belsen who told her story to school groups. Mengele selected the 14-year-old Altmann and her niece to live, while on that same day her father was gassed, along with 23 other members of her family. "As horrific as Auschwitz was," she said, "Bergen-Belsen was so bad that anyone who survived it lived forever. There were mountains and mountains of dead bodies everywhere." As for a semblance of hygiene, "there was none whatsoever. You stepped over bodies wherever you went. In the filth, people would get typhus and tuberculosis." Altmann remembers turning to a friend to speak. "A minute later, she was dead." A niece came down with a full-blown case of jaundice. One had to do unimaginable things to survive. "To earn an extra bowl of soup, I volunteered to dispose of dead bodies."

In March 1945 alone, some 18,000 prisoners died in the camp from various causes: beatings, executions, starvation, disease. Indeed, food rations had been shrinking throughout Bergen-Belsen since late 1944. By early 1945, prisoners sometimes went without food for days. Fresh water was also in short supply.

In Bergen-Belsen Frimet contracted typhus. Said one witness who was a neighbor of hers before the war, "Frieda was no longer the same woman I once knew. The joie de vivre that she once had disappeared." And the beatings continued there. She recalled one incident when Frimet stole a potato from the kitchen and was caught by the SS guard who ran the kitchen. "I lost consciousness and was full of blood" from the beatings that followed, she reported. The terrible conditions in the camps resulted in serious infections and the need for a major operation on her sinuses in Sweden the same year that I was born.

My mother had other memories of Bergen-Belsen, mostly for which I could find no evidence. But as I have learned, that doesn't mean they didn't happen.

For instance, my mother once stated that she and 80 other women from Bergen-Belsen who were sick were sent to be killed in the gas chambers at Auschwitz. Somehow she eluded death and was instead sent back to Bergen-Belsen to work. An expert I consulted believed that was unlikely, at least in that time period, since no sick transports were being sent from Bergen-Belsen to Auschwitz in November 1944. As noted, the gas chambers for murdering the sick in Auschwitz were no longer operational, as the camp itself was being liquidated and any evidence of its killing machines, including its crematoria and gas chambers, was being destroyed before the Soviets arrived.

During her final days at Bergen-Belsen, my mother recounted yet another close escape from death. It became our bedtime story, night after night.

Here's what she told us.

In the final days of the war, the SS guards were eliminating the remaining camp inmates in order to erase the traces of their horrific culpability in the murder of thousands. Soup was being offered to the prisoners, as were meals they hadn't had in months, meals that were welcomed. However, my mother said she decided not to accept the food because she had dreamt that her mother, the sainted Ruchela, who was murdered in the ghetto a few years before, came to her every night, warning her that there was something wrong with the soup. "Have this instead," her mother would say, delivering food to her in a dream, so much that she had no appetite or need for anything more.

Despite being nothing but skin and bones, suffering from typhus and shaking from every manner of mistreatment and malevolence, Frimet said she awoke in the morning and wasn't hungry at all. After all, her mother had already fed her. What was more, she found herself still alive.

The other girls in her barracks, she said, had no such visitor, only their own desperate hunger to assuage, so they ate what the SS guards had prepared. The result, my mother reported, was that many of them died terrible slow, painful deaths from the ground glass that their tormentors mixed into the soup.

As I said, this became our bedtime story for some time. It conveyed its own lessons, replete with danger and brimming over with fear: an unfortunate way to feed a youngster's imagination. It turned out that it had probably never happened as my mother recalled, at least not then. More likely it was the product of her own dreams and nightmares, reconsolidated and reconstructed in her reimagination of life and death in Bergen-Belsen in March and April 1945.

Meanwhile, it certainly was true that in those last days before her liberation, orders came down to give prisoners poisoned bread so that when the British soldiers arrived, they would only be met by dead bodies. Fortunately, not all those orders were carried out effectively. But her suffering continued. During interviews for reparations years later, she recalled, "I was so hungry that I dug up carrots that were frozen in the ground. From that I came down with some kind of mouth sickness, as sacs filled with puss appeared in my mouth. Along with my typhoid and stomach problems, I just lay there until the English came."

At last, on April 15, 1945, the long journey into Hell and oblivion ended for both Frimet and Szlama. British forces found most of the 60,000 prisoners in the camp to be seriously ill and discovered around 13,000 unburied bodies. The British forced the remaining SS guards to bury the dead in a mass grave.

Bergen-Belsen was the first major Nazi concentration camp to be liberated by the Western allies. After the war it became the largest DP camp in Germany. Most of its residents would eventually emigrate to Israel (then called Palestine).

An estimated 37,000–50,000 prisoners died in Bergen-Belsen during its existence, and even after liberation, some 14,000–28,000 former prisoners were too ill to recover and died from starvation and typhus at a rate of 500 a day. My mother contracted a serious case of typhus. The British burned down the camp to prevent the spread of that disease while the remaining prisoners were relocated to a series of nearby DP camps for processing and to seek to recuperate at least from their physical injuries and afflictions.

According to her Swedish medical records, when my mother arrived in Sweden she was suffering not just from typhus but also from jaundice and severe malnutrition. However, perhaps because her case was not as severe as other typhus cases, she was not sent to the special typhus quarantine camps set up near Stockholm. Instead she stayed in Malmö, the port where she arrived, in a quarantine hospital.

What allowed some small fraction of the Jews to survive? Luck, coincidence, a will to survive, their faith in God, themselves or others, a desire to see their families again and ultimately, perhaps, a persistent (if perhaps unconscious) will to defeat the Nazis and all they stood for, simply by surviving.

BEFORE LEAVING POLAND

October 12 was the anniversary of the day Christopher Columbus is believed to have discovered the Americas. It was therefore an auspicious day to make yet another discovery of my own, though this one was focused on the Old World my parents had lost, along with everything and everyone in it: what Roman Vishniac called "A Vanished World." Jakub Goldman, my grandfather, was always a mystery to me. I knew hardly anything at all about him. My mother never spoke of him. Yet my middle name, Jakob, came from his. And our grandson would be given his name as well.

Here are my journal notes from our October 2018 visit to Poland about the first time I "met" Jakub Goldman and other family members, right before we left.

This was a special day. I got to meet my grandfather (my mother's father, Jakub Goldman), a distinguished-looking gentleman, as well as two of my uncles and an aunt on my mother's side. Naftali was one of the youngest in her family – he looked young; a handsome older brother Abraham, who bore a striking resemblance to my mother; and his wife Ann. This was all thanks to a visit to a Kraków City Archives not too far from the Old City Square, where we met our guide Matan in the morning and where he uncovered their applications for Kennkarten (German ID cards) and in my grandfather's case, a registration of his dated October 1940 for the Kraków Ghetto.

A picture of my grandfather, Jakub Goldman, far right, taken in Kazimierz shortly before he was sent to the Kraków Ghetto. (Photo from Yad Vashem Photo Archive, no. 3958_39.)

Two days later we unexpectedly met Jakub again. Here's what I wrote in my journal:

It is our last day in Kraków. As it turned out, a very heavy and emotional morning.

First we walk in an unusually thick fog to Oskar Schindler's factory on the other side of the river. The factory itself, which made enamelware as well as ammunition for German guns, faced the outskirts of the Płaszów labor camp, which was to eventually be transformed into a concentration camp. Inside, it is less a factory than a walk through the history of Kraków's Jews, especially leading up to and then during the war years and the Holocaust. We learn his story.[1]

We followed the story with film and pictorial views of the Jewish Quarter before the war, and then life in the Kraków Ghetto, built not far from here, and ending with Belzec and Auschwitz and Amon Göth, the violent and sadistic commander of Płaszów. What was most remarkable was a picture we happened on of scenes from those ghetto years. It was a street scene featuring a group of people, including one soulful-looking older gentleman wearing a fedora (as my father used to) who looked exactly like my grandfather, Jakub Goldman, who we met just two days before in the Kraków City Archives. Later I would look at the head shot of him we saw at the archives, and a picture of this picture from the museum and was convinced that it is the same person. Remarkable, unexpected, especially emotional at that moment of discovery and every time since as I think about it and what it represents.

As it turned out, I discovered much later from a curator at the museum that Jakub Goldman's picture in the museum was not taken in the ghetto, but in Kazimierz, near the Old Synagogue where my mother was first married or near a flea market abutting the Old Synagogue during a German military sweep of Jews, checking identification documents. It dated from March 1941, the month that Kraków's Jews were expelled from their homes and imprisoned in the ghetto. Wherever it was taken, it was him, and for me that was more than sufficient.

I can't wait to tell Noah and Eric and Matan and eventually Jacob of this discovery. Jakub Goldman was transformed from a title, the father of my mother, to a name, Jakub Goldman, to suddenly a face on an ID card – a distinguished-looking gentleman – to a person living in the streets of Kazimierz, seemingly haggard and worn for wear, but keeping his demeanor – a person alive and engaged. And then to actually visit Płaszów and see where he may have met what would be his end. A journey of a lifetime, over many people's lifetimes, in just a blink of an eye.

In these many pictures and rooms and hallways and exhibits, we once more saw the horror endured by the victims (including an eight-year-old Roman Polanski), we heard the testimony, read about and met heroes of the underground resistance – Poles and Jews – and once more witnessed the bestiality (maybe there is no better word for it) of the Nazis.

Yesterday we visited the 'before' – Kazimierz and the Old City – including visiting the building my Aunt Genny lived in with her first husband and their daughter, who was nearly on her way to becoming a teenager before her life ended in the Mauthausen concentration camp.

Today we saw the documentation of all that, learned a bit more through videos of Schindler's efforts and then after three hours in Schindler's factory, it was enough.

We went outside, the fog having lifted, and we watched runners participating in a Kraków half-marathon under the sun and clear blue sky. Took a walk and checked out of our hotel and coincidentally even had the same driver to the airport who had taken us for the day to Auschwitz at the start of this — the most important leg of our journey.

PART VI

THE POSTWAR YEARS: SWEDEN

SEARCHING FOR LIFE AFTER DEATH

What were the odds that Frieda and Szlama would have made it out of their respective hells alive, even if broken?[1] Before arriving in Sweden, each of them had endured years of unending terror, imprisonment in one form or another, mental and physical anguish and unimaginable loss.

Some rough calculations will put a finer point on the daunting challenges they faced. Of the four major concentration camps my parents were in (Auschwitz, Bergen-Belsen, Bunzlau and Płaszów), not counting the sometimes equally horrible and deadly slave labor camps and ghettos, the odds of surviving one, let alone all four to the war's end, were very much against anyone. On average, around 20 percent of the prisoners brought to an extermination camp like Auschwitz were selected for forced labor. The remaining victims were murdered, mostly in the gas chambers.[2] One out of seven survived Auschwitz, one out of four survived Bergen-Belsen and one out of three survived Bunzlau or Płaszów.

Then there was the larger picture encompassing the slaughter of loved ones and the greater Jewish population. Poland's Jewish population in 1939 comprised about three and a half million souls, the most Jews in any country in Europe except the Soviet Union. By the end of the war, 90 percent or more of Poland's Jews had been murdered. In Europe overall, two out of every three Jews had been murdered.

By the war's end, only some 110,000–120,000 Polish Jews remained alive in camps in Poland and Germany. Most of them were transferred to DP camps after their liberation. Approximately 200,000 more Polish Jews had survived in Russia, but many of them ended up being sent to gulags in Siberia. That leaves more than three million Polish Jews who were slaughtered. According to that simple calculation, as Polish Jews my parents had only a three or four percent chance of survival throughout the five-plus years of the war, excluding those who had survived in the Soviet Union. The odds were even worse, considering that my father spent nearly the entire war – more than five years – in ghettos, slave labor camps or concentration camps while my mother lived for more than four years under similar circumstances. How many of the up to 120,000 people in those DP camps fit into that category? Probably fewer still. Yet Szlama and Frieda somehow came out on the other side.

At some time or another, each of us comes to an inflection point. It could be a point of no return, no turning back, no exit. A road taken or not, traveled or ignored. For some, that point is clear: we meet somebody and it changes everything, or a talent we find deep within us incites a spark that burns bright for years. Sometimes things just happen to us. Sometimes we make things happen. We all have our own stories, but somewhere in them, if we dig deep enough, we will discover points of light, even in the shadows or darkness. In this story, we find two people climbing out of an abyss. Each becomes a point of light for the other. Neither imagined how that could happen, or who that person would be. To extend the metaphor, no light shines bright forever, or in the same way. As you will see, even after my parents found each other, years later they would still question the road they had taken, where they ended up and with whom. It has always been complicated.

Certainly my parents had much in common even before they met. Born in shtetls to large but poor Orthodox Jewish families, they came from similar backgrounds. Their families made a living in the way most Jews did at the time, as merchants and traders or as craftsmen. Both found themselves refugees at a young age during World War I. Their families had moved to bigger cities and thus expanded their horizons, perspectives and, at least in theory, their opportunities. Both attended Polish schools, but only for short periods. Both married older spouses. Both came into adulthood during the growth of Polish nationalism and an accompanying intensification of the antisemitism that was a part of their lives, sometimes more so, other times less. They experienced it peaking during and immediately after World War I, and then again in the mid- and late-1930s. Both appreciated the benefits and possibilities of greater assimilation, including expanding economic options for my father and broader social and cultural options for my mother's dreams of another life.

Both lost nearly everyone and everything they held dear and found themselves virtually alone at the war's end, with no interest in returning to their ruined homeland. Both instead became refugees once more, this time in Sweden. They were the ones who had managed to survive. I still can't fully fathom how. I'm not sure they could process why they did either.

From the outside looking in, their relationship seemed mostly to be about needing each other, filling each other's empty spaces in order to start living again. It seemed less about the magic of their encounters and more about necessity and having someone.

They had very different personalities. Neither had an education beyond elementary school, but my father always seemed very good at math and was interested in learning. He loved to study the Torah and read the *Jewish Daily Forward* in Yiddish from cover to cover. He was intensely interested in foreign affairs and of course, all things Israel. He loved making jokes and laughing whenever possible. My mother was much more insular and self-involved. She was interested in how things looked and how others would perceive them. She craved acceptance but acted otherwise, seeing every other person as a potential enemy who wanted to destroy her and take away whatever she had (mainly my sister, me and her husband). Each of my parents represented a different approach to survival.

Given their differing personalities, capabilities and interests, it was likely something even more important that led to their love: their shared history. That also meant sharing their traumas and losses. Their shared experiences gave each a unique understanding of the other's difficult journey in life. That perspective may also have helped them to forgive, if not to forget. For all the shouting and arguing, they shared a deep, sometimes unconscious and piercingly powerful sense of empathy gained through suffering and loss, at least when it came to each other. They remained a couple perhaps because they had found no one else who could understand or even appreciate them in quite the same way. Their relationship was fraught, but staying together was ultimately more important than remaining alone.

After their liberation in mid-April 1945 in Bergen-Belsen, for the next two months they found themselves living in transit refugee camps in Celle, Germany. They hadn't yet met. And while each hoped to find lost relatives, whether in Poland, Germany, the US or Palestine, another country decided to make the more immediate decision about where they would go next. They were chosen to recuperate in Sweden.

Right after the war, Sweden decided to accept about 10,000 Jewish concentration camp survivors, including up to 6,000 survivors from Bergen-Belsen, to recuperate but not necessarily to resettle there. They were initially screened by the Swedish Red Cross and the United Nations Relief and Rehabilitation Administration (UNRRA), created in 1943 to aid refugees who came under Allied control. Other agencies and groups would help my family later, especially the Mosaiska Församlingen, which today is the Judiska Församlingen (Jewish Congregation of Stockholm), the World Jewish Congress

(WJC), the Hebrew Immigrant Aid Society (HIAS) and the American Jewish Joint Distribution Committee (JDC), among others. Helping these survivors would require a village of organizations based in Stockholm, Paris and the US.

A treasure trove of information was unearthed at the Swedish National Archives in a special section of the archives devoted to records of Jewish refugees dating from the immediate post-war period. Some of it, especially my father's correspondence with various organizations and individuals in Yiddish, Polish and German, was especially surprising. One letter sought advice after my father fell in love with my mother in Mölle, a small coastal village on Sweden's west coast, while they were living in separate foreigners' or aliens' camps. There was also a series of letters exploring the disappointing news about my father's dowry from his first marriage. I've mentioned those already.

As for their emigration from Germany to Sweden, it wasn't clear how each of them was chosen to go to Sweden or what happened to them after the six months that Sweden deemed sufficient for their recuperation, or at least for their stay in Sweden. As stateless aliens they were allowed to stay only temporarily and pass through Sweden on their way to somewhere else once they were medically healed and physically fit, insofar as that was possible in such a short period of time. Perhaps they were supposed to return to their Polish homeland or move on to relatives in the US or Palestine, if they could get in. Sweden obviously did not consider itself the default new homeland for these unfortunates.

Meanwhile, Sweden was undergoing a labor shortage. During the war it had remained neutral while its Scandinavian neighbors were invaded, so after the war its economy was relatively unharmed. Now that the war was over, it was well positioned to grow. At that point Sweden could have used an infusion of relatively cheap labor, especially in its low-wage but growing textile industry. Indeed, about 30,000 Polish refugees came to Sweden from their own war-ravaged country, not to recuperate but instead to seek longer-term employment. As for my parents, they had no papers to confirm who they were or where they came from. From what I could learn, they were issued Polish passports in 1948, but those documents were not recognized by the US government. With that, their early plans to emigrate to the US met a bureaucratic wall.

A NEW KIND OF CAMP

According to materials from the Swedish Alien Commission, their individual journeys of recovery and resettlement became clearer between the time they arrived and the time they met, fell in love and found a homeland, if briefly, or more precisely till a homeland found them.

Key to this journey after the war was the system of camps to which they were sent. I learned a great deal about these camps through one survivor family's experiences, recounted in Göran Rosenberg's *A Brief Stop on the Road from Auschwitz*. Rosenberg's father and mother, both Polish Jews, had survived the concentration camps and eventually were resettled in Södertälje, Sweden, where Rosenberg was born and raised and is today a well-regarded writer and journalist. Sadly, his father later committed suicide after suffering years of depression.

My parents had spent the war years in a different camp system consisting of slave labor and concentration camps. It is not unreasonable to suppose that the experience of encountering another series of camps was met with growing anxiety and some trepidation.

These latest camps represented what seemed to be a patchwork system. Some had been repurposed from refugee camps established in Sweden during World War II for fellow Scandinavians, mostly resistance fighters, government officials, police and even some Jews fleeing Nazis in other Scandinavian countries. Others consisted of hastily constructed barracks in the woods surrounded by fences and barbed wire. Some were school buildings, military academies or even hotels. The ones my parents were sent to were mostly located in southern Sweden, often in smaller towns and villages, most of them in relatively isolated, even bucolic surroundings. There were some 150 aliens' camps in all.[1] The survivors were moved from one camp to the next, awaiting decisions that they sometimes made themselves but sometimes were made for them by aid organizations working with them to determine where they would eventually settle, what they would do or which country they would emigrate to.

Questions arose around the camps and the status of these survivors. For example, Rosenberg reported on what was essentially an uprising, or at least a vigorous protest, staged by some of the newly arrived refugees.

On August 17, 1945, *Svenska Dagbladet* wrote that about 40 "inmates" at Öreryd, a "Polish camp in Småland," had panicked and set out on a march to Stockholm to protest against the camp conditions. The police stopped them at Mossebo, about five kilometers north of Öreryd. The newspaper noted: "The forty who did not want to stay apparently fell prey to some kind of concentration camp psychosis. They are all very young, in the age range 16–20. They claim, among other things, that they did not receive sufficient allocations of food or tobacco in the camp."

On August 29, 1945, the head of an unnamed aliens' camp wrote in the daily *Göteborgs Handels- och Sjöfarts-Tidning* that the only "more general dissatisfaction" he had noted related to food. "As a rule, this is because they are unused to Swedish food – they find black pudding and fish balls particularly hard to come to terms with, and most of them find it impossible to appreciate the Swedish habit of putting sugar in all kinds of dishes. A more intractable problem is how to teach the refugees not to waste food; some kind of hoarding instinct seems to force them to store up supplies, which then go dry or moldy and eventually end up in the pig bucket. The refugees' unstable emotional state provides fertile soil for what might be termed camp psychoses, which take various forms. Sometimes it is individuals suddenly feeling themselves unjustly treated or persecuted by other camp residents; sometimes a general sense of alarm spreads rapidly, with anxieties about the future, the fate of relations..."[2]

Indeed, the status of the Jewish survivors presented a challenge for the Swedes as much as for the individuals themselves throughout that period. After all, Rosenberg explained, "You aren't immigrants, not in your own eyes, nor in the eyes of Sweden... You haven't come here of your own free will or under your own steam, but again by being transported from one camp to another, from a camp in Hell to a camp in a land of vast forests which, out of a combination of magnanimity and guilt, has offered you a temporary stop while you're waiting to journey on to somewhere else."[3]

After absorbing Rosenberg's observations, I realized just how complicated the situation was after the war's end, both for Sweden and for those stateless and homeless Jews who arrived there in the middle of 1945. While Sweden had certainly made a generous gesture, it seems not to have been fully prepared to deal with these survivors, especially over the medium-to-long term. It is doubtful that any country could have begun to understand what these survivors had experienced and the impact it had on them. Also, the country had only a tiny home grown Jewish population. Only over time would it learn how to treat these strangers or absorb them. How did you give new life or opportunity to those who, as the opening poem of this book notes, have touched death, not once but many times over too many years? There were missteps by everyone.

As Rosenberg explained, "You are transit migrants or *repatriandi* in Swedish."[4] There seemed to be something of a negative connotation to the term repatriandi. Such people were expected to be repatriated, to have a home or at least a homeland to return to. Clearly, my father and mother no longer had such a homeland, nor did many others. Therefore, he concluded, "You live a life without a past and without a future."

Some journalists and aid organizations recognized several of these issues early on. "Already on July 3, 1945, an editorial in Sweden's main daily newspaper, *Dagens Nyheter*, notes that the minister of justice has received a request for the benefit of a large group of stateless individuals to set aside the rule requiring a minimum of ten years' residence to qualify for Swedish citizenship. Among the UNRRA refugees that the Red Cross has been bringing here for some time, there are a number of people with highly uncertain futures, for example Polish Jews with no links to home, fearful that they will be sent from one antisemitic environment to another."

Rosenberg continues: "Jewish concentration camp survivors become, in short, a human category all their own. Shipwrecked, you call them in one of your letters."[5] "Floating wreckage, I read somewhere else."[6]

"Some of the shipwrecked still fear that in all probability they should be dead and therefore declare themselves to be something other than Jews, which makes it somewhat difficult to keep a tally. Some of them see forebodings everywhere. *'Förbjudet att luta sig ut,'* says a small metal plate screwed to the window frame in every Swedish train compartment, forbidding passengers to lean out. Some of the survivors see only the letters spelling *Jude* (Jew in German) and draw their own conclusions."[7]

What did they have in common with others in the same situation? They were all survivors, a term, Rosenberg concludes is "for people whose main attribute is that they're alive when in all probability they should be dead."[8]

They certainly yearned for a homeland again, a place where they could belong. But where? And how? And when? Look at people like my mother or father back then, and all you see are question marks.

As late as September 1946, 45 percent of Jewish survivors in Sweden wanted to travel on to Palestine, 28 percent to the US and eight percent elsewhere. Only 16 percent wanted to go back to Poland or their home countries, and a mere three percent wanted to stay in Sweden.[9] Yet in 1946, both Palestine and the US were all but closed to these Jewish migrants. What choice did they have but to do what they did best, that is, to survive, this time maybe for a longer time in Sweden.

For all the distress their relocations surely caused them in those first few years, I will always have a special place in my heart for Sweden and the Swedish people. After all, it was my birthplace. When there was nowhere else for my parents to go after Bergen-Belsen, Sweden did open its doors quickly, if at times not with the sensitivity that one might have hoped for. That was more than could be said for nearly anywhere else in the world. My mother always spoke of the kindness, help and honesty of the Swedes she met during those years. I remember my parents corresponding with some of those former neighbors and friends for several years after we came to the US. In addition, in late May 1998 on a family trip to my birthplace, the discovery of some of my own roots formed the foundation of what I would discover while composing this memoir. Jennifer and I have been back to Sweden several times since then. Our grandson Jacob joined us on one of those visits a few years back. He just couldn't get over how nice the Swedes were. Nor could we.

SZLAMA: ALONE

After his liberation from Bergen-Belsen, my father was housed at the Cambrai Barracks, formerly used by German soldiers, in Lübeck, Germany. There the Swedish Red Cross and UNRRA had established a transit hospital for liberated inmates from Bergen-Belsen who were going to be evacuated to Sweden for recuperation.

I'm actually not quite sure how my parents were selected for transit to Sweden. Perhaps they were among the sickest. My mother certainly had a number of serious health issues upon her arrival. More likely, though, they were good candidates for this experiment in temporary migration because they had indicated that they had relatives in the US or in Palestine, where they hoped to emigrate. At that point they were not interested in staying in Sweden. At the same time, when my father was asked upon arriving in Sweden why he did not want to return to his Polish homeland, his answer was simple: "I have no relatives there. Everything was lost."

Before boarding the ship to Sweden, he also told his initial interviewers at the refugee DP camp in Celle, Germany, that his hope was either to go to the US, where he had several first cousins living in Brooklyn and Queens, New York, or to Palestine, where his wife's brother Pinchas and possibly other Kotlicki relatives lived. My father's US relatives were the Zuckermans, two brothers and two sisters (Hyman, Milton, Esther and Sally) who, with their parents, had fled anti-Jewish pogroms in Poland during and right after World War I.[1]

Szlama made the Baltic crossing with his Bunzlau concentration camp friend Urbach on a Swedish ship called the *KP Ingrid* on or around July 18, 1945, according to records of the American Jewish Joint Distribution Committee. They landed in Helsingborg, on the west coast of Sweden just north of Malmö. From there, while I couldn't find records for Urbach, I discovered that my father was sent to a hospital inland in Hässleholm to get medical attention and begin the process of his physical recuperation. A great many in Bergen-Belsen had been sick with typhus, so he was quarantined there for a minimum of three weeks to play it safe.

A description from the press described the condition of the new arrivals: "All came to Sweden broken to some degree, physically and psychologically. Swedish media reports on the arrival of the survivors to Malmö were filled with descriptions of their shocking appearance. Skeletal, filthy, tattooed with serial numbers, dressed in rags and prison clothes marked with various designations. In short, they had been degraded to animals," a journalist wrote in *Expressen* in June 1945. "Around 90 percent of the UNRRA refugees had tuberculosis. All were quarantined for at least two weeks, and many were hospitalized for extended periods. Quite a few didn't long survive their rescue."[2]

These are the names of people Szlama listed as likely contacts for his possible resettlement outside of Poland, as recorded before he left for Sweden:

- Isaac and Chaim (Hyman) Zuckerman, Brooklyn, NY.
  Hyman was a first cousin in the US; Isaac was his father.
- W.H. Zykbersztajn (Zuberstin?), Tel Aviv, Palestine.
- Szymon Friedman, Tel Aviv, Palestine.

- Pinchas Esttlicki (Kotlicki?), Palestine. His first wife's older brother had emigrated to Palestine from Dąbrowa in 1920.

After his hospital stay, my father entered the Swedish aliens' camp system, all the while trying to figure out which country or relatives might sponsor him. He wrote to his cousin Hyman in the US for help and registered with the US consulate in Stockholm the following year. In 1945 and 1946 my father went from one foreign camp to another, crisscrossing southern Sweden. The facilities were meant to be holding pens of sorts, where these aliens could recuperate physically and take the opportunity to arrange their passage elsewhere.

As for my father, his journey across Sweden began in the Sunnerstaholm camp in Bolinäs, a small town on a lake in east central Sweden. He arrived there on August 17, 1945, a month after his ship had landed in Sweden. His head must have been spinning. My guess is that he didn't know what to make of these camps, having just left the disorder, despair and disease-ridden uncertainty he had met with in the DP camp in Germany. What could be next? Could he control his life again, even modestly? Could he start over, trying to erase the worst of the past? What about his family? Did anyone survive? He had petitioned the World Jewish Congress, the International Tracing Service and other agencies for help to find out more about those he had lost and lost touch with, and to gain some certainty. He listed two of his sisters, his wife and his two daughters as victims he hoped could still be located, but from what he saw around him, he knew in his heart that finding them was extremely unlikely.

He was confused. On the numerous forms and questionnaires, he kept telling different interviewers different birthdates, birthplaces and dates of his imprisonment in the various Nazi camps. How was he going to survive now? How would he earn money? Maybe he could find a way to recover the dowry his wife's family had promised him. He would look into that when he could. He had sent letters to his cousin in New York immediately upon arriving in Sweden but hadn't heard back.

Consider the world in which he found himself, foreign and alone, or as Rosenberg emphasized, "without a past or a future." What if I found myself in my father's shoes? Could I act? What would I do?

He stayed in Bolinäs for almost two months, which gave him more time to think. The air was clear, the lake was nearby and he was in the middle of the countryside. He didn't have to compete with hundreds or thousands of fellow inmates for food or a place to sleep. Now that his daily needs were covered, what he needed most was a plan that would keep his hopes alive.

His experience at the next camp, Tappuddens in Furudal (about 80 kilometers to the west), was a bit different. Still sometimes unsure of his birthdate, he arrived on October 10, 1945 (either a day before or a week after his actual birthday, depending on which date he was using at the time).[3] He was 34 years old and it was a birthday, for a change, finally worth remembering and celebrating. His fellow aliens at Furudal were all Jewish survivors, whereas in Bolinäs there had been both Polish Jewish and Polish Catholic migrants. By the time he got to Furudal, the Swedes had come to understand the need to better segregate the Polish Jews in these camps from the rest of the Polish population, since instances of antisemitism had arisen. The two groups also had very different needs and objectives. In Furudal, he was given a two-month crash course in English in preparation for his highly anticipated emigration to the US.

After a trip by rail of more than 700 kilometers to the south, he came to Mölle, a charming fishing village north of Malmö, on December 10, 1945. In Mölle he was housed in a more basic foreigners' camp established outside the town. He was there for two months.

FRIEDA: ALONE

My mother was also sent to Sweden to recuperate. She left on the *SS Karskaer* from somewhere near Lübek on June 27, 1945, and arrived the next day in Malmö with her sister, Genia Beitscher, who had been by her side through most of their time in concentration camps, and with what her papers indicated was a younger cousin named Fania Czarnocka.[1] In fact, Fania was not a cousin or any relation at all, but she had been noted in my mother's travel documents. This was yet another case of mistaken identity related to a different Frida Friedmann travelling a nearly parallel journey beginning in Auschwitz, through Bergen-Belsen and then to Sweden.

Upon being interviewed shortly after her liberation, Frieda indicated that her plan was to go to America, specifically to Brooklyn, New York, where she said she had relatives. I am not certain any of that was true, at least not until she met my father, who indeed did have relatives in Brooklyn. Instead, ever the survivor, she had gotten names and information about Brooklyn from other liberated prisoners. She mentioned Abraham Hutter (Entenberg), Moses Entenberg (Hutter) and Rachel Singer (the latter being her mother's maiden name) as people who might be in Brooklyn and would therefore be able to sponsor her. She also mentioned Barbara Hutton (possibly she meant Hutter) as another name of someone she knew in Brooklyn. In that early interview, she also indicated that she thought at the time that her husband Abe and her brothers Abraham and Naftali might still be in Kraków. But it eventually became clear that Abe, Abraham and Naftali had all perished.

My mother had developed a bad case of typhus in Bergen-Belsen and was not at all well upon her arrival in Sweden, so her first stop was a military school that had been converted into a quarantine center called the Malmö Epidemic Hospital. Her sister, my Aunt Genny, also needed medical attention and was sent to a hospital in Jänkäping.

In fact, by the time she arrived in Sweden, doctors there diagnosed Frieda as also suffering from chronic fatigue syndrome as well as what they called physical and psychological fatigue syndrome. She also exhibited a variety of stomach disorders. She held on to aspects of those disorders for much of her life.

Frieda (in the middle) with other survivors outside the quarantine hospital in Malmö.

Frieda remained in the hospital in Malmö for about a month and a half, partially in quarantine. She was also treated for bronchitis, severe jaundice, severe malnutrition and severe gingivitis and had to be fitted for dentures to replace teeth, some of which had literally rotted away while others were lost in the beatings she had received.

She was then sent to a school that had been converted into an aliens' camp outside of Malmö, where she received a two-month crash course in the Swedish language.

Very early on, there arose issues that would follow some of these survivors throughout their lives. Rosenberg points to comments made by the Nobel Peace Prize-winning sociologist Alva Myrdal, who worked in Sweden providing international postwar aid and reconstruction services to refugees. Myrdal offered her own perspective on these aliens' camps, and her observations seem particularly apt with regard to my mother's experiences. In the US, and perhaps even while still in Sweden, my mother developed serious eating disorders and an unhealthy focus on eating. She was quite thin and fought an ongoing battle with bulimia. Myrdal highlighted the extreme anxiety that developed in concentration camp survivors when it came to eating, observing that it sometimes manifested itself in the behavior of survivors in the aliens' camps.

"The victims of brutality themselves become brutalized," she wrote. "When life is reduced to its bare minimum, primitive selfishness is the only natural response.... Women whose reason should tell them that they will get enough food, and that there will be food for the next meal and for the next day too, cannot believe it because of their old terror. They save every crumb left over from the table. They pick dandelion shoots and other things to eat. They collect the pigs' potato peelings. They rake up every dry little pea that has fallen on the ground. They even continue to steal from the camp stores."[2]

By August 20, 1945, my mother had joined other Polish refugees at another aliens' camp set up in the Grand Hotel in Mölle. She stayed for about a month and a half.

Mölle's Grand Hotel was home to about 430 Polish refugees like my parents. Interestingly, according to some correspondence discovered by the *Kristidsstyrelsen*,[3] the hotel could have used more bars of soap and soap powder for its residents to wash themselves and their clothes. Each resident was allotted only two bars of soap to last nine

weeks, along with a little soap powder for their clothes. All these
necessities were in short supply and quite expensive at the time for
Swedes and refugees alike.

COMING TOGETHER

It was in Mölle that Szlama first encountered Frieda. To quote from the letter that opens this memoir, "I made the acquaintance of Frieda Friedman (my wife's name was Chaja Friedman). After only several days we began to fall in love with one another and spend our time together."

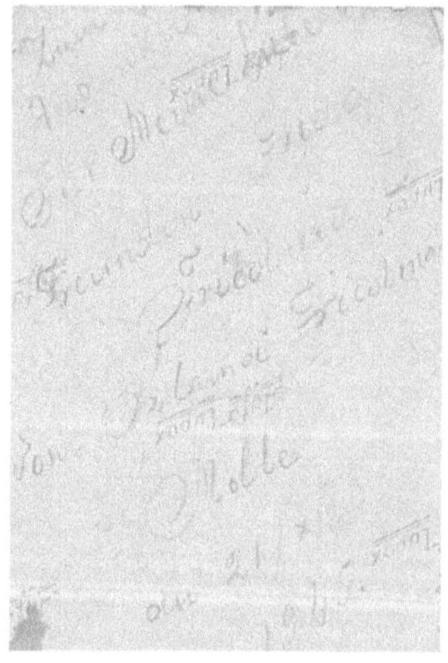

Front & back of a picture of Szlama (on the right) with his friend Urbach that my father sent as "a memory for my dear friend Frida" on December 21, 1945, not long after they first met.

My mother had been moved from the Grand Hotel to a different foreigners' camp in Mölle the day after my father's arrival. That was where they met. She stayed there until mid-January 1946. Szlama remained till the end of January and was then transferred to yet another aliens' camp.

At last, however, a plan was developing for them both, and it began with their rediscovery of the possibility and the joy of love. The two of them spent a month together before they had to separate, whereupon they promised each other they would find a way to be together again sometime soon. For the first time in a very long while, they were feeling a human emotion that was positive and good. They had found companionship and a shared past, and above all else, in each other they saw the promise of a future.

How exactly did they meet? Well, my mother had a story about that – maybe true, maybe not, maybe a little of each, as was the case with most of my mother's stories.

As noted, my mother's married name at the time was Friedmann and my father's surname was Frydman, sometimes spelled Fridman or Friedmann on official listings of survivors. She told us they were both in a hospital in Sweden when she noticed a list of other patients, including one named Friedman (or maybe it was Frydman). On seeing the name, she thought it might be her lost husband Abe. She had last heard of him in 1944, when a fellow inmate in Auschwitz told her someone else had spotted him in the Buchenwald concentration camp.[1] It wasn't Abe Friedmann in that room, of course, but instead someone named Szlama.

It was as though Frieda had gone to a Lost and Found department in a Swedish hospital to ask if anyone had found her husband, an Abe Friedmann, and the Lost and Found Department had responded, "Well we don't have an Abe Friedmann here, but would Szlama Frydman do?" The rest, of course, is my history, my sister's and theirs.

During that month, my mother and father heard each other's stories and shared their pain, their grief and their dreams with each other. I can only imagine how wonderful (and at the same heartbreaking) it was for both of them. Finally, after so much pain, there was joy.

Then my mother left. Not for another camp, but for a job.

My guess is that the Jewish aid group that was trying to track her contacts in the US and develop a plan for her emigration had no luck finding anyone Frieda had suggested, given that the contacts either were somewhat bogus or simply could not be found. Maybe the Swedes decided that Frieda might as well be resettled and placed in a job in Sweden for the time being. She had been a seamstress, and helping hands were welcome in that growing industry. In late December 1946, she was hired to work in the yarn department at Wallbergs Textiles in Halmstad, a city of 70,000.[2] There she was assigned to a coed refugee residence in the eastern part of the city, called Frennarpsgarden, earning about 50 kronor a week.[3]

As for my father, he was formulating a new plan for the future but needed advice. Hence the letter excerpted at the opening of this book, penned in Mölle to Willhelm Michaeli in Stockholm. In it he sought advice on how to get his newfound love to America. He dated it a few days later and mailed it upon arriving at his next and last camp assignment. This time he was placed in Kjesäter, where he arrived on January 31, 1946.

Kjesäter, a well-established camp, was originally created to host Norwegian refugees escaping their Nazi invaders. Opened in 1942, it was the main assembly and transit point for those refugees, some of whom were political activists, members of the resistance and Jews fleeing deportation to extermination camps. At that time, Norwegian Jews who were intercepted by Swedish border patrols were given emergency visas and then provided with directions and bus or train fare to larger cities and towns. Kjesäter held about 800 refugees at its peak. My father found himself very far from Frieda, who was now about 500 kilometers to the southeast.

The Kjesäter Aliens' Camp. (Photo credit: National Archives of Norway)

It was now mid-February 1946. His official six-month scheduled stay in Sweden was up. What next? He and Frieda had exchanged addresses and letters, and he knew where she lived and worked in Halmstad. Though he continued searching and waiting for responses to his frantic queries about his first wife and their children and from the US about his hopes of emigrating, he decided he had to get to Halmstad.

First, he got an extension to stay longer in Sweden. Like all aliens without passports, he remained under the supervision and control of the Swedish criminal police and needed their permission. Second, he was also given a job as a dishwasher at the Hotel Feller, later the Hotel Grand. It wasn't much, but it was in Halmstad.

The hotel, built in 1905, was just across the street from Halmstad's central train station. While Frieda was still at her coed residence, Szlama shared a room and twin beds with three other Polish Jews who had been liberated and made the crossing to Sweden as well. The job allowed him to reunite with Frieda and start to plan what would come next.

A second job as a worker at the Franckes SKO shoe factory in Halmstad followed. He earned 65 kronor a week, doubling his wages, which gave him the opportunity to move to Frennarpsgarden, where Frieda lived.

The happy couple in Halmstad in early 1947.

By October 6, 1946, Szlama and Frieda had moved into their own apartment, a flat above a bakery at the intersection of Skeppargatan and Brogatan. Things were moving quickly, and by December they had set a date for a wedding: Christmas Day, December 25, 1946. Again, they had to get permission from the Swedish criminal police to journey to Malmö, which had the only synagogue in the area. They were able to invite some refugee friends and coworkers from the factories, as these guests were off for the Christmas holiday. They were married by Rabbi D. Grünwald at the Malmö synagogue, which happened to have been founded by Polish Jews in 1871.

So for a change, life was suddenly good. Frieda was pregnant with their first child, the couple had two incomes that provided a living wage and their own apartment, and they could finally see an even brighter future ahead.

In June 1947, my father initiated a serious correspondence seeking to claim the property that was to have been transferred to him as part of the dowry promised him when he married Chaja. He was spurred on by a Yiddish-language article he saw in the Stockholm Jewish community newspaper *Unser Blatt* about the rights refugees had to assets left in Poland. At the Mosaiska Församlingen in Stockholm, a case worker, also named Frydman, had contacted an attorney in the Będzin/Dąbrowa area to locate the appropriate records. Szlama's aim was to sell the property and use the proceeds to help his growing family eventually start a new life in America. Unfortunately, after seven months of correspondence between Stockholm and Poland, my father gave up. The transfer of property had never happened, or if it did, it had never been recorded properly.

My sister Rachel was born on July 17, 1947. A few days later, the family's first apartment was destroyed in a fire that spread from the bakery downstairs. Two days later, the new parents and their infant moved to Furuvägen 24. Frieda gave up her job at Wallbergs two weeks before Rachel was born. I was born two and a half years later on April 29, 1950.

With Rachel in Sweden in 1948 or 1949.

The only event of note that I remember my mother discussing after that (apart from her general view of how kind and generous nearly all the Swedes she met were) was the fact that she dropped me on my head when I was just an infant. I don't know why my mother told me that story. Maybe it was to explain why I had a distinctive mark, now faded, on my forehead, or maybe, on occasion, why my brain had turned to mush.

She conceded that she wasn't very good at taking care of us in those early years. Fortunately, kind Swedish women helped as much as they could. She called these women *schwesters* or sisters (in Yiddish). They were probably nurses (*Krankenschwestern* in German), perhaps from a Swedish hospital or the Red Cross. I also think my sister, being older, suffered more later in life because of my mother's long years of malnutrition, from which she hadn't fully recovered by the time Rachel was born. My mother tried to nurse her, but I doubt that nourishment was sufficient. Rachel always has had great difficulty with her teeth, which may in part have been a result of my mother's condition. I was more fortunate, since when I came into the world, my mother had more fully recovered, at least physically.

After Frieda decided not to return to work, Szlama saw an opportunity and approached Wallbergs for a job. He started on August 25, 1947, nearly doubling his salary, and continued working there in the spinning department till a week or so before we left for America on December 28, 1951. On my family's visit to Sweden shortly after my mother died, we actually went back to that factory. It had been transformed into a go-kart racetrack. We met Gunnar Bjornfors, a staff manager at Wallbergs at the time. As he remembered it, "I was young and it was somewhat exciting to meet all these people, [i.e., my parents and the small number of Jews employed there.] We knew they had suffered a lot during the war."

My father (left) at work in Wallbergs in Halmstad.

In Sweden, both Szlama and Frieda discovered and seized opportunities to recall and sometimes reimagine their lives, including important dates in the past, where they came from, their first families, their work and their concentration camp experiences. My father had the chance to remember his first marriage may have taken place a year earlier than was recorded and consider again the last time he saw his first family. My mother was able to recreate details from her young life, such as her schooling, her friends, her first husband's successes and their imagined dance studio. She was even able to change her birthdate. Perhaps, by beginning to use a different maiden name, Singer, she was finding a way to separate from her father and her perceived "illegitimacy." She also developed stories about how she survived and the miracles that surrounded her to help her survive the war years, stories that better suited her. Their time in Sweden was a chance to step back, reconsider the past, wipe the slate clean of any lingering shame, disappointment or loss and instead write new stories, thus perhaps finding new ways to live with themselves and to love each other.

I was surprised to discover that my father had decided, almost from the very outset of his time in Sweden, that he wanted to emigrate to the US. His prime motive, he said, and I believe him, was that in order to stay employed in Sweden, he had to work on Saturdays, his

Sabbath. That rule was certainly in force at the hotel in Halmstad. In one application for emigration, he wrote, "Lately I was forced to work on Shabbat in Sweden. If possible, I will not do this [in the US]. It cost me my health, and this is a great percentage of why I want to emigrate to the US." He added, "In the US I plan to lead an observant life." It would turn out that although he didn't work on Saturdays in the US he made up the time, often working on Sundays instead, along with the other five days of the week.

I was also surprised that his primary motive was not to find a better life economically, gain a greater sense of security or be with the small family that remained to him, that is, his cousins in America. Given what my parents had experienced and their modest expectations, life in Sweden was pretty good. Nonetheless, early on my father was writing letters to the *Mosaiska Församlingen*, asking for help to fill out forms and arranging financial support for his resettlement in the US. Through these various applications, I learned several other things as well. For instance, his first cousin Hyman Zuckerman, mentioned earlier, tried to use his status as a US Army war veteran and reservist to speed up the emigration process. It didn't help.

The letter below, sent a year after my father's liberation, was from his cousin, who was trying to find a way to help. It is translated from the Yiddish and was written on New York's Mount Sinai Hospital stationery, where Hyman was a cardiologist. Hyman inserted some Polish words as well.

May 6, 1946

Dear cousin Shloime,

I received a letter from a very good friend of mine, Robert Zimmerman, who lives in Hartford, Connecticut, who has a cigarette (papierosy) business. He is very rich, and has a very good business and good profits. In brief, he has completed the papers for both you and Frieda. The papers were sent directly to the Consulate – Visa Division in Stockholm. I confirm that the papers are very good. I am also writing a special letter to the Consul about this. I don't have much money, but I was a high-ranking

For whatever reason, it took my father six more years to follow his dream and land on American soil with us. He officially registered for emigration with the American Consulate in Stockholm on May 30, 1946, and changed his application after he married Frieda and again after my sister and I were born. In 1948 he applied to the Polish Consulate for passports for both himself and Frieda in order to travel to the US. Those passports, dated April 29, 1948, were renewed in 1950 and 1951. However, I gather that they were not used because the US government at the time refused to recognize them, possibly because the second Red Scare in the US was under way and Poland had become a communist satellite of the Soviet Union. Instead, the four of us were left stateless and traveled to the US on temporary "alien passports" issued by Sweden.

As indicated, throughout this period, even after resettling in Halmstad and getting married, my parents remained under the authority of the Swedish criminal police, who still restricted their movements mainly to Halmstad. They couldn't even travel to cities like Gothenburg or Stockholm without specific permission. Asking questions of consular officials and filling out forms for the US government in order to get visas and emigrate was extremely difficult from a distance.

Fortunately, several Jewish relief organizations[4] covered the costs of our passage, provided us with a modest amount of money for living expenses for a few months and attested to the US government that they would ensure that our arrival would not become a financial burden to the United States. In the end, we lived with my father's cousin Esther and her family for about three months before the relief groups (or Hyman) found a job for my father and an apartment in Brooklyn's Coney Island that we would call home for nearly a decade.

Finally, our family emigrated from Sweden to the US. We sailed from Gothenburg on the *MS Gripsholm*[5] on December 28, 1951, and arrived at the Swedish American Line dock on West 57th Street in Manhattan on January 10, 1952. Passage for the four of us, tourist class, paid by the American Jewish Joint Distribution Committee, was 2,980 kronor, about $548 per person. My Aunt Genny, who changed her given name from Genia to Gertrude, had left a few months earlier, having first married another survivor, Philip Waisbort (Waisbrot), in Sweden. They were sponsored by her new husband's sister, who already lived in the US.

Form 1-418
TREASURY DEPARTMENT
United States Customs Service
UNITED STATES DEPARTMENT OF JUSTICE
Immigration and Naturalization Service
(Rev. 1-5-48)

Form approved
Budget Bureau No. 43-R019.1

MANIFEST NO.

MANIFEST OF IN-BOUND PASSENGERS (ALIENS)

Class .... from .... , Dec. 8th, 19 51

on ...... M/S Gripsholm ...... (Name of vessel)   arriving at port of New York   Jan. , 19

JAN 10 1952

List No.	Family Name — Given Name / Destination in United States	Age (Years)	Sex (F M)	Married or Single	Travel Doc. No. / Nationality	Number and Description of Pieces of Baggage	Whether Can Read/Write	Tax Charges and List of Master, Seamen and U.S. Officers
1	ESTREICH Estera / c/o Abraham Birnbaum, 2187 Holland Ave., Bronx 60, N.Y.	25	f	s	I-561146 Stateless	6 HB	yes	306 153
2	FAICH Henry / c/o Anna Brown, Sommerset Ave., Cor. Robert St., Mastic, L.I., N.Y.	47	m	m	I-393793 Denmark	3 HB	yes	154
3	do Eleonora / do	45	f	m	I-393794 Denmark	do	yes	do
4	FELDMANN Fanny / United Service for New Americans, 15 Park Row, New York 7, N.Y.	24	f	s	I-1068206 Stateless	3 HB	yes	155 USNA
5	FLEISCHER Bernhard / c/o Benjamin Friedman, 207 E. 3rd St., New York, N.Y.	40	m	m	I-655480 Poland	4 T 3 HB	yes	156 HIAS
6	do Helena / do	26	f	m	I-655481 Poland	do	yes	do //
7	FELDSTED ANDRESEN Öivind / Economic Cooperation Administration, Washington, D.C.	32	m	s	V-381370 Denmark	2 HB	yes	157
8	FODOR Jan / c/o Max Gottlieb, 18960 Cherrylawn, Detroit, Mich.	31	m	s	I-373719 Stateless	4 HB	yes	158 (USNA)
9	FORSELL Otto / 95 West 162nd St., Bronx 52, N.Y.	30	m	s	I-864471 Finland	1 HB	yes	159
10	FRYDMAN Szlama / c/o E. Henzel, 2720 Kings Highway, Brooklyn 12, N.Y.	40	m	m	I-1068239 Stateless	9 T 4 HB	yes	160 USNA
11	do Frida / do	39	f	m	I-1068427 Stateless	do	yes	do
12	do Rachel / do	4	f	s	I-1068428 Stateless	do	no	do EXEMPT
13	do Max / do	1	m	s	I-1068440 Stateless	do	no	do EXEMPT
14	GLAJTMAN Samuel / c/o Herman Katz, 600 West 112th St., New York 25, N.Y.	35	m	m	I-373773 Stateless	3 T 4 HB	yes	161 HIAS
15	do Rozsi / do	26	f	m	I-373775 Stateless	do	yes	do //
16	do Rut / do	2	f	s	I-373774 Stateless	do	no	do EXEMPT
17	GRANER Chawa / c/o Rosa Oranek-Manutzky, 158 Harrison St., Paterson, N.J.	27	f	s	I-1066998 Stateless	5 HB	yes	162 USNA
18	GREEN Doris E. / c/o Werner O. Berg, 10425 So. Lowndale Ave., Chicago, Ill.	25	f	s	I-561409 Sweden	1 HB	yes	163
19	GRINSPAN Dawid / c/o Leopold Heffner, 12 E. 88th St., New York, N.Y.	45	m	m	I-655427 Stateless	8 T 6 HB	yes	164 HIAS
20	do Fryda / do	34	f	m	373636 Stateless	do	yes	do //
21	GUSTAFSON Sven / 742 Newport Ave., Chicago, Ill	28	m	m	RP-1680850 Sweden	1 T 1 HB	yes	145
22	GUSTAFSSON Ulla / 4323 5th Ave., N.E. Seattle 7,	31	f	s	I-561432 Sweden	4 HB	yes	146

The MS Gripsholm's *passenger manifest, listing passengers Szlama, Frida, Rachel and Max Frydman, 1951.*

PART VII

IN THE USA

THE CONEY ISLAND YEARS

The Frydmans at a company picnic around 1956.

At last, the dream had come true for Sam and Frieda.[1] He was 41. She was 42, though officially she was now 40. It seems as though both of them had seen America as their future from the moment of my father's liberation from Bergen-Belsen and my mother's initial DP interview, even before they met or began to come to grips with all they had lost. My mother seemed to have made up names and places in Brooklyn to prove she had relatives there. My father did in fact have relatives there. When they first talked in Mölle in late 1945, Sam had shared his dreams with his future partner. She found that she wanted the same things. Sweden was just another stop on their long and seemingly impossible journey from survival to elsewhere.

They had now arrived at their elsewhere. Unfortunately, they were virtually penniless, didn't speak the language except for a few words, had no idea where they would live or how and had two young children to support. Rachel, now four and a half, could understand some Swedish and was fairly fluent in Yiddish. I was nearly two, and since I had to communicate with my parents and Rachel, Yiddish was also my first language.

We were lucky to have made contact with my father's cousins. They were helpful and well-meaning, though without significant resources of their own at the time. The refugee agencies were as generous as they could be. Fortunately, Sam and Frieda had each built up reserves of resilience and adaptability to draw on, which would help them start all over again in yet another new place and another new life. Unfortunately, that memory bank was also filled with nightmares and horrific experiences deeply embedded in their souls. Too much of the road ahead would be defined by all that had come before, as is the case for most of us. But for them, what had come before was not what most of us have experienced. It was surely a new beginning for them, but it was nearly impossible to jettison their very different brand of baggage.

After disembarking from the *MS Gripsholm*, we spent our first week in the US on West 57th Street in Manhattan, sharing a single room at the Henry Hudson Hotel, arranged and paid for by HIAS.[2] Then, for several months, while my parents, our cousins and the refugee agencies tried to figure out what was next, we moved in with Esther Zuckerman Henzel's family at 9720 Kings Highway in the Flatbush neighborhood of Brooklyn, where Esther, her husband Abe and their children Judy and Manny shared their small apartment with us.[3] They were a lovely, kind family.

Later we would visit them regularly. Esther and her brother Hyman helped us navigate the practical aspects of adapting to a new country. My father also relied on Esther for her patient counsel and calming influence, which worked as an outlet for him through many periods of turbulence in his relationship with my mother. Rachel liked our visits because Judy, who was older, was sensible and warm. She shared her dolls willingly, and I relied on Manny because he had a Lionel train set that offered me great if only all-too-brief afternoons of joy when I was young. I had few if any toys. What I liked most as I got older about the Henzel family was that they seemed normal. We clearly were not.

Eventually, one of the Jewish agencies found us a small apartment of our own in Coney Island, a neighborhood located on a peninsula at the southern tip of Brooklyn and famed for its amusement attractions, beach and boardwalk. We lived in Apartment 1B at 2905 West 15th Street, around the corner from the Coney Island terminus of a number of subway lines.

Our apartment was on the ground floor of what I could generously describe back then as a somewhat rundown, four-story building between Mermaid and Surf Avenues, two blocks from that boardwalk and public beach. On the ground floor facing the street were a Chinese laundry and Sal's barber shop.[4] Across the street was a vacant store where a gypsy family moved in. My father sold my red tricycle to them for $5 because he needed the money. The building was also next door to a relatively famous Italian restaurant named Gargiulo's.[5] It was a stone's throw from Coney Island classics like Nathan's Famous Hot Dogs, Steeplechase Amusement Park, the Cyclone roller coaster, the iconic Coney Island Parachute Jump and a giant Ferris wheel called the Wonder Wheel. There were also lots of penny arcade games nearby. I remember many of the attractions but should add quickly that we were not allowed to go on any of the rides. Too dangerous. A waste of money we didn't have. I went on the Cyclone with Jennifer right before we were married, and went on the Wonder Wheel perhaps once as well. The only ride we were allowed to go on as children was a nearby merry-go-round.

Our apartment was in the back of the building, where several windows faced an alleyway where garbage cans were stacked and where the rear entrances of several stores, including a photography studio and a shoe store, were located. Because we were on the ground floor facing a quiet area, our apartment was broken into several times while we were out. We could tell because the would-be thieves came through the windows and broke the frames. They got what they deserved, which was nothing, since there was nothing in our apartment worth stealing or worth much of anything to anyone else. Besides the subway there was a movie house nearby, the RKO Tilyou Theater, built in 1926, as well as several other movie theaters. I remember walking many times by the fire exit doors of these theaters and encountering people sprawled on the stairs, drunk, asleep or both. I don't remember ever going into them, but we did see a few movies at the Mermaid Theater further up on Mermaid Avenue and 25th Street. I specifically remember seeing *Them*, a movie about a giant marauding ant that came out in the 1950s. I was terrified.

When we were young, the main activity in the summer was going to the beach. Coney Island Beach was quite famous. Between Memorial Day and Labor Day it attracted literally millions who arrived by subway, mostly from other parts of New York. It was also free of charge, allowing summers to be spent away from our small hot apartment. There was barely room to move on the beach, even though we would get there early to stake out a spot with our blanket near the Atlantic Ocean. When we got home we would take a bath with white vinegar to try to remove the sting of our bright red sunburns. We smelled like bad salad dressing when we got out. My many visits to dermatologists for all manner of skin cancers are the legacy of those early sunburns. A melanoma my mother developed on her face when she was in her 80s was attributable to those same sunburn years. On Tuesday nights, the special treat was a fireworks show out on the water that we could hear from our apartment and see by just going out and down the street. We eventually became quite jaded and skipped many of those remarkable displays.

Back then, the fulltime residents of Coney Island were a mixture of blue-collar workers, mostly Jewish and Italian. Today, after a massive urban renewal project that demolished most of the smaller houses and apartment buildings and replaced them with high-rise, low-income projects, the population is largely Black and Hispanic.

The public schools that I knew about and that served the area were PS 80, an elementary school that we attended briefly, Mark Twain Junior High School and a bit further away, Abraham Lincoln High School, from which Rachel and I both graduated. In addition, there was a Catholic parochial school and church called Our Lady of Solace, a yeshiva for first through eighth grades and an adjoining Orthodox synagogue. The nearly three-mile boardwalk stretched from one end of Coney Island, where there was a wealthy gated community of relatively large private homes called Sea Gate, to the other end, which extended past our apartment to the end of Brighton Beach, a largely Jewish area that attracted a great many union workers from the Garment District in Manhattan. Beyond that was another wealthy community of private, though not gated homes called Manhattan Beach. The beach stretched along the waterfront virtually uninterrupted from end to end.

My impression of our neighborhood in Coney Island was that it was poor and rundown. That was certainly true of our little area near the elevated subway and amusement park rides. At our end, it seemed to be mostly commercial and geared toward day visitors, but about a mile west of us the neighborhood became more middle-class, bustling with small grocery and butcher shops, fruit stands, delis and luncheonettes. While I was young, we rarely ventured to the end of the main shopping district on Mermaid Avenue, where more Jews lived. The population where our family was located was mostly Italian. There was an Italian bakery and a small grocery whose owner my mother called King. I recall that he had several gold crowns on his front teeth that I could see when he smiled and a big refrigerated section full of farmer cheese or pot cheese, as he called it, which he would scoop out for us. When I was in second or third grade, I also went there to buy cigarettes for my mother and ginger ale for my father, as well as the occasional quart of milk.

Our apartment consisted of three very small rooms. First, there was a living room where both my parents slept on a kind of trundle bed. The top bed was covered in some sort of green wool to make it resemble a couch. A second bed underneath would be rolled out at night. We called it a couch because it stood against the wall at one end of the room. At the opposite end was the real convertible couch, where I slept. Both sofa beds were purchased at the Abraham & Straus department store, also called A&S, which we considered a relatively upscale store in downtown Brooklyn. I'm not sure where we got the money to buy anything. I suppose the refugee agencies provided a small stipend to get us started and our cousins helped out. I only remember two other pieces of furniture in that room. First there was a 17-inch Dumont console TV positioned at the center of the wall opposite the entry foyer. We bought it in 1955 or 1956, and it would have been a luxury for us at any point as it cost about $180. The second furnishing in the living room, added in 1960, was an old, black upright piano that stood against the far wall. Straight ahead when you entered, you saw two windows that looked out onto the alley.

Then there was our tiny kitchen, with its metal table and four chairs that barely fit, a sink, a stove and a Frigidaire refrigerator.

On the right (as you faced the windows), there was a little hallway with a small bathroom and a bathtub where my mother would soak for hours (and sometimes fall asleep) while smoking cigarettes. She was a chain smoker and liked Newport (sometimes Salem) Filtered Menthol Lights. The bathing and the cigarettes seemed to calm her. We sometimes worried that she would drown in there since she stayed for so long and we could hear her snoring. So Rachel and I took turns banging on the bathroom door and asking if she was okay. She said she was, but we came to know better. The four of us only took baths. I never even thought about taking a shower till I heard friends talk about getting ready for junior high school. Really! My mother liked to hold court in the bathroom while she was in the tub. She would call us in to talk. I even remember my father sitting near the tub and sharing a cigarette with her. It was a tiny room, and she would cover herself with washcloths placed strategically for modesty's sake.

Actually, there was nowhere to hide in that little apartment, and although secrets lurked inside each of us, we were not heavily oriented to modesty. There were no doors to knock on before entering, except for the bathroom. I don't even remember a door on the bedroom, Rachel's room, which had enough space for a full-sized bed and the black steamer trunk where we kept our most valuable worldly possessions, which had accompanied us from Sweden. That room had one window facing the alleyway.

My mother could never rest. She had an energy, a compulsiveness mixed with anger, an unsettled quality that clearly impelled her to yell, scream, shout. It was as though she was asking anyone to hear her cries, to right the wrongs in her life, to return to her what she had lost in her youth, or more likely, never found. She seemed to live on impulse as the voices she heard forced her to shout and to act.

The bathroom here, and also in our next apartment, was also where she would hide out to smoke on the Sabbath. Smoking, using electricity or performing any other manner of so-called work on the Sabbath was strictly forbidden by Jewish religious law and custom. But my mother was addicted to smoking, so she smoked on Saturdays as well as every other day of the week. My sister and I knew well what she was doing, as the evidence of her transgressions could be smelled throughout the apartment and she often forgot to flush the toilet, where she disposed of the cigarette butts. It wasn't until my father was in his mid-seventies and possibly starting to manifest the personality changes inherent in early Alzheimer's disease that he insisted, during a visit to our house, that he could no longer live with my mother because he had discovered cigarette butts in the toilet on the Sabbath. "She was smoking on Shabbos," he complained to me, clearly grievously wounded. He told me he needed to immediately obtain a *gett*, a document of divorce drafted and delivered from a husband to a wife under Jewish law. I told him she had been doing this since we were young children in Coney Island and asked how he didn't know what we all could see and smell. Frankly, after all these years, I told him, it was too late. He left, speechless.

Rachel got her own room because my father believed that a girl deserved her privacy. As the boy, I had no privacy. Nor did my parents, who seemed to have given up any right to privacy amid the deprivations of their earlier lives. They didn't get their own bedroom until we moved to Brighton Beach in 1960. I got my first bedroom, shared with Jennifer, of course, when I got married in 1971.

The rent was something like $40 a month, and while I have forgotten much about those early days growing up in America, one late Sunday afternoon stands out in my memory. My father was at work when we heard a loud banging on our apartment door. Our mother told us to quickly get into the louver-doored coat closet in the entry hallway, which was about six feet wide and a foot deep. Telling us not to make a sound, she turned off all the lights in the apartment. I was not much more than five years old at the time, and I remember being frightened and confused. We stayed in that closet, virtually holding our breath, for what seemed a very long time. A man's insistent voice at the front door called, "Open up! I'm here for your rent. It's late." Then he banged on the door several times again. I'm not sure if my mother knew this was going to happen, but she did seem prepared for it. Maybe her reflexes simply kicked in when she remembered the searches she and her family had to endure in Kraków after the Nazis invaded. Anyway, the banging eventually ceased. We could hear footsteps moving away. I don't recall that happening more than once, but I do know it happened. It has stayed in my memory ever since.

Fortunately, that brief scare did not become a normal part of our lives in Coney Island, though money was always a concern and fear of all manner of things was encouraged. I soon became afraid of anyone who wasn't Jewish, thanks to my experiences at the yeshiva where I was placed. My mother told us that certain foods could harm us, like peanut butter and white bread. Whenever we came home from a social occasion, my mother would perform a *keinehora* ceremony to ward off any evil eye we might have encountered. More on that custom soon.

From my mother's perspective, every place was a battlefield and every person, especially a fellow Jew, was a potential enemy. Jealousy was to be found everywhere, and if there was a target, from her perspective it was going to be one of the Friedmans.

Our mother's aim was to protect us with whatever weapons and forces she could muster. We had little money, and I never was clear about what we had that anyone else would want, since a tiny apartment and clothing that too often came from fire sales signaled prospects for the future that were not terribly promising.

Apparently, however, we had targets painted on our backs. On the rare occasions when we went out to attend a bar mitzvah, wedding or some other social gathering, or even just visit the few other refugee families we had gotten to know, we were being scrutinised. My mother was certain that others wanted what we had. I would gladly have given what little we had away simply to reduce the paranoia that pervaded our household before or after any social outing.

For instance, several times that I remember and more times that I don't, we had occasion to travel by subway to Borough Park or East New York for Hasidic weddings. Milton Zuckerman, the most religious of my father's first cousins, would get us invited in order to be kind and expose us to life outside our apartment. At such affairs, men and women were separated for the entire evening. Once, I recall, the male invitees brought the groom up from the basement of a brownstone adjoining the wedding venue. He had been fasting for the past 24 hours and looked like he was going to pass out, as some of the men were nearly carrying him upstairs. He had been praying, perhaps mostly for food, given his condition. I was starving, but bowls of chickpeas were the only food on the small tables upstairs. I had hoped for a better alternative to my mother's cooking, but it didn't look promising.

In any case, bride and groom were duly joined together. The men danced with other men, and the women danced with other women. As a young boy, I was shooed away when I stood on a chair to peek over the barriers at the girls and women, but I didn't turn to stone, or into a chickpea either. People seemed pretty happy, and I didn't notice anyone paying any special attention to us one way or another. We didn't stay long because the subway ride back to Coney Island was a long and sometimes dangerous trip at night. We had to be careful not to disturb the drunken men sprawled out on the seats of the train, or their comrades sleeping on the steps of the fire exits of the movie theaters across the street from the subway in Coney Island, just around the corner from our apartment.

Once we arrived home, thankful to have survived another subway ride, but before we could even take off our party clothes, such as they were, my mother would run to the sink, fill a glass with warm water, throw in some bread crumbs, sprinkle in some salt and rush over to us. Then she would dip her index finger into the glass, and with it, touch our temples and foreheads and then circle our heads with the glass several times, saying something like "ptooh ptooh ptooh" while spitting lightly into the air. She would conclude the incantation by saying the magic word *keinehora*. Her aim, of course, was to protect us from the envy or jealousy of others, that is, from the evil eye.

Keinehora is a contraction of three Yiddish words: *kayn, ayin, hara,* literally "not (kayn) the evil (hara) eye (ayin)." *Kayn* comes from the German for "no," and the *ayin hara* comes from Hebrew. The evil eye is one of the world's oldest and most widely held superstitions. Its place in Jewish lore is rooted in classical Judaism and Jewish folk religion dating to the Bible, the Talmud and rabbinic Midrash. There is a rich history, particularly from the Middle Ages onward, of often bizarre and elaborate folk practices (invocations such as *keinehora* being a rather tame example) aimed at thwarting the malicious intent or effect of the evil eye.

The evil eye itself stems from the Greek theory that the eye can shoot rays that strike with harmful or deadly force. The Babylonian Talmud claimed that there were rabbis who had the power to turn a person into a "heap of stones" with just a glance. There are also connections with liquids, including water, wine and saliva, which were thought to protect against the evil eye as a weapon or a shield. This may be one origin of the practice of spitting three times in response to expressions such as *keinehora*. Scholars note that fear of being the object of other people's envy is "the common societal root of fear of the evil eye" across diverse cultures. The Babylonian Talmud warns the owner of a beautiful coat to keep it hidden from the potentially envious eyes of a visitor and cautions against overly admiring another's crops, lest the evil eye damage them.[6]

Clearly, from my mother's singular perspective at that wedding, all those envious people had gotten a look at us in our lavish attire with our bright, smiling faces and decided, yes, we want to be like them. Or even worse (or better, depending on which side you were on), we want to be them. Better still, we want them. My mother was also protecting us from potential child kidnappers and run-of-the-mill thieves.

Her chants worked, because we were never kidnapped. Our clothes and other worldly possessions were never taken, and certainly not by the guests at the Hasidic wedding. Therefore we were safe, thanks to my mother and her magic. If they wanted our poverty, we had fooled them by successfully saving that poverty for ourselves. If they wanted our upright piano, well, I don't think they could have gotten it out of our house. We didn't have much else.

We were not out of the woods. There were other scares, over which her chants had no control. For instance, when we were still quite young, I remember my mother having to be in the hospital for a week or so. My father had us stay with an American family called Rosen who lived in their own house somewhere in the more affluent part of Coney Island. I remember Mrs. Rosen as an attractive blond with a deep voice who chain smoked, much like my mother. They had a daughter named Leah, and even then I thought she was pretty. My father would show up at the door at night after work, mostly to just say hello, make sure everything was okay and thank the family for caring for us. It turned out that my mother had a fibroid tumor that had to be removed, followed by a hysterectomy. We never discussed any of this, but I do recall thinking her stomach/abdomen looked big and round for someone so small and who ate so little.

Otherwise, there was a certain rhythm to our lives during our Coney Island days. My father's roadmap was seemingly simple. He recited his morning prayers (speed praying, I should note) and laid tefillin, a pair of black leather boxes containing Hebrew parchment scrolls, placed on his head and his left arm (facing the heart), along with leather bands wrapped around the arm and hand, which had symbolic meanings. He did that six days a week (every day except for Saturday), and then went to work, usually around 6 or 6:30 in the morning. My mother would prepare his lunch and a thermos of coffee, which he placed in a small dark blue plastic satchel. He wore a fedora, since as a religious Jew he believed his head should always be covered, even at work, out of respect for God. At home he put on a yarmulka. He generally didn't expect that of me. I began the same prayer routine, but only after I was bar mitzvahed and while still living at home.

When I was a child and he came home from work, I always grabbed the satchel and started rummaging through it, asking him what he had brought for me from work. He did his best to find some little knick-knack that had been damaged or discarded. On the Sabbath, as Genesis commanded, God rested and so did he, but only after he went to shul. When I was older I accompanied him, but as a young person I went to a service at the synagogue for kids called the Junior Congregation, often with my sister. As a family, we rarely ate meals together except on holidays and sometimes after my mother lit candles on Friday nights. Otherwise, we ate when we were ready, mostly wolfing down food as my mother offered it. Once we got a TV, we watched it; otherwise, my sister and I would do homework and read books. We both loved to read and took books out of the local Brooklyn Public Library branch, which was only a few blocks away. I remember my joy at being old enough to borrow books from the adult section instead of being limited to children's books.

As for my mother, she cleaned, ironed, shopped, prepared meals and sewed. I remember her using an old Singer sewing machine. Of course, she was also responsible for making sure we took care of ourselves and got to and from school safely once we were old enough. I remember her walking me to bus stops and subways on my trips to school, beginning in elementary school and continuing through junior high. My guess is she did the same with Rachel. I actually didn't mind her coming along with me, especially when I was older. It was a time when we would just talk and catch up, a quiet time when my mother wasn't trying to direct our lives or argue or criticize one thing or another. She would wait for the bus to come, and we would have a few minutes together. It wasn't quite like the time I had with my father on Saturdays in synagogue, but it came close. My mother wasn't posturing in front of others, showing off or telling her stories. She was just being a mother wishing her son well, making herself feel worthwhile as she protected me. It was sweet, warm and loving. As I think about it now, I wish I had expressed appreciation more back then in my own mind and also to her.

Several nights a week, Frieda and Sam would take a bus to PS 225, a public school in Brighton Beach,[7] to attend an adult night school. There they learned to read and write in English and studied enough about United States history and practices to eventually help them pass a citizenship exam on March 21, 1957, a little more than five years after we had arrived in the US.

I remember the day I learned that I had become an American citizen. Citizenship for Rachel and me depended on whether our parents had obtained their Certificates of Naturalization. Although we officially also became citizens in 1957, we didn't get Certificates of Naturalization until they came in the mail more than a year later, dated July 30, 1958, when I was eight years old. Before that day, whenever we took the D train from our home in Coney Island to the city, my parents would insist that I crawl or stoop down under the turnstile to avoid paying the 15-cent fare. No one but me seemed concerned about that. I was embarrassed that I was somehow cheating and sneaking onto the subway.

That certificate changed everything. My parents were no longer Polish. I was no longer a stateless, alien refugee. I was an American, like the other kids. I remember it as a great day in my life. My own certificate featured a picture of me in a white shirt wearing my clip-on bow tie. I had even signed the picture Max Jakob[8] Friedman in my neatest script. My father had officially changed his first name to Salomon and our family name to Friedman the previous March. The Certificate of Naturalization even noted that it was issued during the 183rd year of our country's independence. The document came printed in a nearly indecipherable longhand script, much like the writing of facsimiles of the Declaration of Independence we would receive in the mail for free as a promotion from the John Hancock Life Insurance Company. We had all gotten dressed up for those pictures, and my mother had her hair done. All of us had half smiles, maybe not knowing if a smile was even appropriate, but also signifying that confident yet also nervous feeling that such formal and life-changing occasions can engender. We looked hopeful.

On that day, I asked my father whether, from then on, he would start paying for my subway rides so that I would no longer have to sneak onto the trains. After all, I was an American citizen, with certain new obligations, maybe even more expensive ones. He said okay, at least for that day.

Yet as these new horizons began to open, certain clouds continued to pass through our lives, not always, but still too often.

The first constant that stands out, sad to say, was the arguing, yelling and fighting that seemed to pervade our days and sometimes continue into the nights, with only brief pauses, whenever my mother and father were together for more than a few minutes. I realize I may be overstating this somewhat, but to us young children, these encounters seemed omnipresent and most upsetting. They were loud and too frequent. No wonder this discord is the clearest memory I have of my childhood and its instability. Rachel would agree. We were frightened when it was happening. In retrospect, I feel sorry for both my parents for having to engage in this way. It seemed that my mother began the arguments and my father was the one who was forced to disengage. However, there also were times when my father began the row.

Frieda would often start the encounter by highlighting something she thought my father had done badly or failed to do as well as she would have liked. It was nearly always related to money. It could have been that my father wasn't making enough and should have been demanding more from his bosses, or that money hadn't been spent wisely. It could have been that other people they knew seemed to be able to go on vacations and enjoy their money more, while our family did nothing. As time went on, the argument would relate to the house they later bought and moved our family into, a house with three apartments besides our own that we rented out to tenants. Our parents' issues mutated into problems involving these strangers: we had set the rent too low, or they expected too much for their money, or they kept breaking things and we had to fix them. Recriminations arose over why we even had these tenants at all and what a mistake my father had made by buying that sort of house. There was also a lot of comparing our lives with those of other people. There was blame to be assigned for whatever was not quite what my mother wanted, hoped for or insisted upon. It sounds one-sided, and perhaps it wasn't at all. Whatever it was, it stands out as a constant reminder of the recurring turmoil, especially inside my mother, that led to these kinds of actions and responses. Now, though, I am seeing it in retrospect. In those days I just wanted the fighting to stop and the noise to quiet down.

I remember one fight all too clearly. In this case, it was initiated by my father. I remember it as the worst fight they ever had. Their faces turned bright red and the shouting went on at great length as the decibel levels increased continuously. There were moments when my mother claimed she would faint, and my father clutched his chest as though he was going to have a heart attack. It sounds crazy now. Believe me, it was crazier then.

Why all this? My father seemed extremely upset about my mother having called a plumber to fix something that he thought he could have taken care of. The cost of the repair was something like $5. I remember how my sister and I tried to be heard above the din and begged our parents to calm down before they hurt themselves. After all, it was only $5. Neither would relent. The encounter ended with Sam running out of the apartment. That was often the way these arguments ended. My sister remembers to this day that she was always terrified that after my father left, he might not return.

When my father finally did come home hours later that day, Frieda was wise enough to let the argument pass. More often, though, she would continue the fight, even into the night, while my father tried to get to sleep. She herself was unable to sleep soundly. Those fights were the clearest signposts of the harm done to both these souls, perhaps irreparably.

Money was always an issue, the more so in our early years because we lived paycheck to paycheck. Throughout his 25 years of work, I don't think my father's paycheck ever amounted to much more than $250 a week. Over time, a few other sources of income developed. Once there were savings to invest, there was the interest he gained on his bank accounts. Later, there were rental income from tenants, Social Security payments after he retired and modest reparations payments from the German government to address the years my parents worked as slave laborers, obviously without pay, during World War II.

They received no specific compensation for the loss of their loved ones. After all, how does one value the loss of a human life? Had they owned valuable possessions and been able to prove they were seized by the Germans, perhaps they would have gotten something more. My father was certainly unsuccessful in claiming the dowry that had been promised to him. In any case, the payments from the German government began around 1954-5, starting at about $32 a month each and over time increasing to about $180 a month for each. There were some small lump sums during those early years as well, which helped them afford the downpayment on a house. The reparations were meant to cover their slave labor, any material claims and physical and mental health effects. Interestingly, they even received some small amount of compensation for the specific number of days they were forced to wear armbands with the Star of David before they were imprisoned. Unfortunately they never received any help for their psychological injuries, if that was even possible at that time.

Ultimately, their losses were incalculable and irreplaceable. From their immediate families alone, my mother lost her parents, five brothers and a husband, while my father lost his mother, three sisters, a brother, a wife and two children. And of course hundreds of cousins, aunts and uncles, their partners, children and extended families. In fact, I would sometimes wonder when those checks came every month via air mail from Germany, denominated in Deutschmarks (D-marks) and taken to the Lincoln Savings Bank to be converted and deposited into their savings accounts, what memories they would continue to spark not only about what was lost, but who was lost, and what never could be regained.

Those payments were of course directly linked to the second ongoing theme that ran through our lives: the Holocaust. Specifically we would react to my mother's relentless repetition of concentration camps stories with feeble if innocent attempts as children to hide any mention of the Holocaust from both our parents. My sister and I understood from a very young age that something very bad had happened to them, but only our mother would discuss the specifics of her concentration camp years. Indeed, she did so endlessly. My father didn't want to hear about it and would ask not to be reminded, which became an additional source of clashes and friction between them. From our innocent perspective, it was important to shield them from anything on TV related to Germany, World War II or the Holocaust. We turned off the TV news if a story that included concentration camps was featured, or when a documentary or broadcast aired related to a particular wartime or Holocaust anniversary. Any coverage of any war was also to be avoided. It bothered my mother less than my father to hear about those years, but it was still another sore nerve to avoid touching for both.

A third topic of conversation, consternation and conflict for many years, sad to say, affected mostly Rachel. It related to my mother's conscious and unconscious efforts to shape Rachel's life as if it were her own. As we came to understand later, our mother had vested in Rachel elements of her own childhood and then her own young adulthood, which Frieda sought to affect. Rachel was to become what my mother imagined herself as or wanted to be. But while Rachel was naturally quiet, my mother had imagined herself as outgoing; thus, Rachel had to become outgoing. Rachel liked to sit at home and read books, but our mother wanted her to be more social and have more friends, and so it went. Rachel became the target of all my mother's *mishegoss*[9] for too long. I stood on the outside looking in most of the time, remaining under the radar. I would sit with Rachel and try to comfort her when she was upset by all this. Later, my mother decided that Rachel should be a schoolteacher, something she seemed naturally disinclined to become. She is very bright and could have done a great many other things earlier in her life. But because my mother had cast her in that role, for two and a half years Rachel worked as a second grade teacher in Brooklyn until she couldn't stand it any longer and became a stay-at-home mom. Only after she turned 40 did Rachel find a new career for herself as a speech language pathologist, which better suited her personality, temperament and interests.

Food, Glorious Food

Finally, the emphasis placed on food in our household wasted enormous amounts of precious energy. Again, given my parents' experiences when they were younger and literally being starved almost to death in the camps, it was all understandable. Regardless, it was often unbearable to be a child in that environment. It was unsurprising that my mother spent inordinate amounts of time using food as a weapon, withholding it, insisting on it, hoarding it, hiding it, criticizing others for their eating habits and more. She suffered the most, but the fallout was everywhere.

We grew up chubby. We would eat too fast in case the food was taken away. Our mother hid food from us. When any of the few friends or relatives they had arrived bearing a box of Barton's or Barricini's chocolates, it would immediately be hidden on a high shelf somewhere in the kitchen, out of reach of my sister's or my hands, let alone our mouths. We actively searched for treats when our parents were out of the house. I remember holding chairs for my sister to stand on so that whenever our parents left our apartment for a walk or to visit someone, Rachel could scavenge the kitchen cupboards trying to find the snack stash. My mother also forbade us to eat certain foods, like white bread or peanut butter, asserting that they caused cancer. No wonder I ate a whole 18-ounce jar of Skippy peanut butter with a spoon the first night I was on my own in my dorm room at Columbia. Later, both my sister and I would find ourselves worrying excessively about how much our children did or didn't eat.

Looking back, it is clear that my mother suffered from bulimia. She ate very quickly, not realizing how much she had eaten for someone with such a small frame. Then she would go to the bathroom and throw up. She did this pretty often. It turned out that she knew what she was doing and knew at some level that she had an eating-related problem. Also, when we went to someone's house or any kind of gathering, especially as she got older, she would take food. We would watch her gorge herself at bar mitzvahs (food was allowed at those) and then rid herself of it when she got home. She would sneak food into her pocket or pocketbook. Eventually she started lining her pockets and handbags with aluminum foil. It was less messy that way. As she got older, she regularly hoarded food from the senior citizens' center or even from her own daughter's house. The tendency became more noticeable after Rachel moved to Mobile and we attended bar mitzvahs and other celebrations with our parents at the local Reform temple. There would be a great spread of food prepared by members of the congregation for a celebratory kiddush. My mother would position herself at the head of the line to get food, eat it quickly and then put more of it into her handbag. One piece in her mouth, one piece in her pocketbook for a later time that might never come. Again, the camps had taught her what she needed to survive. Sadly, that lesson never left her side.

Meanwhile, eating other people's foods and paying for the privilege, well, that was an entirely different matter. I was reminded of it years ago when I read a piece in *The New York Times* about a man in New York who had never eaten out in a restaurant. The *Times* found him and decided this "Ripley's Believe It or Not" human being was worthy of an 800-word article. Jaws may drop everywhere at the thought that this was possible in a city that once boasted more than 30,000 restaurants as well as countless bars, snack stands, clubs and private dining rooms of one sort or another. But it wasn't at all startling to me. It's what we did, or should I say, what we didn't do ever, when I was growing up.

Until I started hanging out with friends in high school, I had never eaten in a restaurant, whether paying for myself or going with family or friends. Neither had my sister or my parents.[10]

Why didn't we ever eat out? First, from my father's perspective, because either the restaurants were not kosher at all (we all agreed that my friend's Chinese restaurant fell under that umbrella), or were not kosher enough (everywhere else fell into that category.) Second, from my mother's perspective, no cooked food was as good as her cooked food. Now, everyone, including my mother, had a right to their opinion, but my kids, my wife, my sister, her kids, and maybe even my father, if he was being honest, as well as just about anyone who ever ate at my mother's house, would agree that her food was not haute cuisine. In fact, it was rarely haute or even hot.

Once I was old enough to know better, I realized that more often than not her food was overcooked and then quickly brought to a chill on the kitchen window sill. The food rarely had even a faint hint of seasoning or taste and usually fell into one of three categories: broiled chicken, broiled roast beef, or a version of meatballs that was neither shaped into balls nor bore any resemblance to such a dish elsewhere. Once, during a particularly rebellious time of my life in high school, I actually told my mother I could no longer stand her cooking. It was always the same food, again and again and again. Malcolm Gladwell called it the tipping point. My mother told me to leave the house and consider not coming home again. We got over it, but we never got over the food.

By the time I had a wife and kids and we were invited for dinners at my parents, the operative approach was to distract my mother so that all the food served to my family was put onto my plate and quickly ingested by me. After all, she was my mother, so the burden of eating her food and surviving the likelihood of an upset stomach from the broiled chicken roosting on the window sill was all mine to bear. I will acknowledge that my son Eric did have a fondness for certain of her dishes.

Perhaps another main reason we never ate out, even at a kosher deli or some Jewish restaurant on the Lower East Side, was that we were very poor. I've considered that, but it has never seemed like the most compelling of reasons. After all, McDonald's and other fast food restaurants, some diners, the old Horn & Hardart Automat and even places like Tad's Steak House in Manhattan, where steaks could be had for only a few dollars, including baked potato and ice cream, all catered to people who had little money. It was more than just money that stopped us from ever partaking of restaurant food.

It was something more elemental. Actually, maybe it was pathological. While we were growing up, it was generally unacceptable for someone else to cook food that my mother felt was her responsibility to prepare. Someone else was taking away her raison d'être, her defining moments. And although the fact that it cost money entered into the equation, it was more a question of "Who needs it?" Our taste buds had been dulled by her cooking, so I don't think we would have known whether what we were eating was good or not. We never had much of a point of comparison. Moreover, the idea of being served instead of serving was anathema to my mother's genetic code. Since she felt that her cooking was better and healthier for us than anyone else's, allowing anyone else to prepare food of course meant we were risking life, limb, stomach and colon.

In the end, food was a way for her to control some part of her life: she could refuse it, push it, manipulate it, create it, and withhold it from us and from herself. It was a reliable way of controlling our lives as well. We watched her go through unpredictable, erratic starving binges (anorexia) mixed with mild bulimia.

I don't blame her, at least not now, for some of the strange food quirks and food manias she bestowed on her children. She spent her young years starving in concentration camps, risking her life to steal a morsel of raw potato. When we were young, she told us again and again how she would scrape the dirt from a brick she had dug up, hoping to catch a bit of a root vegetable clinging to its stony surface. Food was a defining feature of life, one that wasn't always easy to get. Once it was gotten, she did everything she could to master the food and make sure we understood that she was in charge of it.

As mentioned, we rarely ate together. Meals were things to do, not times to celebrate or enjoy, except on certain Jewish holidays. Thus, eating out together in a restaurant also made little sense. When all was said and done, our collective eating habits were formed by our collective refugee mentality. My brother-in-law, a Buddhist, once admonished me after one of his meditation retreats for eating so quickly, without mindfulness. Mindfulness in Brighton Beach? Get real! As refugees, we all wolfed our food down, certain that on some subconscious level emanating from a genetic array passed down from the pogroms and impoverished shtetls of central Galicia, this was indeed to be our last meal.

When *The New York Times* regards someone who has never been to a restaurant as some sort of anthropological artifact to be held under a journalistic microscope, I guess I just chuckle and then immediately start my virtual search for that hidden box of chocolates.

Moving on from our eating habits to our everyday lives in Coney Island, my sister and I attended a public elementary school and then were pulled out to attend a local yeshiva.

Those yeshiva days deserve special mention. They certainly hold a less-than-fond series of memories for me, and maybe for my sister too.

It all began when my father, normally a sweet, kind man who tried to look out for his children's best interests as much as he could, acted impulsively in one specific way that clearly has stayed with me all these years.

In what I saw as a horrible spur-of-the-moment decision, he decided I was to leave public school mid-year and attend yeshiva instead. My sister would face the same awful punishment, though she had done nothing wrong, as I seemed to have. At least she got a reprieve and didn't have to start till the following September. For a change in roles, it was my mother who sought each year to rescue us from what I considered a prison sentence.

It was December. I was in first grade and Rachel was a third grader. We both attended PS 80, a typical New York public elementary school on West 17th Street between Mermaid and Neptune Avenues, a short distance from where we lived in Coney Island.

The apartment next door to us was inhabited by the super's family. They were Italian. He had a son, possibly my age, maybe a year older or younger. His name was Sal, and he was a nice kid. My mother loved it when we had friends, so she encouraged our visits together. What attracted me most to Sal that December evening was his Christmas tree and the presents strewn underneath it, some of which had been opened. The tree sat in the center of his living room and faced the door that opened up into the hallway of our apartment house.

On that fateful day, my father came home from work around six or so, and for whatever reason, the door to that apartment was open and I was sitting with Sal under his Christmas tree. These were small apartments, and there was nowhere else to play except near that tree.

That brought our public school careers to an end, for a time. I had attended Mrs. Blockner's kindergarten class the year before. I sort of liked it, except when my mother forced me to sing two songs in front of the class with her in attendance: *Love and Marriage*, made famous by Frank Sinatra when it was introduced in 1955, and *That Doggie in the Window*, recorded by Patti Page. I don't remember why, but Frieda was captivated by both songs and drilled me into memorising them and performing both, in my not-very-lovely voice, in front of my classmates and her. I didn't know what the word mortified meant, but on that day, that is certainly what I was. Even so, I don't recall having a bad time at PS 80 until then, or when I returned nearly five years later. Rachel and I each skipped a grade during our elementary school careers, which was a common practice for smart kids at the time. I assume the elementary school curriculum was not particularly challenging.

Anyway, the very next day after my father saw me with Sal under the Christmas tree, he told my mother to take me out of public school and enroll me in Yeshiva Shaarei Zedek, a Jewish day school attached to the Orthodox synagogue that we attended on Mermaid Avenue and West 23rd Street. There was no discussion, but much later it seemed that from Sam's perspective, I had come under the influence of Christian rituals in a way he could not abide. I sort of get it now, given what he went through, but I certainly didn't get it then.

Being wrenched out of the class seemed like an extraordinary punishment for sitting and playing with a friend. I thought it was cruel and unfair, but all I could do was cry and then do whatever was expected of me. To this day I don't know how to apologise to my sister for what I recall as ruining several years of her life. To her credit, she says it wasn't that bad.

Actually, I don't even remember today why I hated yeshiva so much. In retrospect, it was probably for several reasons. First, I never understood what I had done so wrong. Second, I found yeshiva to be a violent experience. I abhorred violence as a child (and still do), especially back then, perhaps because I heard so much about the violence in my parents' lives. I just couldn't relate to fighting, even among kids. I had heard too much fighting between my parents. I also remember that some of the teachers in yeshiva seemed to use force gratuitously. Public schools forbade corporal punishments, but private religious schools worked by a different set of rules. For instance, my fourth grade social studies teacher would get our attention by jabbing our arms as he walked by, using two fingers that clearly were made of steel. As for my fifth grade Hebrew teacher, I believe he had been thrown out of the Israeli Army for being too aggressive, which seems like a contradiction in terms, given what the Israeli Army was famous for. He even used to challenge my classmates to attack him as he walked up and down the aisles so he could practice his martial arts skills on us.

Furthermore, the kids in my classes, especially in the Hebrew classes, were also pretty aggressive and too often totally uninterested in learning. In public school, the best students would be grouped together. At yeshiva, you would have kids who were in eighth grade in English classes and at third-grade levels based on their abilities in Hebrew classes. Some pretty big kids in my fifth grade Hebrew class were advanced in English, but had been left back in Hebrew. It was often intimidating.

Finally, there was the competition that appeared to be encouraged by the teachers. Each of us had to be the best. It was clear who our greatest competitor was in any class, and our job was to outdo him or her. In my case, it was a kid named Julius who we called Julie. He wore a red cardigan, and I decided it must have some sort of superior powers, so I asked my mother to get me one. She didn't. Julie also cracked his knuckles, something I had never experienced before, but immediately mimicked as a competitive learning aid.

Over time, I came to learn that some of my English teachers weren't too bad and the English language principal was pretty decent. Still I felt that I was missing real life in some way, having experienced it once in public school. In yeshiva, there were only Jews, which my father may have liked, but I became paranoid when I saw other kids in the street who, I decided, could not be Jewish and therefore hated me because I was. Perhaps that was real life for my father in the Polish schools he attended when antisemitism too often was the order of the day. In my case, I became accustomed to being only with Jewish kids; otherwise I felt threatened. That lasted longer than I would have liked, especially since I was wrong about all of it.

I also came to appreciate that not all yeshivas are created equal. Some were actually pleasant and may even have had decent teachers who could have taught in public schools but decided not to. At the time I felt as though our teachers were manufactured in a public school rejection factory. Again, this was all instinct and not at all based on fact.

As I learned later, you do indeed get what you pay for. We were enrolled at the very lowest tuition cost of around $25 a month. Starting at 8:30 every morning, we attended classes for the Hebrew part of our curriculum. After a lunch cooked and served in the basement by Sophie, the wife of the president of the synagogue, we attended afternoon classes in English, math, social studies and other state-mandated curricula until about 4 p.m. Then Rachel and I would walk home or sometimes take the public bus, since as younger students we had a pass that allowed us free passage. We did homework till we dropped. The bottom line was that I hated the entire experience, both English and Hebrew.

A few things about my yeshiva experience stand out more than others. First, I saw older girls like my sister being chased around a table by a dirty old man/rabbi who taught them Hebrew. Where was the Me Too movement when it was most needed in yeshiva? Second, I remember our vaunted class trips: one was to the kosher chicken slaughterhouse next door. We did not watch the actual killings, but they were happening close by and we knew it. Students would examine the integrity of the eggs the hens laid, using a strange kind of ultraviolet light as the eggs were inspected to make certain they contained no specks of blood. An egg containing a blood speck was considered unworthy of consumption by a Jew. Third, I remember taking another class trip to attend the funeral of Sophie's husband. Honestly, I'm not sure that at my age it was necessary for me to touch the pine box in which he was to be buried. I know some kids in public school would go on visits to the United Nations or to the Aquarium, but as far as I can remember, a class trip for me meant the slaughterhouse, a funeral or nothing.

I was finally sprung from yeshiva at the end of fifth grade because I lied to my father, telling him that my Hebrew teacher had hit me and put a long wooden pointer into my ear. For my father, that was a bridge too far.

Earlier I mentioned my mother uncharacteristically trying to rescue us from our yeshiva experience, year after year. I don't really know why she sided with us or how she explained it all to my father. Still, she tried to help us. Here's how that played out. Each year, right before the start of the coming school year, it was my mother's responsibility to go with us to return the schoolbooks that we had been forced to study over the summer. They were also to be our textbooks for the year ahead. If the plan was successful, she would come out without any books. If not, we were sentenced to another year in yeshiva.

On the one hand, my mother worshiped the English principal of the school. Her admiration was connected with several things, among them the example of a successful Jewish woman, a position my mother may have craved but never did achieve, and the fact that my mother had learned the hard way in concentration camps that ingratiating oneself with authority figures was a necessary part of survival.

On the other hand, my sister and I both made it clear, at least to our mother, how unhappy we were. I disliked yeshiva more than Rachel did. We both objected to the sometimes less-than-kind or less-than-competent teachers, many of the other students, some of the crazy rejects posing as rabbis and all the useless homework, especially during summers and school holidays. Apart from the good care she gave my father when he was diagnosed with Alzheimer's disease, I can't recall another time in our lives when we were so gratified by our mother's efforts and admired her courage so much, no matter the outcome.

Thus, each September on the first day of school, we did not attend. Instead my mother schlepped a load of heavy, useless textbooks into the yeshiva office and tried to explain that we didn't want to come back. Maybe she really felt our pain. She certainly was not a religious person, so she may have sensed that we would be better off in public school in the long run. In the meantime, Rachel and I would hide in Bella's candy store across the street from the yeshiva while my mother went in to plead our case.

Imagine the scene in St. Peter's Square in Vatican City after a Pope has died and the College of Cardinals is voting on his successor. During those Papal votes, black smoke comes out of a chimney whenever the Cardinals fail to agree. On the other hand, when white smoke emerges, the crowds offer a great cheer that a new Pope has been identified. Papal smoke may not be the most tasteful analogy in reference to a Jewish institution, but the analogy holds. Think of Bella's candy store as St. Peter's Square and Rachel and me as a mass of onlookers eagerly awaiting a decision of monumental importance, though only to us. Our mother's emergence from the basement office of the yeshiva without our books would reveal that we had gained our freedom for the year and could somehow re-enter the real world around us, where kids played and laughed and seemed to have fun, or at least more fun than we had. Her emergence holding those books, however, represented another year of repression, endless study, competition with others and searching for friends that were not meant to be, in a world that had been carved out from the world in which we otherwise existed. White smoke? Black smoke? What was it to be?

Our yeshiva journey comes to an end when Rachel graduates eighth grade and I leave after fifth grade.

The upshot was that she always came out with our textbooks for the next year. She seemed really very sorry she couldn't help us. It would have been a banner day had she succeeded. I don't know why we thought she would. Maybe because we actually realized how much she loved us and that whether she succeeded or not, she was our mother, standing up for her children. So it could have been worse.

For the most part, growing up was, as you can see, no fun for us. Once we returned to public school, my sister found a way to escape our home lives by immersing herself in her books. I needed a way to escape as well. My escape was wanting very much to grow up and get away.

In sixth grade, I finally had something of an opportunity to see what getting away might be like when I went to work with my father on Sundays for several months. It showed me another side of my father's work life and what he thought being a father was all about. It was a very special, if brief, education.

One day in 1960, my father came to me and asked if I wanted to help him at work on Sundays and get paid a dollar an hour in the process.

I jumped at the chance. I liked my father a lot. He went to work every day, taking several subways to get to his place. He called it "the place." It was actually a warehouse in East New York, Brooklyn, on a street in a poor Black neighborhood off Eastern Parkway, not too far from the Brooklyn Museum, the Brooklyn Botanical Garden, and the main branch of the Brooklyn Public Library at Grand Army Plaza. The place, however, was a world away from all of those grand institutions.

The place supplied supermarkets in New York and New Jersey with housewares, cheap flatware, Pyrex bowls, plastic containers, dishes, kitchen implements, simple plastic toys and popular paperbacks; in other words, the clutter of stuff you see hanging above the shelves apart from most of the foodstuffs in typical supermarkets. Those products made up the addenda of a supermarket. They were convenience goods sometimes related to food, certainly nice to have, but easily acquired elsewhere and not core to the supermarket shopping experience. My father's place was a place that served on the periphery. So was his job.

I was never clear about how he got that first and only job he ever had in America. Back in 1946, Hyman had promised my father a job with a friend of his in New Haven at a cigarette factory. Seven years later, my father was finally in America and went to his interview with a cousin's son acting as his interpreter. As it turned out, he didn't get the job. I don't know why. The job he did get may have come thanks to the refugee agency that brought us over from Europe. Or it may have come from one of cousin Hyman's contacts after the New Haven job didn't pan out. I do know Sam started as a shipping clerk, picking orders that would be delivered by the place's trucks.

He was still essentially a shipping clerk and had been there a good long while when he offered me the job. He had worked hard and was so smart and well-liked that he was given the title of manager, partly due to his age and partly because the owners were well aware of his difficult history. He had refugee written all over him in the way he dressed, the way he spoke and sometimes the way he thought. His salary and his responsibilities were limited. He would never be an outside man. His staff was small. It was me.

I didn't do much at home on Sundays but read, watch TV and avoid arguments with my mother as much as possible, so I gladly welcomed the idea of being with my father, making some money and growing up. Now, it should be understood that even though I was going to make money, the concept of spending money was a fairly limited notion. We just didn't spend money in our household, or else spent very little, and only for the barest of essentials. My mother didn't work outside the home and as I said earlier, my father made little more than $250 a week in his peak earning years. When I was in sixth grade, he probably wasn't making much more than $100 a week. We always seemed to live our lives waiting for the other shoe to drop, the next knock on the door that would bring disaster. Thus, money was to be made, whereupon those who earned it were to scrimp and save. It was never clear for what.

Anyway, back then, saving the money I was to make sounded like a great idea. In those days and perhaps today, any child older than 14 who worked had to have an official paper filled out by the employer and certified by a bureaucrat to make certain he or she was not being exploited in a sweatshop, as though we were back in Dickens' London. I was nowhere near 14, yet I had heard my father say I could work without these papers. It was okay. It was Sunday anyway. I would still get my dollar an hour.

Every Sunday for several months we started out on the D train, changed from the Brighton Express to the Local and then at Prospect Park to the Franklin Avenue Shuttle. Then we went a few more stops to Eastern Parkway, where we would get off and walk quickly through streets where we could tell we were not welcome to get to the place.

Upon arriving, we would immediately go to my father's office, which was actually part of a makeshift storeroom/closet secreted upstairs behind the bookkeeper's desk. There my father kept his lunch, his prayer book, some extra work clothes and any papers needed by the clerks and managers of a warehouse. He also kept his pride and his very private counsel. For him, it was quiet there, peaceful, idyllic, a refuge.

He would then set me to work. Some days the work consisted of picking orders, which meant maintaining a list of things a particular supermarket needed, like three Pyrex bowls, four sets of plastic tumblers and some *ECKO* flatware. My father prided himself on being able to sell that flatware and to get it for us at a discount. He considered it to be of very high quality, so much so that when I got engaged years later, he gave us a set as an engagement gift.

On some days I would add up columns of numbers on a manual adding machine, the kind that had a handle on the right side that you would pull down hard after you pressed down keys that didn't bounce back, but stayed down. You'd pull the lever forward and the numbers were entered. Press the keys for a second number and it was entered as well. Only then would the keys return to their original positions.

Some days I would just follow my father and watch him do all these things. We would take a lunch break, sitting on little stools in the dimly lit closet and sharing some rye bread and cheese. As a special treat, I would be allowed to sip from his thermos of highly sweetened, very light coffee with whole milk added. Sometimes when there was an extra paperback that had been damaged or a toy that had fallen out of its packaging, my father would give it to me to take home.

At the end of the day we would pack up and clean up, and he would pay me: four dollars one day, three another, six another. Payment depended on the hours in which I actually did something, unlike real work in the offices I would inhabit years later.

Each week, upon arriving back at our apartment, I would put the money in an envelope hidden (or so I thought) at the back of the bottom drawer in the kitchen, where we kept stuff we didn't know what to do with, like our electric and telephone bills. Our day-old bread was kept right below that drawer. Some call it stale bread. My mother liked aged and aging bread because she believed fresh bread would give you a stomachache. Given that my mother had quite a history to contend with when it came to food and just about everything else, it was no surprise that just about everything gave my mother a stomachache.

Over the course of time, I had saved at least $100, maybe a little more. I felt I had earned it, too.

One day I stopped going to work with my father. As I recall, it was a fairly abrupt end to my career as a mini-shipping clerk. I hadn't been fired, but my father said the place didn't need my help any more.

That was okay by me. I never thought this was going to be my future. I had my heart set on becoming a chemist so that I could discover the cure for lung cancer and help my mother, who, I was convinced, would contract the disease because she smoked so much.

I was proud of the $100. In my free moments I would take time to open the drawer, take the bills out of the envelope and recount them. It was the first money I had ever worked for, and it was a cushion for my future retirement.

One day I went to count the money, and it had disappeared. The envelope was there, but there was nothing in it. I hadn't spent it. What had happened? I was heartsick.

I questioned my mother, who answered matter-of-factly, "Oh, yes, I took it." She said she needed the money for food or clothes or some such. Yes, she knew it was mine, but it was also ours. "Don't be silly," she said.

I'm pretty sure I didn't forgive her for that until years later. I forgave her for most everything else, but not for that.

Only much later did I get it.

Yes, I was silly. Finally, it dawned on me that the place wasn't paying me that dollar an hour; my father was, from his own paltry earnings. He was trying to teach me something about work, about growing up, about a father having a son and the responsibilities and pleasures that come with that relationship.

It took a father to teach a son to take a broader perspective, not just about himself but about others like his mother and his family, as well as all the necessaries of keeping the family whole. That was when it suddenly occurred to me that when my mother took that money from me, she was only taking money she needed to buy food because my father had given her a little less every week so that he could give me something more that may have been even more important. This wasn't spare money. It was the only money they had.

When you're a boy, your father is just about the most important person in the world. When you have a son or a daughter, your child is just about the most important person in the world. The world you create for that child can be as small as my father's little nook at work or as limited as a warehouse clerk's job. But what happens in that space, in that time, between that father and son can be very large, very special indeed. And at a dollar an hour, it was worth every penny and more.

Thanks to those times at work, I actually decided I wanted to do more paid work, despite the abrupt end of my career in wholesale housewares.

Watching briefcase-toting people heading to the subway on their way to the City, as we called Manhattan, gave me an idea. I found a 9x12 manila envelope among my father's papers, put on my best shirt and clip-on bowtie and regularly took subways into Manhattan by myself. The first time was when I was about eight. My father was at work or asleep, and my sister and mother were out shopping. I remember wandering into office buildings and going up and down elevators.[11] I was playing a serious game of make-believe in which I was finally grown up. Other kids might have played make-believe with toys. We had no toys except for a cap pistol and a game called 52 *Games in One*, so I decided Manhattan would become my toy village. The idea, of course, was to escape to another life. Perhaps, by imagining a world where I could be in control, I was doing the same thing my parents were doing, though on a different, much smaller scale.

Another thing I did when I was still fairly young was to sneak out to the penny arcades and play skee ball on Shabbos, after synagogue, when my father would catch up on his sleep with a long afternoon nap. That was just enough time for me to take a little change from the envelope where he kept his earnings under the seat of an armchair in the living room and escape into another forbidden world. I rarely won anything, other than a growing sense of freedom. Yeshiva had deprived me of freedom, and this was an opportunity to assert some slight level of independence. My mother and sister would do even worse by taking the subway to Fulton Street for a quick jaunt to buy some inexpensive clothing at Korvette's or some other department store in downtown Brooklyn.

The reality of my father's work world, of course, was quite different.

Sam with his friend and work colleague José.

Sadly the war had a lasting effect on my father. The changes in his physical and psychological condition even affected his ability to earn a living – at least from his perspective. Before the war, my father made about 75 zlotys a week in Poland as a commercial clerk, not a bad salary when one considered that many factory workers and farmers made that much in a month. Once he came to America, his gross pay was actually about $55 a week in 1956, a modest salary to be sure. "The Nazis destroyed my economic existence," he admitted in another reparations-related affidavit. In the US he said that his nervous condition wouldn't allow him to concentrate and take advantage of his training in commercial office work. Instead, he noted to the German examiners in the mid-1950s, "I worked in the US in a warehouse, filling orders. I could no longer be what I used to be. Since my wife is also ill and can't earn anything, I am in a bitter situation and dire straits with my family, which is particularly unbearable," he lamented.

However, one of the two co-owners of my father's place, called Supermarket Housewares (FBA Inc.), was a religious Jew named Kaufman, so perhaps some connection in the Jewish community had helped. In any case, FBA Inc. became my father's employer as well as a respite from the stress at home. The warehouse operation was owned jointly by Kaufman,[12] who spoke Yiddish and thus could communicate easily with my father, and Norman Duberstein, a decorated World War II pilot and a secular Jew. FBA Inc. was initially located on East New York Avenue near St. John's Place in Brooklyn, in a particularly rough neighborhood of Brownsville. Today that area has been largely gentrified and it can cost up to $1 million or more for an apartment in some neighborhoods. Back then, it was known more for its poverty and crime than anything else. Quite a few times on those Sundays working with my father when I was 10 or so, residents approached us while we were standing outside at lunchtime to grab some air and called us "whiteys" and "kikes," reminding us that we didn't belong in their neighborhood. When my father was older he was mugged, possibly several times, going to or from work on the subway. I wasn't supposed to know about that.

As noted earlier, FBA supplied supermarket chains in Brooklyn, Queens and Long Island with housewares, small toys, children's books and other miscellany beyond the normal food, cleaning products and paper goods found in supermarkets. My impression was that salesmen visited these stores and warehouse workers fulfilled the orders; then the goods were collected and delivered by FBA drivers. Inside there were also a few office workers who ensured that products from suppliers were shipped to the warehouse and kept all the books and accounts straight. Later, when the neighborhood got too rough, FBA moved to Atlantic Avenue in Jamaica, Queens. I remember that Sam started as the low man on the totem pole, stocking shelves and then moving to picking orders. He had come from a family of merchants and traders, so doing business was something he liked and was good at. Eventually he took on a managerial title because he had proved himself to be smart, hardworking, good with numbers, trustworthy and generally amiable.

He developed two lifelong friendships at work, one with a tall Black guy named Jimmy and another with a delightful Puerto Rican man named José. In many ways, all three were outsiders and thus recognized commonalities among themselves that were not apparent on the surface. Jimmy and José protected Sam in the neighborhood and often came to our apartment to pick him up in their cars so he wouldn't have to take the subway to work. Jimmy, José and their wives all came to our bar mitzvah/sweet sixteen celebration and danced the hora with the rest of us. José gave us a special gift: a Super 8-millimeter film of that party. Sam loved these two men especially, as they had come to understand him better than most. I think that when they saw him coping with the pain of trying to succeed in an unfair, prejudiced world, they saw their own pain. After all, they were all trying to do more or less the same thing.

Thinking back on those days, I recall Frieda and Sam arguing about his work. Frieda thought Sam should get paid more and should insist on it or quit. My father told her he would ask for more, but I don't think he ever did. Instead, he gained self-respect from working and from gaining the title of manager, even though very little more money came along along with it. It seems he concluded that because he wouldn't work on Saturdays and also was a "Greener,"[13] he wouldn't be able to get another job that would offer him the same degree of freedom and respect, let alone the money he deserved. My mother didn't quite understand that he needed something more than money from his job, which she saw as purely transactional. After all, she was the one in charge of spending that money to buy clothes and food and the like. In any case, his work became another opportunity for tension.

I do remember listening to their arguments and agreeing that perhaps my mother had a point when she complained that he was underpaid and perhaps even taken advantage of. I recall how pleased I was when I was slightly older (maybe 11 or 12) and heard he was considering buying a car and learning how to drive. Maybe he could even find another, better paid job that took greater advantage of his skills and experience. He saw that both Jimmy and José had been promoted because they owned cars and thus had the mobility to see customers in parts of Queens or Long Island. He seemed excited by the prospect. However, it never happened. He stayed at FBA until he retired in 1977. When he left, he received an engraved Seiko wristwatch as a gift: "Sam Friedman. In Appreciation. FBA 1977."

BRIGHTON BEACH FAMILY
MEMORIES

We lived in Coney Island for about nine years. Then, in the summer of 1960, we moved a mile or so away to a better neighborhood. My parents purchased 3060 Brighton 14th Street in Brighton Beach, where we lived until my sister married, I left for college and later also got married. The area was predominantly Jewish and Italian for most of those years. In the years after we left home, leaving our parents to their own devices and traumas, and to each other, I felt as though we had abandoned young children of our own. As surely as they were there for us for the first 15 years of their time in Brighton Beach, we were there for them, mediating between their Old World views and the American world as it then was. All the while we sought also to intervene between them, protecting them from themselves, each other, their pasts and an unforgiving universe.

The early days on Brighton 14th Street.

Brighton Beach stretched from Ocean Parkway and Brighton 1st Street along Brighton Beach Avenue to Brighton 15th Street, the unofficial border with Manhattan Beach. Most of Brighton Beach's main shopping street, located under the elevated subway tracks, consisted of small clothing stores, fruit stands and groceries. When we lived there, there was only one supermarket worth visiting: Waldbaum's, at the end of Brighton 11th Street. The adjoining neighborhood, Sheepshead Bay, located at the east end of Brighton Beach, was literally a man-made bay surrounded on three sides by private houses and apartment buildings, as well as some famous seafood restaurants. The bay led out to the Atlantic Ocean. Where Manhattan Beach ended, a former military base had been transformed into Kingsborough Community College.

Brighton was to some degree an extension of Coney Island, so it was also bordered by the boardwalk, the beach and the Atlantic Ocean. The Brighton Beach side streets that led to the boardwalk typically featured six-story apartment buildings, along with a few newer, high-rise luxury buildings that afforded wonderful ocean views and were priced accordingly. Homes between Brighton Beach and Ocean View Avenues were mostly two- and four-family houses like our own. There were a number of synagogues (several Orthodox and one Conservative congregation), a YMHA, the famous Brighton Beach Baths beach club, and several public schools, including Abraham

Lincoln High School on Ocean Parkway. There was also a branch of the Brooklyn Public Library. I attended Cunningham Junior High School a bit further away in the Midwood section of Brooklyn because after completing sixth grade in Coney Island, I had qualified for a special three-year accelerated academic program. My sister went directly into Lincoln after graduating from eighth grade at our yeshiva.

Brighton Beach was first created out of farmland and later, in 1868, transformed into a resort area that for a time would serve as an upper middle-class contrast to the adjoining, more rundown Coney Island. With the advent of subways, and as first- and second-generation Jewish Americans moved in, the area was redeveloped as a residential community in the 1920s. By the 1930s and 1940s it had become a predominantly Jewish area. After World War II it also was home to large numbers of concentration camp survivors. As late as 2011, most of the estimated 55,000 Holocaust survivors residing in New York City lived in Brighton Beach. By the mid-1970s, what was then a largely elderly population had been revitalized by Jews emigrating from Russia and Ukraine to the US to avoid a resurgence of Soviet-era antisemitic persecution and discrimination. That was when the area took on the nickname Little Odessa. The neighborhood was initially Jewish for the most part, but after the collapse of the Soviet Union, thousands of other former Soviet citizens flocked to Brighton Beach, bringing new shops, nightclubs and restaurants, all sporting signs in English and Russian. At that point some of the eating establishments were decidedly non-kosher. Today, Brighton Beach is more Russian than ever. Brighton Beach Baths was torn down to make way for a large number of high-rise condominiums, and our own house is now a one-family home with an awning and iron grates on all the windows.

All in all, Brighton Beach was a pleasant world for us. It offered lots of places to shop, good knishes from Mrs. Stahl's, and a great diversity of housing and therefore kids and adults from many different backgrounds and income classes. My parents saved up (and used their lump-sum reparation payments) and bought our four-family home at a price somewhere between $16,000 and $20,000. My father went on to sell it for $55,000 in 1985, right before his Alzheimer's became more apparent and both my parents were finding that dealing with tenants and an aging structure was more than they were able to handle. They also found that without Rachel and me living there they needed even less space. As it turns out, that same house was recently listed on Zillow for nearly $1 million.

During the 30 or so years our family lived there (from about 1960-1991), our entire block featured a row of similar two-story, four-family brick buildings attached to each other in identical pairs, with alleys between them. You would enter our house from the street, going up a flight of stairs painted a deep red. On the first floor there were two three-room apartments that we rented out. A door at the end of a hallway led down to the basement. There I set up that amateur chemistry laboratory to cure lung cancer. The black steamer trunk from Sweden was also relegated to the basement, where my father now kept his important papers. The basement was also the scene of parties my mother urged my sister to host once Rachel joined, also at our mother's direction, a group called B'nai B'rith Girls, which was mostly a social organization for teenage Jewish girls. Our apartment was upstairs on the second floor. Located at the front of the building, it had four rooms. There was another apartment at the back of the house, which we rented out.

Our apartment seemed luxurious, compared to what had come before. Our expectations, of course, were decidedly modest. Upon walking in, you entered a dining room that could seat eight and that also featured a narrow hutch that held some Kosta Boda crystal vases, bowls and decanters that my parents had brought from Sweden in that black steamer trunk. These were wedding gifts from other refugees and Swedish co-workers back in Halmstad. To the right was the kitchen. The cabinets were a medium light wood and defined what was then called a "Hollywood Kitchen." At least that's what my mother called it. It was a sign that we had made it, or so my mother believed. There was also a small breakfast table and three chairs. A black phone hung on a wall in the corner. One day my mother decided to paint that phone and our piano white. In those days we shared the phone line with one other family. We didn't know them, and I assume they didn't have a clue who we were, but sometimes when we picked up the phone to make a call, we would hear someone else talking. This arrangement was called a party line, which was cheaper than a private line. I do remember that our partner on our anonymous party line was rude enough to pick up the phone and tell us we had been on too long and that she wanted to make a call, whereupon we would have to hang up. I don't think we ever did that to her. That was one difference between being always refugees and being Americans, who seemed to have a better idea of what they wanted and how to get it. Even my mother was a bit shy about such things, except with fellow refugees.

Opposite the bathroom, which was only a little larger than the one in Coney Island, was a hallway coat closet on the left. Once more, my mother found a refuge from her torments and a new bathroom to smoke in and hold court. If you walked further toward the front of our apartment, you would find my room. Actually, my room was once again the living room, home to the convertible couch, where I slept amidst our upright piano, our Zenith TV console and an old armchair from Coney Island. Off the living room there were two bedrooms: my parents' on the right, and Rachel's on the left. New furniture was ordered for each room: white French Provincial for Rachel, dark brown and black Formica for my parents. Again, this was a significant change compared to where we had come from. The bedroom windows let light in and faced 14th Street. The furnishings were better, but the nightmares and arguments that inhabited my parents' room remained constant.

In the living room, there were two windows facing an alley where clotheslines strung between the two buildings were shared by us and our neighbors, a plumber and his family, across the way. My mother would hang our clothes to dry after sometimes washing them on that old washboard standing in the bathtub. At some point, she did switch to a laundromat down the block. Before long my Aunt Genny and her husband Philip had moved to Brighton Beach from East New York (a part of Brooklyn) to be closer to us and again to escape rising rates of crime and poverty. They lived in a two-family house at 2843 Brighton 7th Street and had only one tenant. Philip worked as a tailor at Brighton Beach Mens and Boys Clothes on Coney Island Avenue.

My father collected rent from three tenants, that is, when they were able to pay. It supplemented our family income nicely, even if some of that money had to go toward repairs. Those tiny apartments were a source of various degrees of turmoil. Either a tenant had, from my mother's perspective, misbehaved, which often meant that either the renter was disinclined to share their life's story, or something was broken and needed to be repaired. When my mother called my father at work about some problem at home, he would generally say he was too tired or too busy, so the problem might have to wait. That answer was rarely good enough. Therefore our own "Daily Tenant Show" would become one we dialed into regularly, whereby its issues became another source of family tensions. Nothing was simple or easy.

We were now beginning to enter our teenage years, which brought a whole new dimension to the practice of helicopter parenting. On the one hand, you would think that my parents would continue to be as involved as humanly possible in every aspect of our lives, since protecting and guiding the two of us was what mattered most of all. Our lives had become more complicated, with days packed with additional homework, friends and all sorts of other social interactions. At least the school/academic part was not an issue. Both Rachel and I were self-motivated and rarely asked or even told either of our parents anything at all about our academic lives and projects. Teachers would tell us we were doing great and leave it at that. Our parents left it at that as well.

Rachel, however, even more than when she was younger, still bore the brunt of tolerating my mother's continuing quest to reinvent Rachel in Frieda's own image. She spent a lot of time bothering my sister about every possible thing. She wasn't so sure Rachel needed to wear glasses. Instead, she needed to read less and party more. She needed more friends. She needed better friends and prettier friends. She needed boyfriends. Whatever she did was never quite good enough.

My parents basically left me alone. I could pretty much come and go as I pleased as long as I ate what was served to me, went to shul on Saturdays with my father (which I liked to do anyway) and dressed the way my mother insisted. She bought all my clothes, and I accepted her taste as my own. I always sought the path of least resistance. Much later, when I was just starting to date Jennifer in college, I remember dressing up in what I thought was a very smart three-piece green wool suit. But it was summertime, and I looked like I was going to melt. The pants legs were pegged. The outfit was not cool on more than one level, but it was all I had, and I recall that when my mother bought the suit for me and told me I looked very handsome in it, I believed her. Though my father didn't expect me to wear a yarmulke when we were outside, he did expect me to do so when we were on the Lower East Side, which basically meant any time we were in an environment that he considered relatively welcoming for Jews. His life in Poland had given him enough experience to determine what might be safe.

As we had done in Coney Island, we kept to ourselves for the most part. We would visit Esther's family and my aunt. We also visited with a few other Holocaust survivor families in the area, mostly at their houses, not ours. Frieda wasn't comfortable with American families, but at the same time she was suspicious of former refugees because they clearly were jealous of our good fortune, such as it was. In our earlier Brighton Beach years, Rachel went to some sort of summer camp for poor Jewish girls in Ellenville, New York, for a few summers. I'm not sure what she thought of those times, but at least it offered her some escape from our lives together.

I too had the misfortune of being sent to a religious camp, this one for boys, in Deal, New Jersey. It was horrible, except that we were allowed and indeed encouraged to eat white bread at all our meals, which my mother would never have sanctioned. We were mostly marched around the camp as punishment for one thing or another. During our marches we were easy prey for swarms of yellowjackets. Our biggest treat was going into town to see William Holden in the film *Golden Boy*, about a boy who wanted to be a boxer instead of a violinist. It rang true to a degree. When I was younger, I always wanted to become someone other than who I was. Still, the film was not quite what sparked the interest of 12-year-olds. I wrote a postcard to my parents, saying I was miserable and telling them to come and take me home from the three-week-long camp. Unfortunately, my counselor intercepted the card and I was punished once more by having to march around to nowhere. How would my parents have come to Deal, New Jersey, anyway? They had dropped me off at a camp bus on the Lower East Side of Manhattan, they didn't have a car, and I'm sure they were as clueless as I was about the actual location of Deal, New Jersey.

Around that time, we also went on a few excursions as a family. My Aunt Genny and Uncle Philip joined us on at least one of them. I remember taking the subway to the Bronx to visit Freedomland, an amusement park that recreated the American frontier. It was a treat, except that we weren't allowed to buy any food or go on any rides. Regardless, we could walk around, which at least was a change of pace. We did the same thing at Palisades Amusement Park, but that time we took a subway to the Port Authority Bus Terminal and then a bus to New Jersey. On rare occasions, we traveled to Radio City Music Hall in Manhattan to spend the entire day sitting through three or four showings of the featured film and the Rockettes' stage show. In those days you could stay all day for the price of a single ticket.

Life continued apace in Brighton Beach. We all had our share of family dramas, including my father's ups and downs at work and the added distraction of tenant troubles. When he wasn't working or dealing with house issues, he kept himself diverted by focusing on all things Jewish, especially as they related to Israel. He kept up with the news on the Yiddish-language WEVD radio station and by reading the *Jewish Daily Forward*. My mother did her usual cooking, cleaning and complaining. Life was normal.

Rites of Passage

The next big event came in 1963 with my bar mitzvah and my sister's sweet sixteen. Money was once more an issue, so my parents found a creative way to merge both events into one. I'm not sure if either of us was pleased.

Rachel and me at Brighton Beach, July 1963.

It was April, before President Kennedy was shot but after the Cuban missile crisis. The Beatles were on the cusp of appearing on the Ed Sullivan Show. I was turning 13, becoming a man or at least navigating the bumpy road through adolescence, and nearing the end of eighth grade. A Jewish male's 13th birthday meant only one thing: bar mitzvah. Your knees shake. Your voice, already changing from tenor to baritone or bass on an hourly basis, cracks again as you strain to remember, and then chant, the portion of the Torah you had rehearsed every day after school for the previous eight weeks. You didn't know what you were singing, only that you didn't want to screw this up. Too much was at stake, for example, getting it over with.

Our synagogue, the New Brighton Jewish Center, was similar to many other such modest congregations in many respects, but different in a few. The synagogue was on the main floor, and the women sat upstairs. This was an Orthodox congregation, so separation of the sexes was ordained. So was separation from your pocketbook. By that, I mean that the centerpiece of most Saturday services at the New

Brighton Jewish Center was not necessarily the reading from the Torah, nor the standing and swaying prayers of devotion, nor the mourner's chants of Kaddish, nor the sermon delivered by our aged rabbi. No, the centerpiece was the appeal. Every week there was an appeal for something. Maybe money was needed to repair the roof or the cantor deserved a raise. Perhaps the toilets backed up and something had to be done, or the paint was peeling. If there wasn't any specific need, well, perhaps it was simply time for the appeal. It was, after all, tradition.

Hands would go up, signifying contributions. You would be recognized by the cantor, who stood at center stage on the bimah,[1] calling out names and amounts. He had two helpers who would wander the aisles, sternly staring at everyone in an attempt to embarrass them into raising a hand and making a pledge, or to point out a less-than-enthusiastically raised arm for the cantor. Having little to pledge except my birthright, my father rarely participated in this show of arms.

This went on for too long. As part of Saturday prayers, I accompanied my father to these marathon fundraising events at that synagogue every week, from boyhood until I left for college, when I'd join him again on weekends when I visited. By then, the script had taken on an amusing, even existential life of its own, and even my father thought it had gone a bit too far. We spent some of the sweetest moments of my adolescence exchanging stories or just catching up on life or the news in whispers of amusement while the appeal went on around us.

Meanwhile, back when I was 13 and my time came to be bar mitzvahed, the mercenary but perhaps necessary elements of my religious life and our secular lives remained foremost. I'll get to what I mean by that in moment.

What mostly distinguished the New Brighton Jewish Center from many other congregations was that it ran a thriving business with its catering hall, which happened to be in the basement of the building.

Some years ago I attended an elegant fundraiser with the King and Queen of Sweden at the Metropolitan Club on East 60th Street in Manhattan. Yes, it is a kind of catering hall as well, and yes, money, whether having it and or parting from it, was both a star attraction and a great draw. But what a grand way to make money! Having entered through a regal gate, we went up a small set of stairs to the main reception area, where we were greeted by a performing choir and string quartet. The chandelier that hung in the center seemed larger than our entire apartment back in Coney Island. Then when dinner was served, we noiselessly ascended flight after flight of plush carpeted stairs, past marble and alabaster statuary and through the unmistakably thick scent of money. I privately imagined that when really rich people died, they would ascend to heaven on stairs much like this one, in a club much like the one I was in.

In my case, we didn't ascend to the stars when I was 13; we descended into the basement. It doesn't quite have the same ring, does it? It didn't even then, at least not to me.

For my parents, however, it was perfect, which brings us to the mercenary thought mentioned a few paragraphs back. It was cheap, or let's say economical, prudent or thrifty, and it was convenient. Furthermore, they became even more creative on the thrifty end of things. They had a really great idea for making the day just that much more perfect for both Rachel and me. The clincher – the pièce de résistance or, as we said back in Brooklyn, the proof in the noodle pudding – was that my bar mitzvah, the celebration of my entry into manhood, would be coupled with my sister's sweet sixteen. The fact that she wasn't yet 16 and wouldn't be for several more months didn't bother my parents one iota.

At some level, each of us desired a moment alone in the limelight, some friends of our own to be with us only and some attention devoted to the specialness of a particular time in our lives. Well, none of that entered into the calculation. My parents had hit upon the perfect arrangement. Rachel and I were not amused. If truth be told, we didn't have much money, so this was a practical solution. Unlike those Saturday services, my parents couldn't conjure up a special appeal just to fund our parties.

Anyway, the preparations didn't help matters. The night before, my sister was forced to have her pretty, long blond hair rolled up in curlers and teased into the kind of bouffant hairdo Marie Antoinette wore to the guillotine. And since this was a two-for-one deal, my mother actually put a curler in the front of my own locks for good measure, so that my normal pompadour could become even more pronounced and embarrassingly taller and curlier. Ah, to become a man.

What do I remember most about that entire day and night? I remember that for drinks we had club soda and ginger ale. I remember that we had kosher bologna and salami deli platters with pickles and mustard to eat. Our band consisted of a single accordion player who wore us out with endless rounds of music for dances no one knew how to do. And I remember most vividly that at the end of the event, Gregory G., who I thought was my friend, came up to me and said simply, "This is the cheapest bar mitzvah I have ever been to in my life." Congratulations, Max.

It's not fair that days like that one are measured by how much you spend, as compared to how much you love, or how much you care or are cared for. But that's how it was upstairs in the synagogue when we were getting religion. That's also how it was downstairs, the night before we were becoming men, or girls were turning 16, back in Brighton Beach just before the Beatles appeared on the Ed Sullivan Show and before any of us knew any better.

Around that same time, I had the opportunity to select a very special bar mitzvah present and learn something about class differences and how they become manifest, even as I was crossing a border by becoming a man.

Years before, my father had bought our old black upright piano from a guy he met at work who seemed to know all the good deals. It might have cost $35, a sum that amounted to just $20 less than what he was making each week in the mid-1950s. Looking back, I'm not sure "good deal" is exactly the right phrase, as the seller was the same guy who convinced my father to buy an encyclopedia set from him for $10, which was perhaps a bargain except that it was a 1903 edition of the Encyclopedia Britannica that was missing volume II. Given all that had happened since 1903, I assume it was missing a lot more than that.

My parents apparently thought every cultured family should have a piano and it would be a good thing for my sister to expand her horizons by learning how to play it. I don't know what they were thinking, and I'm sure my sister was far from thrilled at the prospect of more to do and more to learn. We were already attending yeshiva, with its required loads of senseless homework every night and hours and hours of useless memorization on most weekends. Both of us were expected to be the best in our respective classes, though actually, I'm pretty sure we expected more of ourselves than our parents did. Either way, there was very little time for anything else. An out-of-tune upright piano that cost more than half a week's salary at the time could not go to waste.

Neither Rachel nor I was musically inclined, or so it seemed; at least, neither of us could carry a tune. Somehow, however, my mother decided that my sister would get piano lessons and perhaps someday become a concert pianist of the first order, attracting other musicians of all ages and stripes, adding to her credentials for her future life and possibly for a future husband. I was about 10 at the time and Rachel was about 13. The plans were laid. What my mother could never attain or have the possibility of attaining, my sister had to aspire to and achieve. So it was thought, and so it would be done.

The woman who would lead my sister to scale the mountains of musical achievement was Mrs. F. I will not use her actual name for fear that one of her relatives would come after me after all these years. Let me tell you: although I was still pretty young when I first met her, I knew from the outset that she was a piece of work.

I was never quite sure where she came from. She might have been Russian or Austrian. I did know that her thick European accent was unlike my mother's, which was a mixture of many languages and styles, but more like the speech of the haughty women I saw on television playing the Czarina Anastasia or similar foreign upper-class figures, waiting to be seduced by Rasputin or his ravenous colleagues. She wore her hair in a tight bun and held on to a handkerchief that emitted a strong scent of perfume. Her initials were embroidered on it, and I once heard, or perhaps only dreamed, that the handkerchief came straight from Lord & Taylor. Recall that if A&S was high-class in our household, Lord & Taylor was clearly a store for only the very wealthy. It was out of reach, located in that mysterious part of the world we simply called the City. Our shopping universe, when we needed dressy clothes or real furniture, was in downtown Brooklyn at Korvette's, Mays and, if the gods smiled on us, A&S.

In any case, Mrs. F agreed to teach Rachel the piano for $3 a week. While we were still living in Coney Island, she would come once a week for an hour or so and go through scales in a book of musical exercises by Carl Czerny, and then on to pieces like Für Elise, Solfeggietto and several of Mozart's Sonatas. Don't get me wrong: I was not a precocious musical genius who understood any of that, or could even read those titles, let alone the music. I know what was taught to my sister simply because one day, my mother decided the torture would be shared. For some strange reason, Mrs. F once heard me fooling around, banging on the piano and trying to play something I had heard on television, by ear. She thought I had talent, or at least an ear or two.

It was a fatal slip of the hands that I would regret for what seemed like too long. For an extra $2, Mrs. F agreed to come for an extra half hour each week, and I could split the time with Rachel as we or she saw fit.

Over time, my sister was spared and stepped further away from the piano as I became the centerpiece of our little musical world.

Actually, I didn't mind practicing. I sort of liked it. I would memorize pieces and play them fast, faster and often louder than they were meant to be played. All this activity strengthened my fingers, which was important since everything else about me was fairly weak. Whenever I got into one of those silly little macho matches that boys would have with each other, my only defense was my hands, not to punch, but actually to grab my opponent's hand and squeeze it with so much force, crunching knuckles with such vigor, that my opponent, usually that same obnoxious kid Julie or someone like him, would give in and go away.

What I liked least about the piano experience was Mrs. F herself. I was only a kid, but I knew in my own paranoiac way that she didn't think much of us, and especially not of our mother. She would wave her embroidered handkerchiefs in our faces, making a point of wearing what I considered to be expensive clothes that were clean and didn't have the distinct smell of Spic and Span that for some reason seemed to pervade our clothes. My mother cleaned our clothes mostly on the washboard in our bathtub in those days, and I'm sure the floor cleaner sometimes replaced Tide detergent. In any case, Mrs. F would talk to my mother about some other way of living that was completely foreign to us, as though she had just bought some Fabergé eggs from one of her Duchess friends and my mother was too poor and too uneducated to even understand any of it. Mrs. F thought she had somehow bonded with me, as in theory I was the talented and educated one, and we would flaunt our New World ways over my mother. And while I certainly had, as they say today, issues with my mother, I never forgot where she had come from and what she had gone through. No one had the right to question, challenge or ridicule the validity of her meager existence, and certainly not the likes of Mrs. F.

I still cringed when Mrs. F came to our apartment, even after we moved up in the world a little and left Coney Island for the slightly grander middle-class pursuits of nearby Brighton Beach.

My musical career ended when I was turning 13. It was around the time when my mother one day decided to paint our black piano white. I'm not quite sure why, but it was something that seemed to make her feel good. Perhaps the color complemented our new white bedroom set, or just brightened our dreary rooms. Well, Mrs. F did not approve, and she let my mother know it, scoffing at her taste once again. Mrs. F had a habit of keeping time by using a very sharp pencil, which she had my mother dutifully sharpen for her at the beginning of each lesson. She moved it up and down as she sat next to me on a chair near my piano bench. I hadn't realized it until my mother painted that piano white, but Mrs. F was actually writing on the piano as she did this, in small, sharp strokes that moved up and down to the beat of my lyrical pounding and questionable musicality. Once I saw those strokes on the newly painted white piano, I was more certain than ever that this woman harbored absolutely no respect for us or for our piano.

When my bar mitzvah came and other children were getting opportunities to travel or receiving gifts of money or other wondrous presents, I asked only one thing of my parents: that I would no longer have to take lessons with Mrs. F. They couldn't say no. In fact, I now believe that deep down, my mother had very much wanted to say yes for a very long time and rid us of this strange Russian baroness for good. It was music to my ears and hers.

I was free at last. After stopping those lessons, I still played the piano when I could, by myself and for my mother, who would dance when I played Malaguena or the Blue Danube Waltz. When I left classical music and played by ear one of her favorites, Petula Clark's Downtown, my mother would light up. It was then that we all realized that music was not only about the sounds you heard or the emotions you felt, and it was certainly not about how grand your piano was. Instead it seemed to be about an old upright that could not be taught culture, but could nevertheless find a way to sing.

*My parents step out to a wedding. Also attending among the guests
are my father's US first cousins with their spouses: Seated next to
Frieda is Hyman, standing second from left is Sally, fifth from left
is Esther and third from right is Milton.*

The next year, Rachel graduated high school near the top of her class
and then went on to Brooklyn College, where my mother influenced
her decision to pursue a degree in elementary education. Rachel
lived at home, which I thought was a shame. She needed to get away.
But I don't think the idea of her ever leaving home to go away to
college had been discussed or even broached. Rachel and I both
qualified for Regents scholarships, which covered full tuition at any
college in New York State.

A few years later, after I graduated from Lincoln, which I always
remembered as a great academic and social experience, I got into
Columbia College and gleefully seized the opportunity to move into
the dorms there. My father asked me why I was going to live away
from home. I replied honestly, up to a point, saying that I thought it
would be good for my education. He thought for a minute and said,
"Okay, then, you know best." I got the lowest-priced room in the
college. It was $325 a semester for what was called a closet double,
because it was about the size of a walk-in closet. What's more, I
shared the room with someone else, a sophomore from Turkey, who
was also on a full scholarship. Indeed, this closet double had once
been the maid's room (she had it all to herself) for the son of the
dormitory's benefactor.

I also wish Rachel had gone away to college so that she could have explored all the great things she was capable of doing academically. But she was soon to go away for a different reason after she met Elliot Borak, her future husband, at a mixer for college Democrats in Washington, DC. She was a freshman and he was in his junior year at NYU, a pre-med student planning on becoming a physician. They married in 1969. She taught for two and a half years and went on to get a Master's in Education in 1971, while he went to medical school.

In the summer of 1969, I traveled to Europe with some friends on our own "Europe on $3 a Day" plan, and when I returned to Brighton 14th Street, who should I find visiting with his wife and daughter from South America? None other than Isaac Urbach, my father's friend from Bunzlau. It was wonderful to see my father so happy to be with him. I'm sure it brought back difficult memories, but somehow they were totally subsumed by the abiding, deep friendship they shared. On that summer visit to Europe we had decided to visit East and West Berlin, which at the time were fully separated. Nevertheless, I was reluctant to tell my parents that I had visited Germany, thinking it would also bring back horrible memories. However, when I told them what I had done, their response was something like, "So what? Did you have a nice time?" I told them my Yiddish had actually helped get us around in Germany, which pleased my father. His three years in Bunzlau meant three years in Germany, as Bunzlau was just over the border from Poland. And of course, Bergen-Belsen was also in Germany, not far from the DP camps where he and my mother were both processed before being taken to Sweden.

In May 1973, Sam and Frieda decided at last to visit Israel for about a week on a group tour. It was, of course, a country and an idea in which my father had invested a great deal of himself, first in Poland, when he became a Zionist, and then when he toyed with the idea of trying to resettle in Palestine after the war. I'm certain that given the opportunity, he and his first wife would have moved there at some point. Indeed, several of her brothers did just that. After their return, however, the only news I heard about my parents' trip was that someone had come into their hotel room while they slept and stolen whatever jewelry my mother had brought. The slings and arrows of outrageous fortune continued to challenge these two survivors, even after they fulfilled a long-held dream (at least for my father) of returning to the Promised Land.

I realized this was a group excursion and thus that there were limits to what they might have done on their own. Still, knowing what I know now, I am surprised that Sam never tried to contact Chaja's relatives in Israel. After his liberation from Bergen-Belsen, he had their names and possibly some of their addresses and if he had asked me, I would certainly have helped track them down or at least try to find out what happened to them. It was once again apparent that he was determined to leave his past behind him, for all the reasons suggested earlier. What would Frieda have said, had he found his first family's relatives? Could she have endured the pain of my father finding hints of his first wife and children and the memories it might have recreated? We will never know.

While I was in college, we all got together for Passover, which was still our favorite holiday. Maybe it had something to do with the idea of freedom, when the Israelites were freed from bondage and fled Egypt for the Promised Land. Or perhaps it was my family's way of subconsciously celebrating my parents' ability to remind themselves that despite whatever they worried about and sometimes fought over, they had finally gained a large measure of freedom in America. They would remember all they had suffered quite literally in their years of bondage. Certainly they had paid a heavy price, but it was freedom nevertheless. It was a joyous time. My mother would actually laugh as my father made fun of her cooking, and we joked about his praying even as we all talked amongst ourselves. It was a small group compared to the large families they had enjoyed in their other lives, but we were a family nevertheless.

My father was not above finding other things to laugh about. Once, at another Passover seder, he lit up when he found the Afikomen (a piece of matzoh that the children would hide and then negotiate for in order to conclude the Passover service). I was doing the negotiating, and he was playing along. He let some friends of mine who were guests at the seder in on the secret. I was the only one who was unaware. It was funny and fun. You could see in his eyes that all the burdens that weighed on him were lifted, replaced by the possibility of happiness. It was a moment that warmed my heart.

Along with joy came measures of sadness. My Aunt Genny died on February 5, 1976. She was blinded by untreated glaucoma and died of untreated heart failure. Mostly she died of a broken heart, having never recovered or accepted the murder of her daughter in 1943. Of all my mother's hundreds of relatives in Poland, she was the only one who had survived. Aunt Genny was five or six years older than my mother, and the two of them were together for nearly the entire war. Sadly, my mother had a tortured relationship with her sister. My aunt evidently had a decent life with her husband and young child before the war, but both were murdered in Mauthausen after surviving the Kraków Ghetto and Płaszów concentration camp.

The four of us with Aunt Genny in Ellenville, NY, visiting Rachel at a summer camp.

Aunt Genny was much quieter than my mother, to say the least. She was more reserved, and to me she seemed somehow more resigned to her fate, or to never being able to move on. Unlike my mother, she was not a fighter. My guess, though, is that she was popular as a younger woman in Kraków. She had an easier disposition and didn't antagonize others the way my mother might have.

The intensely close but also fraught relationship between my mother and her sister played a big part in all our lives. When we were teenagers we saw our aunt several times a week, once she and her husband moved to Brighton Beach, and we talked on the phone most days. We saw how bad the interactions were between the two sisters but never understood why. My mother constantly criticized Aunt Genny. It was as though doing so somehow made my mother feel better. One thought is that my mother always needed victims who would have a hard time fighting back. Perhaps that was rooted in her horrifying wartime experiences, during which she witnessed abundant examples of those with power and those who were powerless, and saw how some survived while the weaker could not.

At one point, my sister said she heard Frieda say Genny blamed herself or my mother for leaving her daughter with their mother Ruchela, who then was about 65 years old and had no way to protect a little girl who was only five or six when the war broke out. I have doubts about that story, as from what I could learn, Genny's daughter was not murdered in the ghetto or even in Płaszów but instead died in 1943, when she was she was imprisoned with her father in Mauthausen.

Thinking about it, I realize that although Aunt Genny never came to our house, not even for the holidays, she was the only person my mother could link to the past. Maybe my mother simply didn't want to remember the past as it was and erased her memories by targeting the only person who could remind her of it. In truth, each woman lived in a fantasy world of her own. The sad part is that they could have been happier if they had given up on those past lives and focused on what was in front of them. Clearly, they just couldn't make that leap of faith.

Another theory emerged while this book was being researched. It seems that Aunt Genny, my grandmother's older daughter, may have been favored by her parents. In a large family like theirs, the eldest daughter would surely have been given a greater amount of leeway and even some authority over the younger children. Perhaps my mother harbored some resentment toward my aunt. Moreover, Aunt Genny had married much earlier and had a child from that marriage. Her husband was an airplane mechanic, certainly beyond what would normally be expected of young Orthodox Jewish males at a time when most of them became traders or craftsmen, like my mother's father and brothers. So even though Frieda often urged us to watch out for people who envied us, I sense that my mother was actually jealous of her sister. True, all that took place long ago, years before the two sisters arrived in America. Regardless, each of them had suffered great loss and endured drastic change, and past jealousies could have played a role.

Nevertheless, in the present day there was nothing for Frieda to be jealous about when it came to her sister. My mother could see that when it came to their second marriages. Aunt Genny's second husband was no match for my father. Philip didn't have my father's obvious smarts or his generous, warm personality, and he wasn't particularly kind to my aunt, as far as I saw. Also, my mother had Rachel and me, while Genny had lost her only child and lived in a strange fantasy world in which that reality was not accepted. My aunt fantasized about her daughter surviving the war and living in Sweden with her family. At the same time, Aunt Genny collected dolls that she said were for her young daughter. In that fantasy, Genny's daughter was frozen in time and had not aged since the last time my aunt saw her in the 1940s.

If there had once been anything to be jealous about, the tables had turned considerably in my mother's favor. Didn't she realize any of that? Over time, I came to understand that the many hurtful things she did and said were not intentional. Frieda was undeniably damaged by the war and perhaps even before then, having spent her earliest years as a refugee in Prague. So although Frieda sought to control everyone and everything, and would say whatever came into her mind with few filters or forethought, she did so precisely because she had no control. At my aunt's funeral, she screamed at Philip, saying he was to blame for neglecting the many health issues her sister had faced in the last years of her life. The truth is, we were all to blame. Aunt Genny was generally a sweet, quiet woman who seemed unable to hurt a fly. We felt only sadness and pity for her losses during the war and her lifelong inability to overcome them. But perhaps because she didn't make her mark forcefully, as my mother did, we sometimes forgot she was even there. Then and today, we are reminded that the psychological effects of surviving were both apparent and hidden in our parents and our aunt, and later perhaps in ourselves as well. (See Part IX.)

After they got married, my sister and her husband rented an apartment in Stuyvesant Town/Peter Cooper Village, a large group of apartment buildings on the Lower East Side of Manhattan that stretched from East 14th to East 23rd Streets and from First Avenue to Avenue C. It was known for its reasonable rents and boasted a number of larger apartments, established and back then owned by the Metropolitan Life Insurance Company, which had its headquarters in the area. Rachel continued working as a second grade teacher but disliked teaching and willingly gave it up to become a stay-at-home mom. Soon my mother would spend most of her days helping care for Rachel's first three sons, who were born in New York: Hugh, born in 1971, Greg, born a year later, and Jeremy, born in 1975.

Jennifer and I met at Columbia in 1970. She was at Barnard. We came from two very different worlds, but love conquered all, and fortunately, no painful joy was involved. We got married in September 1971 and went off to California for a year so that I could complete a master's in journalism at UC Berkeley while she took time off from her Columbia master's program in library science.

SAM AND FRIEDA: BY THEMSELVES AGAIN

In June 1977, Rachel and her family left New York and moved to Mobile, Alabama, around the time when my father retired from the only job he ever held in America. Her husband Elliot had completed his medical training and naval service and joined a gastroenterology practice in Mobile. I was sad to see her go, and I'm sure my parents felt a much deeper loss. Her absence left a big hole in their lives, especially for my mother, who had spent so many years commuting by subway to her apartment in Manhattan to help care for her growing family. It had to be tough on my mother when her days suddenly became quiet. She had built her life around Rachel, and then around Rachel's children. Once again Frieda faced the challenge of finding a new life. Jennifer and I welcomed the birth of our twin sons Eric and Noah in August 1977, just a few months after Rachel left. We lived north of Manhattan, so it was a considerable schlep for Sam and Frieda to come see us, and between work and caring for twins, it was difficult for us to go down to see them in Brooklyn very often.

At first I thought my mother would be beside herself with worry, anxiety and unhappiness and would respond by loosing her superabundant nervous energy onto the universe and her upset even more onto Sam. What would life be like, without the subway trips to Manhattan and without her focus on Rachel and her family?

That may have been the case for a while, but our mother, ever the survivor, found new ways to channel her energy. After Sam retired, there were several years in which I actually thought my parents' resilience, born of their wartime experiences, helped them experience some measure of happiness. I even sensed that they were doing better than ever with each other. They began to visit us more often, now that there were new babies for my mother to help feed. On every visit. Sam brought candies and Frieda provided two roast chickens that she would buy in Brighton Beach but thankfully did not prepare herself. We made sure to sneak cake to my father while my mother was playing with the boys. We got together for Passover seders in Brooklyn, and when the boys were still young we all met at Jennifer's parents' apartment in Manhattan for Thanksgiving, right after sitting outside with the boys to watch the Thanksgiving Day Parade. Sam and Frieda would come by subway, and after the meal ended we would walk them to the D train at Columbus Circle. Frieda always took the leftover turkey bones home to make soup. This became a tradition for as long as they lived in Brooklyn.

They also discovered the pleasures of volunteering at a local Jewish senior center. Sam prided himself on his work as a waiter serving food to the more elderly seniors. It was kosher, so he and my mother ate lunch there every day. Knowing how my mother operated, she doubtless moved a decent amount of food from lunch into her large handbag to serve for dinner. My father really seemed to enjoy the social aspect of his job, kibitzing with others and feeling good that he wasn't yet as old and worn as they were. My parents also got pounds of surplus American cheese from the senior center. They kept some of it for themselves but brought the bulk of it to us. It tended to end up in macaroni and cheese, one of the kids' favorite foods.

Frieda also volunteered to participate in various senior center exercise and dance classes, finally, after a fashion, getting her own dance studio. Both Sam and Frieda went for long walks on the boardwalk, and my father started going to shul to study and listen to the rabbi discuss that week's portion of the Torah. My mother even agreed to spend several weeks every summer at a senior Jewish camp in the Catskills. Sam liked being with people, and Frieda liked some of the classes. She complained about the food because it wasn't her cooking, which was certainly one of the reasons my father wanted to keep going back to those camps.

The four of us in Mobile celebrating the bar mitzvah of one of Rachel's four sons.

In the years that followed, Sam and Frieda attended the bar mitzvahs of three of their grandsons. My mother was still alive when Sam was bar mitzvahed in 1994. We joined everyone for all those celebrations. Sam and Frieda also continued to visit Rachel and her family in Mobile for a couple of weeks at a time. Rachel occasionally came up for a visit as well. Sam, Rachel's youngest, was born in 1981 in Mobile. It was good to be together again, even if the personal interactions were complicated, especially when Elliot's mother moved down to be near her son and daughter-in-law in her later years. There was a decent amount of competition for attention between them, with Rachel, as always, caught in the middle.

In September 1979, I was in my office at Channel 13 when I got a call from my father's cousin Hyman, who was now a successful cardiologist. My father had suffered a serious heart attack. The good news was that he survived it, and while the damage to his heart was significant, it could have been much worse. The bad news was that he was at Coney Island Hospital, which was not a great place to seek care or medical expertise. At least it was close to home so my mother could visit him. I quickly drove to Brighton Beach to see my mother and then my father. Within a week he was stabilized and released into my mother's care. At that point, Frieda was clearly afraid Sam would die, so she decided she would put her penchant for controlling others to good use. She put Sam on a strict no-salt, no-fat diet. No sweets (at least, not from her), no cooked food that had any taste, but lots of fruits and vegetables and a new regimen of walking even more than they had before, for several hours a day. He lost a great deal of weight, but he never had any heart problems again.

As time went on, they fell into a routine, which was good for their bodies and minds. Shul, the senior center, TV, more shul, walks, naps, more shul, more walks, TV. Frieda watched her favorite soap operas. Sam and Frieda came up to visit us on Sundays at least once a month. We also visited them more often.

In April 1984, I got a call at work from my father, who was letting me know he had decided to sell the house. He didn't say why, and I decided not to ask. I assumed it had something to do with the increasing amount of energy it took for my parents to deal with tenants and the expenses of keeping the house in shape. It had become a burden. In retrospect, I suppose my father was starting to see himself becoming less able to run the financial and other aspects of their lives. He had always been the one shuffling bank accounts, looking for the best bank gifts given to new depositors and finding better Certificate of Deposit interest rates. He enjoyed doing all that and watching his savings grow. But the continuing fights about tenants, the need to find acceptable new tenants when someone moved out, and having to threaten evictions for non-payments of rent had all started to tax his executive functioning, as the neurologists would explain later about the aging brain and early stages of dementia.

Sam sold his house, with his rabbi advising him. In hindsight, I would have gotten more involved had I known about any of this earlier. By the time he told me what he had done, it was too late to offer an opinion. The kids were still young and a new job was demanding all my free time, so I simply congratulated him. It was easy enough to sell the house since the sale occurred at the height of a housing shortage caused by Russian immigrants moving into Brighton Beach who were willing to pay top dollar for anything they could get. I'm sure he could have gotten much more, but it was best to just be done with it and move on.

This sudden sale was the beginning of a downward spiral of his mental and physical health. To this day, I'm still not sure exactly when his Alzheimer's disease could first have been suspected. Could it have been noticed sooner? If so, could we have done anything differently to help him? I really don't think so.

Indeed, it's pretty ironic to be trying and failing to remember aspects of a disease that steals memory, that laughs in the face of memory, that diminishes it, obliterates it, mocks it in all its glory and its pity. Even as I attempt to do so, I find myself in my own aging period of memory slump and sag. These days I have to shrug off the fact that I don't remember people's names or other things related to the peculiarities of being 70 or older.

In a world where equilibrium is supposed to be an immutable law of the universe, where highs naturally go to lows, where atoms rush in to fill the voids and vacuums of emptiness and black holes mock our pedestrian understanding of gravity, a question naturally arises. If there is memory loss, I ask myself, where is the memory gained?

To some degree, that's what I've been trying to do in this story: to recall the moments of my father's journey toward emptiness in order to somehow fill the void he left, more specifically the space around not understanding at all or ever accepting what happened to him and why.

Perhaps the sale of the house and its suddenness should have raised suspicion. Or maybe that key point was two years later, when another seemingly innocent event may have been the beginning of his disease. Early one evening, Rachel called me from Alabama to say she had been talking to our father when he suddenly told her to hold on because someone was at the door. She waited, but he didn't come back to the phone. After a while she hung up and periodically tried to call back. All she got was a busy signal. It had been several hours and she was anxious. She began to think something had gone terribly wrong at 3060 Brighton 14th Street. Perhaps, she imagined, someone had broken into my parents' second-floor, front-facing apartment, taken them prisoner, tied them up, beaten them, and was in the process of forcing them to give up their handful of Lincoln Savings Bank, Dime Savings Bank and Williamsburg Savings Bank Certificates of Deposit and any other precious possessions they may have had.

Her anxiety, her terror and her rational concerns suddenly became contagious. They spread 1,000 miles north and quickly enough became mine too. After another hour of dialing and busy signals, an operator affirmed the phone was off the hook and not out of order. I called a neighbor, who was not home. Finally, I called the police at the 60th Precinct in Brooklyn and asked for their help. Could they send a patrol car to the house? They asked what the problem was. "Oh, I don't know," I considered saying, "a possible kidnapping, hostage taking, torture, robbery, or worse? Take your pick!" In the end I simply told them this behavior was unlike my father, and my parents were old.

"Are your parents ill?" they asked.

"Well," I wanted to answer, "if you define 'ill' by the number of demons that haunted them, their chronic pains dealing with life, my mother's anhedonia and my father's stress levels, then yes, they were very sick."

Instead, I told the police, "Physically, well, my father once had a heart attack." All they could say in response was, "We'll see what we can do."

Half an hour later I got a call. It was my father. The police had just left, along with an ambulance and stretcher, all testing the strength of the rickety stairs to that second-floor front-facing apartment where I grew up.

"Why did you call them?" he asked. "What's wrong with you?"

"We were worried," I told him. "Rachel was worried, so I was worried. You didn't hang up the phone."

"Oh, yes," he answered. "Our neighbor came in to talk and I forgot Rachel was on the phone. Why are you making such a big deal about nothing?"

Maybe he was right. Forgetting is an everyday occurrence for me these days. He was 76, older than I am now. Why couldn't forgetting just be as routine for him too?

That was the first time the topic of forgetting became an issue in my father's life and my own. Later it would overwhelm everything.

Not too long after that incident, I got another call in November 1987, this time from my mother and in the morning, just as I got to my office. That day, I was scheduled to attend a big meeting and then lunch with my boss's boss's boss, who reported to the chairman of the company. As my boss said, this was a command performance. On the phone, it seemed an alternative appointment was in the offing: my mother told me that my father had fainted that morning while praying in synagogue and had been taken by ambulance to Coney Island Hospital. "Do something, please!" she begged.

I tried to calm her down and learn more. Such attempts were usually destined for failure. When my mother was in distress, she gave the word hysterical a new and even more unbalanced meaning. I called the hospital, but in vain. Then I rushed off to Coney Island.

The emergency room at the hospital was full of the strange chaos that comes from confused people who don't speak the language, and from meeting people in charge who may feel overburdened yet are willing to help, or else appear irritated, as though they wished they were elsewhere. The atmosphere seemed to alternate between silence and rejection, anticipation and acceptance, between being told to sit down and then being told to come quickly.

Putting on my best air of authority and assurance in a hospital where English was not a first language for most of the patients, even though common sense and communication were seldom attributes of those who ran the institution, I nevertheless tried to discern from them where my father was, what had happened to him and what I could do.

Adding to the chaos, my mother arrived, having come, she said, by following an angel. She ascribed her ability to get to Coney Island Hospital some 18 blocks or about a mile away from her house, thanks only to the good graces of a stranger who noticed her confusion and walked her there, thus becoming her angel of mercy. I guess we all need one of those in a pinch.

I was soon led into what I can best describe as a holding pen behind the nurse's station. There, people who were not under the direct fire of a heart attack or stroke, whose bleeding was controlled or unseen, whose traumas were still unknown but worth investigating, time and space permitting, were held on stretchers and beds in hallways and doorways. A doctor actually took me to my father's bedside in one of the many hidden corners of this maze. He was still only 76, but he looked very old lying there. Hospitals have a way of transforming the healthy into the sickly as much as they try to do the opposite, or so it would seem. They had removed his false teeth, his yarmulka and his glasses. His hat and clothes were piled at his feet and he lay in a conscious daze.

"Daddy," I said, taking his hand. "It's me. What happened?"

He looked at me, smiled slightly, and said, "I don't know why I'm here."

I turned to the doctor, who looked at his chart and agreed.

"I don't know why he's here," the doctor observed. "The ambulance brought him here because he had fainted. We ran a few tests and will run a few more. I don't think we'll find anything so we'll probably let him go home."

I held my father's hand for a few more minutes and told him everything would be fine.

I took my mother home and told her she should just wait, as he would be home soon, or if not, the hospital would call and we could figure out what to do next. I had to get back to that meeting with my boss's boss's boss and lunch in the executive dining room.

I kept calling anyway.

Right before I left the emergency room, I asked the staff if I could leave money to make sure my father was sent home by taxi or ambulette.

"Oh no, don't worry," I was assured. Medicare would pay and they wouldn't send him on his way alone.

I felt assured, though slightly worried. The scene in the emergency room didn't promote confidence about what would follow. Later that afternoon I was back in my office. Having heard nothing, I called the hospital to see what had happened.

"Oh, we released him about two hours ago."

I called home. My mother reported that he hadn't yet come home. I called the hospital again.

"How did you release him? What ambulette did he take? When?"

"We don't know," they replied. "Maybe he went upstairs to get some medication." I called my mother again. Had he come home yet?

No. Nothing. No father. No answers. Forget it. The hospital had lost my father. But as it turned out, he had lost the hospital, and maybe more.

I excused myself from my command performance, taking with me the appropriately disturbing memories of the glares emitted by my boss, my boss's boss and my boss's boss's boss as I got into the car I'd borrowed from my father-in-law, who lived close by. "Sorry," I said to everyone, "my father seems to have gone missing" or something equally melodramatic. "I have to go and find him."

Back at Coney Island Hospital[1] I wandered the halls, searched the staircases, went to the pharmacy. There was no lost-and-found department for fathers, but I asked around anyway. No one knew anything. It had now been three hours and he was not in the hospital and not at home, which would have been a half-hour walk away, walking very slowly.

I drove up and down Ocean Parkway and Brighton 11th Street, went into his synagogue, stopped at grocery stores and the library along the way home. When I finally arrived at my parents' apartment, planning to report no progress and call the police, there was my father.

He had arrived a few minutes earlier. He said he had left the hospital and gone straight home.

"But Daddy, where did you go for three hours or more? We've been looking for you everywhere."

"I just went home. Right home," he said. "Why are you making such a deal? I'm fine. Forget about it. I'm fine." He was not precisely fine, as it turned out.

The next time we should have known something was up came a few months later, when my father, without warning or discussion, stopped sending us a small monthly stipend. He had regularly sent this small check since Jennifer and I got married, before I started working and then during my first few jobs, when we had very little income. Later my father institutionalized the checks, insisting on sending them even when we were doing okay, with the proviso that it remain our secret. In fact, anytime my mother said he should give us an anniversary gift or a birthday gift, he would say sure, and then wink at me so that I'd understand that those gifts were covered by that check as well. That was fine and always appreciated.

Then, one day, the check didn't come. Then the next month, nothing. The next time we saw him, I said something about the check, with my mother out of earshot, and he just looked at me in surprise. "What check?" he asked. "You know," I replied, trying to assure him that my mother wasn't around to hear, "the check." "There are no checks," he answered, now somewhat agitated. I dropped it. "Forget it," I said. Sadly, he did. It was just the beginning of forgetting more and more.

During that same 1987–1988 period, Rachel too had noticed changes in his personality when our parents visited her family in Mobile. She knew that something was awry on one such visit when my father suddenly criticized her for not being religious enough. Normally he would never do that (even if he thought it). He let a lot of things slide, even when it came to religion. It was the only way he could survive. On another visit not much later, he became extremely agitated and accused her of not sharing some Little Debbie cookies with him and instead giving the cookies to her young children. Where was the playful father she had known? He used to try to defuse arguments in our family, instead of starting them. Something was up.

Months later, the call came at six or seven in the morning, this time from my mother telling me it had taken Sam four hours to get home after morning prayers. It was then that we knew something was terribly wrong. On another day he had simply left the apartment for no reason and not returned for hours, without remembering where he had gone. He had begun wandering. It was time to make the trek to the neurologist and the radiologist to get scans and tests in the hope that it was only malnutrition (I wouldn't have been surprised) or a thyroid problem or even something to do with mini-strokes that a few aspirins could remedy. At that time and today as well, for that matter, the medical approach to this problem has changed very little, at least when it comes to finding any long-term solutions. There were no drugs to help, no places that could really do much good. It was

Alzheimer's disease, an intractable illness that even today remains as hopeless as back then.

After selling the house, my parents moved into another apartment in a building similar to their own, further down on Brighton 14th Street. Problems with the landlord, possibly because they had been landlords themselves, led them to move once more that same year to a bigger apartment building at 3085 Brighton 13th Street, Apartment 4E.

Ultimately, Rachel and I decided our mother could not handle our father's continuing decline on her own, though she was actually doing yeoman's work understanding their finances while I tried to help her manage the practical aspects of their daily lives. Rachel and I decided that the best idea was for them to move down to Mobile to a garden apartment just a short car ride from Rachel's house. My mother agreed. Rachel had more time than I did to watch out for our parents, who could no longer function without considerable help. Her husband Elliot, as a physician, had a profession we thought might prove valuable for accessing medical resources.

It seemed like the only stopgap measure we could think of. Naturally, I felt very guilty about shifting so much of the burden of our parents' upkeep onto Rachel; however, there didn't seem to be any alternative. It was clear that their experiences during the war would have an effect for years and throughout their whole lives, if not for generations afterward. I began to seek an even fuller understanding of this around that same time and then later, as I learned about the psychological impacts of the Holocaust on the families of those who had survived.

PART VIII

A FINAL STOP: MOBILE, ALABAMA

ALZHEIMER'S CHANGES
EVERYTHING

After all they had suffered, along with the effects their suffering had on their children and even on future generations, it was our turn to help our parents as best we could. First, though, there was at least one more *simcha* (celebration) for us to enjoy together in New York. In September 1990, we all celebrated Eric and Noah's joint bar mitzvah, marking one of the last times I heard my father recite his beloved prayers over the Torah, even if haltingly. The diagnosis of his Alzheimer's was clear by then, but I was pleased that he could still participate in saying prayers and hear his grandsons chant their *Haftorahs* and speak about him and my mother, what they had endured in their lives and what their survival meant to our family.

Six months later, in March 1991, Sam and Frieda moved to Mobile, Alabama. I took the plane down with them. It was a difficult experience for all of us. In Mobile, they were once again strangers in a strange land: refugees of sorts, fleeing the aging and disease that represented their present and future. This time there was to be no escape from either.

"I JUST DON'T KNOW WHY"

Frieda thought Sam's Alzheimer's disease was a product of all the beatings he experienced in the years he spent in slave labor and concentration camps in Poland and Germany. She also thought it was caused by the stress of the war and the loss of his first family. She was on to something. Over the next two years, the diagnosis became a prognosis. Past became prologue, and the terror of memory loss mutated into the horrors of language loss, loss of comprehension, loss of bodily functions and ultimately, the loss of my father.

I tried to fly down every three weeks or so, and Jennifer and the boys came too when they could. By then Rachel had gone back to college, and in 1991 she completed a second master's program, this time in speech pathology, a field she loved. While my parents lived there, she worked part-time at a school for the cognitively impaired. As long as my father was alive, my mother seemed more or less stable. Caring for him was certainly her shining hour.

It was hard to see my father become more childlike as his dementia progressed. He would call my sister "that nice lady." He would sometimes call me his father. Once he had forgotten who we were or even how to speak, he seemed more at ease. Even then he prided himself on what he could still do, and how he could contribute.

Though he forgot most everything, he was happy, and he seemed particularly proud that he could still wash and dry the dishes. He wore his torn cardigan. He caressed each dish, patiently, lovingly. It was as though all his memories had moved from his head and his heart to his hands. Perhaps there was some memory of his dishwashing job back in Sweden at the Grand Hotel in Halmstad after he first met Frieda and knew she was the woman he loved and would marry. Unlike my mother, who shouted out, he was saying, "I am still here. I know something. Do not forget me." He did so without any words at all.

The transition to a non-Brighton Beach way of life was especially difficult for Frieda, mostly because her dependency on Rachel increased exponentially. As we had learned over many years, Frieda wanted to be in charge. That was one of the reasons she was so good with my father, caring for him as the child he had become. After all, she was better with children than with adults. Children don't talk back as much, if they can talk at all. Sam was in no position to argue. Those days were over, and the time had come when he couldn't talk at all. Children don't see the layers of memories that cloak each one of us and seem to define us, for better or worse. Rather, they see what's in front of them and either feel love or don't as a result. My father, though, remained playful, nearly to the end. He still found something inside of him that wanted to come out. Whenever my mother turned her back to him, he made faces, as though he were a child again. Then he would turn back and smile at me, knowing he was being a bit naughty.

Rachel was a saint. Once again, Frieda found reasons to criticize what Rachel was trying to do for and with them. Rachel endured this, despite being greatly affected by witnessing her father's decline. She saw it up close every day.

The end came too quickly. It always does. Having lost his swallowing reflex due to the progression of his Alzheimer's, my father died while my mother was feeding him: he aspirated a spoonful of soup that entered his windpipe and then his lungs. We would never tell her that her food was somehow involved in his last moments.

Sam died on March 9, 1993, a few days before a freak snowstorm hit Mobile. He was 81.

Sam was four times a father, in two families. Sadly, he lost his own father as a child and then lost his first family to murderers; yet he ultimately became a grandfather many times over. I can relate, as a father and especially these days as a grandfather, to many of the feelings that imbue those precious roles. Like so much else that happened in his life, I can't begin to imagine what it was like for him, though at least I know more now than I once did. For that, I will always be grateful.

I've mentioned that my father considered himself a religious man. Although he believed in prayer and in the symbols and rituals of Judaism, it was his family that was holiest for him. I'm certain that his deepest regret was that he had been unable to protect his first family. From his perspective, God had given him a second chance to have a family, and he was determined to keep us safe and well, even if it meant sacrificing some of his own ambitions. At the start of this book I mentioned the origins of the name 'Friedman.' When I was young, I thought it meant someone who had been set free. Later I came to learn that it actually meant a man of peace, a man who was happy. For my father, peace and happiness came as one. That was what he wanted out of his life and for his family. He found both the fruits of his survival and the reason he had survived in once again having a family to protect and love, and in making sure they felt that love and security.

Mostly, because of all he had lost, he taught us what he had learned, first without a father and then without a family. He discovered that others were more important than he was, and that love and faith in ourselves and our beliefs were all that really mattered, except for a sweet now and then. He insisted above all that we treat people with respect, that we believe in ourselves and that we love. He saw fatherhood as his highest calling. He wanted to get it right. And at the end of the day, he did. In Hebrew, his name was Shlomo, someone who is wise and peaceful. All he wanted was *shalom*: peace, in his household, in his life and in the world.

It is ironic and sad that my father, who spent so much of his adult life trying to forget all that he had lost, ultimately lost the memory of his entire life to the ravages of a disease – perhaps, as it turned out, an affliction that may have been sparked by those beatings and his other wartime experiences.

Some of the last intelligible words I recall him uttering were spoken during a visit to Mobile. Jennifer, Eric and Noah came with me to see him sometime in late 1992. When we entered the garden apartment to which my parents had relocated, he at first looked closely at us and seemed happy. Then, quite suddenly, he started to cry. Through the tears, he said in Yiddish, "I know I love you. I just don't know why." At least we knew why we loved him. But that wasn't enough to save him.

Naturally, Frieda missed Sam. They had been together for nearly half a century, experiencing the painful joys of their love and their lives. However much they argued over the years, they knew each other so well, and shared so much of what had come before for each of them in Poland, that I can't imagine my mother ever really getting over that loss. Even in the midst of his Alzheimer's she was used to caring for him and thus felt herself worthy and worthwhile. Without Sam, the difficulty of being with her and caring for her increased.

Perhaps because she didn't know what else to do, she continued to fight in the face of her own infirmities. Old habits were hard for Frieda to break, even in a new setting. For instance, whenever Frieda talked to just about anyone, from complete strangers to close family members, she sought to control the space by invading it entirely. It was tantamount to being in a huddle with her, or maybe stuck in a very narrow closet, or more likely sharing a hard, cold wooden shelf on which to sleep with ten other equally desperate women in a barracks at Auschwitz or Bergen-Belsen. At the same time, though, power also meant cajoling and charming and even learning to submit to another person by enchanting them with compliments and praise.

When she wanted to charm you she was coquettish, almost flirtatious. She looked at you and through you, as though you were the only person in the room that counted. That was because she craved your attention and wanted you to listen to her, believe her, respect her and if possible, to either fall in love with her or fear her.

Remember also that she was a survivor. She was very strong when she needed to be. Don't cross Frieda. Remember too that she was very much in her own zone, even when she entered yours. In some ways she was stronger than virtually anyone else she met. At the same time, even in those situations, she could be described as armed and dangerous, after a fashion. What exactly am I talking about? Well, the stories she told you ran a gamut. Often, she would tell you one of her stories about her days as the most popular girl in her school. Another time she would tell you how she barely managed to scrape by with her life in Płaszów after coming face to face with its violent, maniacal camp commander, Amon Göth, accompanying her tale with a weapon. I mean that literally. This quality went beyond her sharp, sometimes indiscriminately violent tongue and her piercing yet gravelly, smoking-induced voice. Much too often, she emphasized her stories by actually waving a very large, sharp knife around in her right hand. To her, that knife was not a weapon but an exclamation point, an appendage left over from working in the kitchen cutting up vegetables or slicing some rye bread. If you didn't know any better, you would run for your life. Sometimes that wouldn't have been a bad idea, but as we always reminded ourselves, she meant well.

At times, things seemed to be okay. She continued to make Rachel's life more difficult, sometimes intentionally, sometimes without realizing it. At least she came into her own in a few ways. She became a local celebrity once word spread that she was a Holocaust survivor. When Holocaust Remembrance Day came along, she suddenly appeared on local television and in the newspaper to tell her stories. Rachel's boys, now grown, would come to visit, and she would once more insist they eat her *lokshen* (noodles), holding her ever present knife in her hand and waving it for emphasis.

Once I took her back to New York for a visit to see Eric and Noah at Yale. She had a good time. The only mishap occurred after we left the pizzeria where we'd all had lunch and were on our way back on Interstate 95. While I was driving, my mother suddenly told me there was something wrong. "Look! I don't have my teeth," she exclaimed, opening her mouth to prove her point. It seemed that she had washed up before leaving and forgot her dentures in the pizzeria bathroom. We turned the car around and fortunately, there they were, sitting all alone on the bathroom sink. No one had decided to take her teeth as their own.

Though we had always known that our parents had been displaced persons more than once in their lives, "displaced" took on a whole new meaning when they moved to the Deep South. There, Frieda actually found a place, maybe because Southerners are taught to be polite. But even as my mother became a Southerner, she didn't become any easier, less frank or more polite. By then, it was all about eating, about her bathroom habits, God help us, and as ever, about her tortured relationship with my sister, who cared for our mother deeply but who our mother only ever saw as a competitor. For what? Youth, innocence, time lost, dreams unfulfilled? My sister gave everything to her, while my mother gave her mostly grief. Somehow, though, mothers and daughters find accommodations for their own relationships, no matter how complex or difficult. When the world is burning around you and your father or husband vanishes in front of you, forgiveness takes on a whole new dimension and a host of new possibilities. For us, it became the only thing that seemed comprehensible in a world gone mad.

Frieda's health had begun to fail, maybe due to a series of small ischemic strokes caused by years of smoking that narrowed the blood vessels in her brain. The melanoma that developed on her forehead, mentioned earlier, had to be removed. She fell and broke a hip. When I visited her in the hospital, I recall that she was strapped to her wheelchair. To me this seemed excessively cruel, but I was later told she had refused to listen to the nurses' instructions to not move more than necessary. She became more irrational in her interactions with Rachel, and at one point she told me she wanted to come back to New York and live with us in Larchmont.

Since her hearing was also failing, or else because she just didn't want to listen to my responses, I wrote her a letter, saying my work situation simply didn't allow me to take care of her as well or as reliably as Rachel could. Jennifer was working too, and by then our boys were in college. I urged Frieda to listen to Rachel and to be kind to her, if for no other reason than that she needed Rachel's assistance. I doubt it helped.

After a while my mother became quieter for a time, absorbed in grief, loss and perhaps also confusion. By then her years of chain smoking, unspeakable home remedies, bacteria-laced chicken on the window sill, years of suffering deeply felt tortures, loneliness and solitude had gotten the better of her heart, lungs, skin, legs, hips and balance. Her body shriveled and her mind gave way. Memory faded ever more from view. I would visit, my sister would be her angel and a few more years would pass.

In any case, Rachel thought a group home made sense. There, Frieda could be with other patients but still live a somewhat normal life in her own room instead of an institutional setting. Frieda tried two different group homes. In the first, she repeatedly broke the rules about smoking, evoking shades of her Coney Island bathroom adventures. In the second, her failing health was such that she could no longer live semi-independently, and Rachel moved her to Bay Manor Nursing Home, a facility that tried to help her but was still a place where my mother fought as hard as she had fought everything else in her life.

It was the best solution, given that no choice was particularly good. I sat with her at her grandson Hugh's wedding in 1997. She had quieted significantly and become more of a bystander than an active participant. For a change, she was too weak to dance or even engage with others, but she was happy to watch the wedding festivities.

Sometimes you take a walk physically, hand in hand with someone you know and care about. Sometimes you walk through time on journeys that come to haunt you and maybe, if you're lucky, to heal you. I have had a chance to take that walk in my mind again. Both times, they were good walks that made a difference in my own journey and in understanding my mother's place in my life and the life of our family. Both experiences brought back a flood of memories about our relationship.

To say that our relationship was not an easy one is to understate the obvious. Then again, anyone's relationship with my mother was often tumultuous and difficult at best, maybe even hurtful. Such were her relationships with my sister, my father and my aunt. My mother would often tell us she saved my aunt's life at the selection at Auschwitz, where they were headed for either the gas chambers or the typhus-ridden slave labor camps. I don't think she let Aunt Genny forget it, either. For all of us, my mother represented the uncontrolled and uncontrollable id, the part of her brain and personality that lacked filters for social correctness, appropriateness or sometimes even for kindness. Most of the time, what we saw and heard and felt from her came with no holds barred, totally bared for all to see.

My mother had lost her youth to the war, her innocence to the killing, her good memories to the nightmares. She saw loved ones and strangers murdered and was forced to steal and scrape or worse in order to survive another miserable day and night, first in the Kraków Ghetto, then in Płaszów, then in Auschwitz and finally in Bergen-Belsen. There was no comprehending or wondering about the pain she felt, nor any end to the pain she seemed to inflict purposely at various times on those she actually loved, perhaps as a direct result of her own pain. In the end, though it sometimes was difficult, and even when we became the objects of her wrath, we recalled her past. Knowing that, we still always forgave her, perhaps not in the moment but eventually.

That was life with Frieda, while we were growing up as children and later as we transformed and grew into our other roles as spouses, parents, professionals and sometimes even as dreamers. When we heard voices cry out "Never Forget!" about the terrors of the Holocaust, it was easy for us to obey because our mother would never let us forget, just as she could never forget her own torments.

Yet there was a sweet side to her, a gentle and loving side that would sometimes move her back in time to a more innocent youth that she had once experienced. It was rarely seen or appreciated by my sister or me when we were young. Our children felt it more because they connected with her almost as though they were of the same age, though not of the same time. She tried hard and gave the bulk of whatever good was left in her to us and especially to them. For all the murkiness and haze of her daily life, there was a simplicity and honesty to her common sense that one could appreciate. She would smile and dance as though she was a teenager again. She never relaxed but was always busy, always on the move. She cooked and cleaned, cleaned and cooked again. She shopped for sales and bargains. She scrimped and saved for the rainy days that would always come. She was superstitious and sometimes surreptitious. She would flout the rules and norms of others and insist that her way was correct. And she had a special relationship with the truth. She could see it in others, but it often would not apply to herself.

She cared and did her best. She had seen more of the worst in people than any of us, except for my father. And she survived it to become the woman we knew.

OUR LAST WALK

As her energy waned and her body and mind lost their will, I visited my mother one day in April 1998. It would turn out to be the last time we would talk and walk in any way that could remind us of what normal life, even our version of normal life, once was.

Our walk was around the periphery of the nursing home, including the parking lot. I pushed her wheelchair and told her again about her grandchildren. Naturally, she was proud of them. All grandparents are proud of their grandchildren. In my family, I found that she connected with my kids, Eric and Noah, in ways only they understood about each other. They were more forgiving of each other than we were of them; they saw things at face value and appreciated each other for the way they behaved toward one another, without the baggage that surrounded our relationships. That was certainly also true of Rachel's four sons, with their relationships forged mostly when they were young and three of them still lived in New York, with my mother coming most days to help care for them.

But on that day in April, my mother smiled more on our little walk (or stroll, push, or whatever you call it) than she had smiled in almost as long a time as I could remember. I took the opportunity to tell her that we were planning a trip in May to Sweden, where my sister and I were born and where my parents first met and found their initial refuge from their past. Again she told me how wonderful the Swedes were to her. We talked about my sister and how much she had tried to be everything my mother had hoped she would be, which was basically what my mother had hoped for herself before the torturers came to Kraków. How good Rachel was, how hard she worked, how much she tried. Through the years, when we had spoken about my sister, kind words were rare and forgiving words mostly were unspoken, even if felt. That day was different, though.

We talked about my work and how she thought I worked too much and should work less. She saw what work had done to my father: it gave him purpose but sapped his strength. It gave him pride, though sometimes false, yet once it was gone, he seemed to have lost more than he gained. She talked about Jennifer and how kind and pretty she was.

I tried to ask my mother more about the past because I knew it was fading fast. I wanted to grab it, the good, the bad, anything at all that would fill in the parts of the puzzle that still confounded or surprised us. At that point I had no intention of writing it down for our children and grandchildren and all the others who knew her or would benefit from her story. Ultimately, I just wanted to know more, maybe because I had decided to visit Sweden for the first time since we had left for America.

However, for the first time in a very long time, my mother was no longer particularly interested in the past. She had harangued us about it and held it over us as a weapon for our entire lives, but on that walk that day, she was more interested in how much time we had left together and in having me there, pushing her in a wheelchair in a parking lot in the Deep South, in the deep twilight of her own life.

When we were very young, my sister, my mother and I would take long walks on the boardwalk at Coney Island. She would drill us on our multiplication tables as we went from one end of Coney Island to the other. For a treat, she would sometimes get us a knish or a soft ice cream cone. The days were sunny then, and there were springs in our steps. She liked to walk fast. In those days, we were at the beginning of many walks. In April 1998, the day was calm and still, with a breath of cold in the air. It was to be the last of our walks.

On that day, our time and our walk together were oddly peaceful. In many ways it completed a journey for me, and perhaps for her as well. Under other circumstances, and in another life, perhaps all those walks that came before, indeed the whole journey that came before, might have been very different, even peaceful. At least this one was.

It was a strange way to end a life together, a life I remember filled mostly with screams and yelling and anguish. After all, my mother spent her entire life fighting for her family and for herself in the only way she knew: with a dogged persistence of voice and a tenaciousness of spirit we will never see or know again. She was an original who slipped past death many times in the flower of her youth and who in many ways died nearly every day afterward in what should have been the blossom but instead became the withering of her years.

My mother died the next month on May 2, 1998 at the age of 88. The day before I flew down, Rachel said she had smiled when she heard I was coming. But by the time I arrived that morning, her eyes had rolled nearly all the way back into her head. Her voice, always made deeper by the cigarettes she smoked all those years, crackled and cried in what the nurse said was her death rattle. Her lungs were filling up, and it sounded like a final, horrific game of marbles was being played in her chest. Then they stopped, and so did she. I had been holding her hand. My sister was holding her other hand. All I could do was turn to my sister and say the words you don't know how to say: "I think Mommy is dead." Finally, it came time for my sister and me to walk out once more to that same parking lot, more alone than ever before but perhaps more together than we had ever been. We were two orphans trying to understand what had happened to us in the middle of our lives and at the end of our parents' lives.

Beyond some facts and conjecture, we may never know much about who Frieda was before we knew her, so we guess, recreate or willfully forget, much as we do with many of our own memories. Each time we revisit memories, something seems to change; something is lost, and something else is gained. Some of that happens through a process that might be called an informed imagination. Some of that allows us to recreate lives lost, as though they were formed and then found once again. Memories are what stay with us when all else is gone until they too disappear.

At the end of the day, my mother always sought to live the life she thought she might have had if nothing had gone so terribly wrong as the Holocaust. Upon reflection, though, it seems to have been more than that. Her entire life had been at odds with her hopes. Her first husband, the antisemitism that surrounded them, the poverty they often had to endure, their status as refugees and outsiders: through it all, she always felt she was something she didn't want to be. None of it ever felt right enough. She had great expectations that seemed always unattainable.

Yet for all the tensions between my father and mother, and despite the great mismatch that they were, love always remained, even if it did so as a painful joy for them both. Regardless of all that, she remained devoted to my father, especially after he had his heart attack and then later, when he was stricken with Alzheimer's disease. She washed him, bathed him, changed his diapers, held him close.

Those last few years were horrible most of the time, for her and certainly for him. They were at a place in their relationship when she no longer could rely on him but found inescapably that he could only rely on her. She was at her best with babies, who needed only the most elemental things: to be held, to be loved, to be fed, to be taken care of. My father fit into that category at the end. There was no longer any competition between them, nor any expectations about what might have been. He relied on her, and that was what she required most: to be relied on, to be needed, to be listened to, to feel important. It was Frieda's finest hour, and despite all that Sam had lost, there was a part of him that knew that. From the moment Sam met her, he knew he loved Frieda, and over time, he came to know why. So did she.

It took me more than two decades to begin to understand still more about how that happened, and about so much more.

PART IX

AN ENDURING LEGACY

PSYCHOLOGICAL EFFECTS OF THE HOLOCAUST THROUGH THE GENERATIONS

Where does this journey leave us? It would be remiss of me to try to answer Jacob's questions about survival and its effects on our family without first taking a look beyond our own story to the stories of other survivors of the Holocaust and its lasting effects on the survivors themselves and the following generations. Throughout this book I have provided glimpses and examples of side effects of the Holocaust on Sam and Frieda's behavior and on our own lives as their children. Here I offer some additional observations in a brief glimpse of some of the science and research behind survival and its enduring legacy. In so doing, I hope to expand perspectives and look a bit into the future of our family and the families of other survivors.

This section represents just the tip of a very large iceberg connected to a burgeoning knowledge base regarding the psychological effects, both good and bad, of survival. This field of knowledge has been explored in hundreds of books and studies at great length, offering a great deal more scholarship and insight than I can begin to provide. At the same time, ending this journey without at least reflecting on how these effects have touched our family, including my sister and me as second-generation survivors, our children and grandchildren, and maybe even generations beyond them, would do a disservice to Sam, Frieda and the memories and impressions they left behind. I managed to discover some of the logic undergirding their behaviors and learn some of why they and we became who we are. However, much remains a mystery and probably always will be.

In part, the search for answers and how to get them first emerged shortly before my parents moved from Brooklyn to Alabama in 1991 in order to access the kind of assistance they required at that point. As it turned out, I too was looking for ways to cope in my own life at the time. The solutions, along with new questions, linked directly to my parents and the ways their past influenced my own psychological development and that of others in our family.

Back then, I attended a work-related retreat outside of Boston where my colleagues and I met with an industrial psychiatrist to learn how to better handle difficult personalities and situations at work. In my case, I came prepared to discuss an abusive, bullying boss. In the course of our discussions I shared some of my personal background, briefly mentioning my parents and, as I often did, characterizing them as survivors of the Holocaust who had been badly damaged by their life experiences. I reported that I dealt with my boss mostly by working hard enough and trying to do well enough to minimize his complaints and bullying behavior. I also relied on humor to help defuse hostile encounters with him. I concluded that I was holding my own and could outlast the bully. I had no plans to leave the company and let him win.

The psychiatrist cautioned that although my strategy seemed successful on its face, years hence it would likely have lasting negative consequences for my self-esteem, my desire for self-fulfillment and the way I would look back on my professional career and life. "Max," he said, "you have done an excellent job of mimicking aspects of your parents' survival instincts. I warn you that one day, you will look back and realize that merely surviving was not a sufficient reason for living your life and gaining satisfaction from your professional career. Surviving won't be enough for you, even if clearly it was and had to be for your parents." He advised me to look for another job. I didn't. I probably should have.

Looking back further on those years and thinking more about what surviving is and isn't, I recall one of my early memories as a child accompanying my parents to see a psychiatrist involved with a group called the United Restitution Organization. Established in 1948 as a legal aid service, it helped European victims of Nazism living outside of Germany file claims for financial compensation for their suffering, loss of liberty, health, professions and employment. About 250,000 victims submitted these claims, my parents among them as described a bit earlier in this book.

In addition to their initial interviews and whatever documentation could be mustered to prove their claims,[1] they also had to appear for regular interviews with psychiatrists in New York City to prove they were still alive so that their modest reparation checks would continue, and also to keep track of their mental state, though in fact they were never treated for their many manifestations of psychological trauma and distress. It made me wonder about how the lasting effects of their Holocaust experiences affected the second generation, that is, Rachel and me, as well as the generations that followed us.

There is no sensible way to create a picture of who Sam and Frieda were after the war without pausing to examine the psychological and physical fallout of their years of horrific loss, constant terror and torturous imprisonment from 1939 to 1945. A great deal has been written about the Holocaust's psychological effects on survivors and their children and grandchildren. More recent studies have even examined generations beyond those. What did my parents undergo psychologically? What was it like to have Holocaust survivors as our mother and father, who in the natural order of things were supposed to guide us, protect us, nurture us, teach us and love us in our young lives, but who were unable to do all those things as well as they might have otherwise? A large part of this book has provided some idea, based on my and my sister's experiences and observations. I decided to see what the experts had to say. Having culled information from what is a large and ever-growing body of research, here I offer a modicum of what I learned.

Love us, they did. We could feel it. But we also witnessed their terrors and their inability to parent us. One question we still can't answer has always stood before us: How much of who they were, as adults and as our parents, was directly related to Holocaust experiences, and how much was who they would have been even before the war, or if there hadn't been a Holocaust? The psychiatrist they visited was supposed to try to bring clarity to that question, or at least help them answer it. I'm certain he never came close. Readers of this memoir can judge a bit more for themselves. What is covered here about their past may at least offer some additional perspectives on who they were and what they had already experienced when the war began.

When it comes to the Holocaust years, reminders of the kind of suffering Sam and Frieda endured are unnecessary. However, a quick summary that describes what most survivors went through, taken from a 2010 analysis by Israeli researchers, might prove useful. "The atrocities of the Nazis against Jews and other minority populations during the war were horrific. Victims were rounded up and transported like animals to concentration camps, where they endured continuous threats to life, depersonalization, and loss of significant others. They suffered from horrendous living and working conditions, starvation, and diseases, and those who survived were subjected to atrocious experiences."[2] What were the enduring effects of these traumatic experiences over time? Not surprisingly, they came in at least two forms: the negative effects that one would expect, but also certain clearly positive attributes of survivors that helped them survive and sometimes even thrive after the war. The negative attributes were clearly significant. Frankly, Frieda and Sam exhibited them to varying degrees throughout their lives and definitely in the years when we children were there to witness them.

On the negative side, our parents obviously suffered various symptoms that are consistent with Post-Traumatic Stress Syndrome

(PTSD), and more particularly in their case what has been called Survivor or Concentration Camp Syndrome. The symptoms, most of which we definitely saw in Frieda on a daily if not hourly basis, included nervousness, irritability, mood swings, emotional instability, sleep disorders and a variety of health complaints, including headaches and stomachaches. We also heard her reexperience traumatic events through tales of the camps, evincing a numbed emotional capacity that meant she rarely exhibited happiness, understood jokes or humor and seldom laughed. She had little empathy for others. And of course there were the nightmares suffered by both our parents. They came frequently, and we kids knew they were happening because we could hear them scream.

Speaking for the second generation, the effects and practical impacts of being the children of survivors were everywhere in our daily lives. For instance, Rachel recalls sometimes coming home complaining about a problem she had at school, or with a friend, or some other personal concern. Rather than hear Rachel out and accept her youthful emotional upset, my mother would instead simply launch into the reasons why Rachel's problems could never compare to the challenges she suffered in the concentration camps. Frieda's typical response was something that has been reported of many other survivors. "You think that's a problem?" she would ask. "What about seeing the girl standing next to you shot in the head by someone standing at a window overlooking where you were?" The shooter she was remembering was Amon Göth, the commander of the Płaszów concentration camp, where my mother was imprisoned. "Your problems are nothing compared to what we went through during the war." On one level, of course she was right. On another, why compare that horrific world of wartime Poland with the more normal, if often fraught, everyday life of a child in America? Instead of offering Rachel advice or at least sympathy, Frieda minimized my sister's feelings and emotions again and again. My father stayed out of the fray altogether. Rachel felt guilty for having such "selfish" thoughts, in the face of my mother's past. That response would affect Rachel throughout her life.

The stories my mother told us still resonate. To this day, Rachel gets extremely anxious whenever she has to have blood drawn, sometimes to the point of fainting. She knows why. "When that tourniquet is put tightly around my arm," she says, "all I can think of are my mother's descriptions of people she watched being hanged in the camps. That tourniquet somehow becomes that rope around my neck. I can't seem to help it."

Thankfully, our parents' experiences before and during the Holocaust also had at least some role in imprinting positive attributes in the next generation. Studies of survivors often point out the obvious ones: resilience, tenacity, perseverance. Thus, while the bad news is that trauma can be transmitted across generations, the good news is that resilience can too, along with traits like adaptability, initiative and tenacity. Attributes like these, which enabled survivor parents to survive the Holocaust, may be passed on to their children and beyond. That was true in our case as well. In addition, studies have shown that Holocaust survivors and their children tend to be task-oriented and hardworking. They also know how to actively cope with and adapt to challenges. Strong family values is another positive characteristic displayed by many survivors and their children.

Then there is the research on how traumatic stresses like those experienced by Holocaust survivors not only remained with them as PTSD, but were also transmitted to their children through varying levels of cortisol, a stress enzyme we all have in our bodies. That was the most intriguing of the various studies I encountered. A study reported just a few years ago in *Scientific American Mind* noted that stress hormones of descendants of Holocaust survivors were so altered that their parents' traumatic experiences might "hamper their offspring's ability to bounce back from trauma."[3]

The study focused on the profound impact a person's experiences can have, not only on themselves but on their future children's lives. Studies by Professor Rachel Yehuda and her colleagues in the growing field of epigenetics and the intergenerational effects of trauma have shown that the stress hormone profiles of people who survived the Holocaust differ from those of their peers, perhaps predisposing the former to anxiety disorders.

Yehuda's team and others previously established that survivors of the Holocaust have low levels of cortisol, a hormone that helps the body return to normal after trauma. Those who suffer PTSD have even lower levels. Both categories applied to my parents. Yehuda also was the first to report distinct biological changes in survivors who have PTSD symptoms: they had elevated levels of norepinephrine, a stress hormone. Researchers believe many of the symptoms are due to a sympathetic nervous system that is too easily aroused.[4]

PTSD is a mental health condition triggered by a terrifying event or series of events either experienced or witnessed. Such events were regular occurrences in the lives of my parents, sometimes every night for long stretches of time. Symptoms include flashbacks, nightmares and severe anxiety, as well as uncontrollable thoughts about the event. The syndrome itself relates to an inability to recover from the immediate effects of such a trauma. Yehuda's research over 20 years points out that often, "adult children of Holocaust survivors still define themselves in relation to their parents in a way which is unusual for people of that age. Looking at the literature revealed many articles intent on dispelling the 'myth' of damage to the next generation. People want the story to be that survivors are resilient and their offspring are successful against all the odds."[5] She found that cortisol may have something to do with those long-lasting or indeed, pan- or multigenerational effects.

It is not completely clear why survivors produce less cortisol, but Yehuda's team recently found that survivors also have low levels of an enzyme that breaks down cortisol. The adaptation makes sense: reducing enzyme activity keeps more free cortisol in the body, which allows the liver and kidneys to maximize stores of glucose and metabolic fuels, an optimal response to prolonged starvation and other threats they had clearly experienced. The younger the survivors were during World War II, the less of the enzyme they have as adults. Fortunately for us, our parents were adults when the war began. My father was 28 and my mother 29.[6] This echoes the results of many other human epigenetic studies that show that the effects of certain experiences during childhood and adolescence are especially enduring in individuals and sometimes even across generations. Epigenetics, after all, is the study of heritable changes in gene expression or cellular phenotype caused by mechanisms other than changes in the underlying DNA sequence. For example, something happens to a gene to make it function in a different way. That new function is passed on to the next generation. My parents may have been adults when they suffered camp traumas, but changes in my sister's and my own cortisol probably still occurred, resulting in, for example, our ongoing difficulties with anxiety and my sister's increased propensity for panic attacks.

Cortisol is central to our "fight or flight" response to stressful events or situations. Stimulation of cortisol production is a response to both stress itself and the containment of stress. Cortisol initiates the response, but after a few hours it works to return the hormones to a more normal level. Initial hormonal responses are ultimately modulated by what we think. This leads to a question: Can individuals control the magnitude of the stress response? It seems we can use our thoughts to influence our response to stress. Trying to calm down after a traumatic event is actually very good advice. Some thoughts decrease distress and in particular the amount of adrenaline released, while other thoughts increase distress. This is important, as adrenaline is involved in the creation of memories of the event and contributes to the development of intrusive memories at a later date. What explains these differences in thoughts? Yehuda points to cortisol and the amount various people may have thanks to their genetic makeup.

What led her to that conclusion was the discovery that although there was no difference in the actual exposure to trauma in the adult children of Holocaust survivors compared to a control group, there was significantly more PTSD among the offspring of Holocaust survivors. Looking further, it was found that the offspring of parents who had experienced PTSD were the group most likely to have

PTSD themselves. This differed from anxiety and depression in that simply having a parent who was a Holocaust survivor was enough to register a higher incidence of PTSD, whether or not the parent displayed similar symptoms. Fortunately, Rachel does not have PTSD or anything close to it and neither do I; however, our anxiety levels can sometimes be overwhelming, often over the slightest things. Our parents, however, did suffer from PTSD or something akin to it. They were not formally diagnosed.

In another study, Yehuda found that compared to a control group matched for age and background, half of the survivors she studied still had PTSD, marked by symptoms like frequent nightmares, repetitive anxiety dreams, insomnia, intrusive and disturbing thoughts, hypervigilance and being easily startled.[7] "My parents woke up howling almost every night. For a long time as a child, I thought all parents did," Art Spiegelman, author of *Maus*, recalls about his own parents' experiences during the Holocaust.[8] Certainly that was our experience as children with our parents.

Another intriguing connection relates to a study in rats showing that a lot of licking and grooming by the mother can change cortisol levels. This excessive grooming may in fact be "smothering" rather than "good mothering." Many Holocaust survivors display similar overprotective and hovering behavior, and a relationship between cortisol levels and maternal overprotection has also been demonstrated; however, no such relationship is seen for paternal overprotection. Did Frieda provide Rachel and then me with these lower cortisol levels? Was Rachel affected to a greater degree, having been born first and only two years after my mother suffered some of these traumatic events?

Such observations and questions also led Yehuda's team to consider whether epigenetic changes could be involved. Even small changes can have large consequences, because they can change the expression of the gene and thus alter its functioning. For example, changes that happen as a result of parental starvation may in fact be preparing the fetus to tolerate similar conditions when it is born.

However, if food is in fact abundant, the result of the changes could be obesity and metabolic syndrome.

A number of implications can be drawn from Yehuda's work, including that the effects of trauma can be passed on to the next generation, that these effects probably develop to prepare the next generation for coping with adversity and that some of these changes may begin in utero. In fact, it appears that pregnancy and the early postnatal periods may be critical in future manifestations of how second generation children cope as they grow older. Some of the biological effects may be mediated by disrupting parental behaviors that relate to the parents' own traumatic experiences.

An important message is that although epigenetic effects are enduring, they may also be reversible. Current research carried out by Yehuda reveals biological changes before and after psychotherapy. This is important, as it gives people hope that once they are ready to change, change is possible. If the environment can affect genes and produce symptoms in one direction, then it is likely that a different environment can produce a similar effect in the opposite direction.

A study in 1992 focused on the fact that resilient traits, such as the adaptability, initiative and tenacity that enabled some Jews to survive the Holocaust, may also have accounted for some of the successes they may have experienced later. In their own ways, even after the war, both our parents clearly had to adapt to extremely difficult circumstances in Sweden and later, when we came to the US. They had to demonstrate initiative to find ways to fit into communities, find and keep work and cultivate tenacity as they sought to persevere against all odds for most of their lives. They persevered with each other as well, realizing that despite their differences they had to stay together, not only for their children but also because they had come to rely on one another. They might at least have passed some positive aspects of these characteristics on to their children.

Another researcher, Dr. Eva Kahana, a sociologist at Case Western Reserve University, observed that we need to remember that survivors were more than just that. "We needn't look at survivors as pathological specimens," she noted. "They are normal people who have endured something horrible, human beings who are responding in surprisingly positive ways. Yes, they may have nightmares and psychosomatic problems; they have been traumatized. But at the same time they have lifted themselves."[9] Indeed, it has been suggested that positive traits in Holocaust survivors tend to be overlooked and that Holocaust survivors may actually be more task-oriented, cope more actively and express more favorable attitudes toward family, friends and work.[10]

All true, but even as they sought to move on, the damage done to our parents remained obvious. For example, my mother walked a fine line between demonstrating the positive attributes of tenacity and perseverance and being an extraordinarily difficult person to deal with. She would harangue us and our father, saying the same mostly critical things again and again. She repeated stories about her concentration camp experiences, her opinions about how we should find friends and her view of all the things my father did wrong.

In ways that resonate, Emily Dutton points out aspects of the second generation's responses to the traumas their parents suffered. In "Survivorship and Shame," she writes: "The afterlife of traumatic knowledge and experiences has been absorbed and internalized by the second generation. As the son of one survivor acknowledged: 'Somehow I've taken on a survivor's identity and feel so much like it all happened to me that I must feel the sorrow and take it away from my parents. I feel that my life is an assignment, a mission to make up for my parents' losses and give meaning to their survival.'"[11] After hearing that psychiatrist's question back in Boston, Dutton's conclusions sound all too familiar.

PART X

COMING HOME

BACK TO SWEDEN

My own part in the story of Sam and Frieda began in Sweden when I was born. It seemed only fitting to return, just a few weeks after my mother died, to the place where Sam and Frieda met and where Rachel and I were born.

It was then that Jennifer, our sons Eric and Noah and I first embarked on a journey to find my roots. I wanted to fill in some of the blanks on my birth certificate, written in Swedish and issued on April 29, 1950 to a couple named Szlama and Frida Frydman in Halmstad, Sweden, for a baby named Max.

From the time I was still very young but could understand and recall my mother's words, her view of my relationship with Sweden was formed by my hair color. My mother told me repeatedly that I had blond hair *because* I was born in Sweden. The same went for my sister, who also had blond hair. Frieda's view of Mendelian genetic character traits was simple: while some genes may be inherited, her assumption was that some genes were transferred directly from the environment, as though we were being infected by the world around us, in my case by lots of Swedes with naturally blond hair and in her case, I fear, continual disappointment with the world and her resulting paranoiac view of it. Alas, my own genetic infection never seemed to spread the trait for being tall, or for having blue eyes like my parents and my sister.

I took my first journey back to my birthplace in May 1998. I had always had questions about this place, where I spent not even two years, but it still held a magical, even romanticized sway over my life. Better to talk about being born in Sweden than about being raised in Coney Island just yards away from the boardwalk, Nathan's Famous Hot Dogs, the Parachute Jump and the Cyclone roller coaster. My mother and father always talked about Sweden in idyllic terms too, as though it was a paradise lost. Considering what they really had lost, Sweden did look a bit like paradise. But if that was so, why did they want to leave so soon after arriving from the hell they had just endured? Perhaps because they hadn't chosen to go there. Sweden, like so much else at that point in their lives, was never their choice. In any case, I just wanted to see it for myself and connect with the pieces of my parents' lives that had always been lost to me.

What did my birthplace look like? Who were the people who knew my parents or perhaps even knew my sister or me? Could they tell us anything more about the people who came from the camps, what they had gone through and where they were going? Could it help me in some way to understand my own journey over these past decades? Was Sweden my first home, or simply the place where I first rested my head?

A young reporter, Tony Balogh, himself the son of refugees from the 1956 Hungarian Revolution whose family also migrated to Sweden, noticed an email I had written to the Halmstad City Hall requesting any information at all about my past. All I had was a birth certificate in Swedish. I indicated that I wanted to visit Halmstad and learn more if possible. If we came, he asked, could he write my story for his newspaper? In return, he would explore my roots with me and for me.

Thus our days in Halmstad were spent touching the landmarks of my early life, escorted by the reporter and his girlfriend. Here's what our tour of highlights from our life there sounded like:

"Here's the second house where you lived at Furuvägen 24," Tony told me. "Your parents' first apartment at the corner of Brogatan and Skeppargatan caught fire and was destroyed when you were still very young."

Yes, I suddenly remember my mother talking about how they lived above a bakery until it burned down.

"It's in the industrial part of town, near the train tracks. And here's the building where your parents first met. They came from the camps and after being hospitalized for a time for malnutrition and typhus in Malmö. All the survivors were placed in a coed dormitory, where they would live until they found places of their own and people of their own." The building, called Frennarpsgarden, is now a kindergarten.

"Here's the hospital where you and your sister were born."

I remember my mother telling us how kind the Swedes were to her in that hospital particularly. This was certainly a landmark where human beings had shown my mother kindness, something that had happened only a few precious times in her life, at least from her vantage point.

"Here is the factory called Wallbergs, where your mother first worked for a short time until she gave birth to your sister. Your father worked in a shoe factory near your home and then got a job at Wallbergs as well and stayed there till you left for the United States. It was a textile factory. And here is your father's boss, Gunnar Bjornfors." We meet a man who remembers my father as a hard worker and a good man. He says he felt sorry for the 15–20 Jews who had come to work for him here. He hopes he had shown them some kindness. The factory is now an indoor go-kart raceway. Shoe prints are embedded in the floor. I step where my father once stood at the beginning of his new journey.

Then, my father's former boss has an idea. "There is one camp survivor in all of Halmstad who remained, named Paula Zuback. She worked at the factory. Her husband was a butcher and got sick so couldn't make the journey elsewhere. They stayed. Maybe she'll be willing to see you." He calls her on his cell phone and we drive to her house. This part of the trip comes as a complete surprise to my reporter friend, to my father's old boss, to all of us. We hold our breath, not knowing what to expect. What we will see, hear or learn? It is an extraordinary experience because we meet Paula, a Holocaust survivor from Poland who had stayed in Halmstad. She and her husband are the only Jews remaining from those years. Her husband had a heart condition and therefore, she said, was unable to travel to Chicago, where they had hoped to resettle. They had a son, Jakob, and Paula's husband had opened a butcher shop in Halmstad.

The woman who answered the door was stooped and spoke only Yiddish to me. I understood her at least. She was heavier than my mother and had a look about her that combined suspicion with anticipation, a cautious welcome and a yearning to be loved. She was not my mother, but she was of my mother's life, time and place. Her home looked much like ours in Brooklyn. There was a television at its center, and the couches and chairs were covered in clear, crackly plastic. We sat together at the small round kitchen table, and she told us to eat, to eat more, to drink. She held my hand and caressed my face.

Paula Zuback, a survivor who we discover knew my family in Halmstad, uncovers pictures from our past.

Yes, I was home again.

Her son came over to translate to her Yiddish from our English. I explained to him as best I could who I was and why I was there. Paula looked at me deeply; she looked through me. She thought and thought and then started to cry. Yes, she said, now she remembered my mother, my father, my sister and even me, from nearly half a century before. I started to cry. Everyone did. She remembered the past with a clarity that defied memory.

One second, she indicated, holding up a wrinkled, determined hand. It was what my mother did: gesture and command. Then she whispered to her son, who went upstairs and returned with an old brown leather handbag bursting with cracked black and white photographs. My heart skipped a beat, and I sensed Paula's did as well.

She showed us a picture. "Yes, I remember your mother Frieda," she said. "She was so young. We were all so young. But nothing was ever good enough for Frieda, though. She complained a lot. She always had a hard time. How is she?"

"She died last month," I told her.

Paula's heart sank as the reunion suddenly became smaller. The picture took on new meaning.

"Here's your father. He was always smiling, making jokes. He was a sweet and intelligent man. I always wondered how the two of them could get along. They were so different. How is he?"

"He died five years ago."

Her eyes closed, as though in a silent prayer of mourning. "And here is your sister. Your mother always said she ate too much and she would get too fat, yet she kept feeding her."

I looked at the picture. It was the same picture we had at home back in Brooklyn.

"How is your sister?"

"My sister is fine. I'm sorry she's not here. She still worries about what she eats."

"And here you are, just a little baby."

I looked at the picture, not sure if it was really me. It didn't look like me. But this place, this person, those other pictures? They all looked like a part of me.

How am I? I'm home again. Not in this building, or in the city of Halmstad, but in a part of my past I had imagined but had never seen, a place that had now become a real part of me. As Paula showed us those pictures, I couldn't help but recall my mother's habits regarding the photos she kept with her. I found many shots with people cut out from the photos, people she didn't like for some reason or who had offended her in some way. It seemed she had found yet another way to refashion the memories she wanted to keep. The memories and people she had decided to edit out were removed in the most practical way she knew, with a pair of sewing scissors.

We also went to the local parish office of St. Nikolai's, which held records of my parents' birth and other records, including their arrival in Halmstad. We bent over dog-eared books about people who, worn out by war and their past, sought to find a way to build their lives again, sometimes over bakeries that burned down, forcing them to seek to live again elsewhere. All their names were inscribed in fading ink and in those worn memories. They had just moved on. Now it was time for me to do the same.

Looking at our family records in 1998 at the local parish office in Halmstad. With me were (from left) Eric, Jennifer and Noah.

LOVE THAT DEATH HAS TOUCHED

Sam and Frieda in happier times.

My mother always told me to start each journey well, with energy and purpose. "Put your right foot forward, like so," she would demonstrate, just to make sure I understood. "And then follow with your left," she added, just in case I was somehow confused. Then she would hook her arm into mine and march us forward. Like so. She would probably give the same advice at her own journey's end: do your best to be remembered.

There were other bits of wisdom she liked to share. "Stand tall and straight. Don't walk with your head down and back bent. People won't respect you. Look like me." She demonstrated, standing stiff and proud, eyes forward, all five feet of her. When we were young and she didn't think our posture was good, which also meant our attitude wasn't good because we weren't listening to her, she made Rachel and me walk while balancing stacks of books on our heads, starting against one wall and crossing to the other side of the room. Straight and tall, so the books didn't fall and we didn't falter. "Don't go sideways either," she would say. "Instead look straight ahead. Then you will be successful and people will respect you." As was her custom, she would say all these things again and again.

Good advice, but as you have seen in this memoir, my parents never had the chance to travel the straight and narrow. Their lives were too often defined by the unexpected, by others, by circumstances beyond their control and sometimes beyond anyone's imagination. They endured twists and turns, some unimaginable, some even descending through the circles of Hell. Yet they came out the other side.

My father had fewer pieces of advice to offer, beyond the practicalities of the kind of house we should buy (brick, and at least a two-family, so someone can pay rent and cover expenses) or where to safely put our money (CDs). Instead, his approach to the more important stuff was not to do as I say, but to do as I do, that is, be quiet and humble. He put his faith in faith itself, in the goodness of people to do what was right and in the mysterious ways of Hashem, of God. Sometimes it worked, sometimes not. He trusted his children to lead their lives as they saw fit. Mostly he cheered us on from the sidelines. Finally, he put his faith in praying for the future of the Jewish people. He had suffered too much to do otherwise. He was interested in the world, but less interested in directing it than my mother was. Having lost everyone in the family he once had, he mostly focused on doing what was right for this second family of his.

We relied on him as the breadwinner, but also as the calm beyond the inevitable storm that was our mother. He tried to avoid engaging with her, but that mostly didn't work. Still, he held out, trying to be who he was, not who she wanted him to be: someone more ambitious, more successful, just more. He wanted to be more as well, but his more was more thoughtful, more understanding, quieter. There was also a large part of him that wanted to be a little less. Less involved. Less in your face. He liked to laugh and tried to look at the bright side of things instead of being reminded again and again of the dark side of life. He didn't need reminding of that. He said more than once that all he wanted out of his life was some peace. Well, he came to the wrong marriage for that. And he had endured too much pain – yes, even painful joy – to ever be the person he had once hoped to become. His youth was too often defined by hardship, loss, privation, turmoil and terror. He didn't want to go back. He couldn't abide going back.

All in all, my mother sought to relive her past while reimagining herself. My father sought to forget his past and thereby to save himself.

I've spent the last many pages and the past five years trying to figure out who these people were before they came to be the way we came to know them, each in our own way. For those who are meeting them for the first time in these pages, you probably have the picture by now. I hope I have done my parents justice, opened up some eyes and fresh perspectives and touched some hearts with their story, their struggles and their triumphs. Sam and Frieda's story is both universal and very personal.

Our pasts affect all of us, influencing who we become and how we build our lives. What distinguishes Sam and Frieda's story from many others are the existential threats they faced again and again over the course of their lives.

The aim of this memoir is to honor their memory and restore their humanity by reconstructing their story as best I could. Having started with virtually nothing, I have journeyed a long distance to present two lives and their times. I hope I have succeeded in that, at least to some extent. I leave it to readers, be they my family, friends or others who have decided to learn more about these two ordinary and yet extraordinary people, to take what they wish from this story.

I now better understand some aspects of their lives, but others are totally puzzling. And despite my fresh appreciation for the way some people persevere against all odds in the worst of times, I realize more than before that there is always a price to be paid. At a more universal level, my takeaways from Sam and Frieda's story are the importance of resilience, the critical nature of luck and fortune in life, the ability of all humans to reinvent themselves anew and, as always, that we can't change reality itself but only how we perceive that reality.

An extraordinary thing about their lives was that they repeated so many of their early experiences later in life. Frieda started out as a refugee, homeless at the age of four. She remained a refugee even after the war ended, rarely living in the present, and instead escaping to the past. Having had no childhood, she sought to create one in Rachel. My father became fatherless when he was less than four years old. He then took on the role of father and provider, not once but during three periods over the course of his life: first, when he was still too young at age 13, then with his first family in Poland and finally, with us. While experiencing these challenges, my parents learned that sometimes facts were fungible: they would have to be quick on their feet to survive in a harsh world, so sometimes reality turned out to be in the eye of the beholder. They continued learning that lesson throughout their lives. Were they in training to be the survivors, a role that would too often define them?

And what about the answers to Jacob's questions, which helped to catalyze this journey? Have my parents passed survival skills, genes or traits on to their children, grandchildren and yes, great-grandchildren? Has their suffering and perseverance made me or any of my offspring stronger or better? I think so, to some extent. These traits may or may not have been passed on through DNA, but their story, in and of itself, completes that process and helps to close the circle of their lives.

They taught us not only about the power of love, but also about what happens when love is unrecognized, lost or touched by pain and death. How do we continue? Painful joy was sufficient for them because it was all they could experience. We are fortunate to have much more, especially if we are willing and able to recognize the gifts that love and family offer, and not take them for granted. Sam and Frieda did the best they could. Maybe even better than that. As for us, we can always do better.

Only very late in their lives did I begin to understand them. With this memoir, I understand them a bit more. I learned through them to question what was real and what was perhaps reimagined, and to better understand how and why it happened.

Sam and Frieda were ordinary people who led extraordinary lives. We didn't think so at the time. They certainly didn't. But I believe it now. I hope this book remembers them respectfully and expands our understanding of their lives and times. May it also serve to keep their memory alive in our children and grandchildren, and maybe even after them. The question is no longer how they survived, but how much they were able to create as a result.

They say it is not the destination but the journey that matters. Maybe surviving is sufficient. Maybe survival is what each of us does every day, celebrating each moment in our own, less dramatic way. It is not about what we have lost, but what we have found to take its place.

In many respects, writing this memoir has been a joy because I learned so much. It was also an emotional roller coaster, in part because I wanted to learn more but couldn't. What I did learn was alternately fascinating and horrifying. My nightmares began from the moment I started, and night sweats followed, not every night, but still on too many. But once again, even that experience provided a window into what it might have been like for my parents when they couldn't shut their thoughts out either. Their thoughts were much more real and constant than mine.

If there is a lesson to be learned from Sam and Frieda's story, incomplete though it is and always will be, it is not so much what was or even what is. It is what might still be.

Painful joys defined their lives and help us understand them. Despite the hardships they faced, the challenges they encountered and their unbearable pain and loss, Sam and Frieda chose life. They chose to fight back, one quietly, one shouting. They clung to hope and faith, however they defined them for themselves. They chose to reimagine and recreate what was lost. It's a complicated journey, but it's also what each of us does in our own way every day. And in the end, without Sam and Frieda, there would not have been us.

ACKNOWLEDGMENTS

There are so many people to thank for helping me on this journey of what turned out to sometimes be painful joy.

First and foremost, I thank my wife Jennifer, my love, my partner in everything and an all-around dream come true for more than 50 years, for sharing her love with me, as well the pain and joys of this voyage of discovery and learning. She also has been my kind, honest, talented editor and proofreader, wise counsel and fellow traveler experiencing Frieda and Sam once more and demonstrating her compassion and empathy for them and for me, especially during these last five years.

To my sister Rachel, who shared her memories, painful and funny as they sometimes were, as well as her insights about Sam and Frieda as parents as we grew up and grew older together. Of course, as they grew older and my father was stricken with Alzheimer's, her generosity of spirit and love were ever present, especially in those last difficult years when we moved our parents to Mobile so she could watch over them in their time of greatest need, and then after our father died and our mother experienced even greater difficulties of body, mind and spirit.

To both our sons, Eric and Noah, who participated in this project in numerous ways, sharing my journey, advising me, listening in to my moments of discovery and disappointment, learning about their grandparents and demonstrating their compassion and love for them over many years.

I thank Eric for sharing his own book project, his meticulous proofreading, and exchanging insights with me as another budding author. I thank Noah for doing his best to teach our grandchildren about their Jewish heritage and the family they never knew. To Noah's son, our grandson Jacob, I continue to be grateful for his abiding interest and sensitivity, and for asking the right questions at the right time to spur me on. I will be ever grateful to Emma, for entertaining us with her talent and refreshing us with her innocence. And I was encouraged by the emotional response and interest of my daughter-in-law Yanqing, sparked by our visit to Yad Vashem.

To Matan Shefi, of the Jewish Heritage Institute (JHI) in Warsaw. A former Israeli submarine commander with Polish roots, he had moved his family to Poland and later helped greatly with my research both through the JHI and as a guide, companion and teacher on our visit to Poland to see where my parents lived and where their loved ones were murdered. Throughout, he would always remind us that nothing we saw or heard was simple. "I think it's more complicated than that," he would observe. He was so right.

Thanks also to Marta Mackowiak of the JHI Genealogy group, for her initial research in Poland and tracing of early family histories.

Through my friend and former colleague Colin Baigel and his South African high school classmate, Stuart Bennett, we were fortunate to meet and learn so much about the Holocaust years and my parents from Bennett's son, Giles, a wonderful person and brilliant academic researcher who lives in Munich and works at the Institute for Contemporary History's Center for Holocaust Studies. He provided many contacts through which to learn more, interpreted and shed new light on various documents and helped guide me from the earliest days of this project and throughout its many drafts. He also provided invaluable insights and suggested revisions for a late draft of this book, all the while highlighting the complicated nature of the facts and their interpretation. In addition, he met us in Kraków for our difficult, tearful, never-to-be-forgotten visit to Auschwitz. When I thanked him for coming down from Munich to help us try to understand the incomprehensible when we visited Poland, and to share in our own tears, all he could say was: "It was a privilege for me to accompany you." The privilege was ours.

To Julia Collins, who generously gave of her time and talent to offer a professional and invaluable initial review of this book when I completed my first full draft. One specific insight of hers was instrumental in changing the book from a family-only project to an effort that could be of interest and value to anyone. All she wanted in return was a box of chocolates. I can't thank her enough. Maybe additional boxes of chocolates will help.

To Rick Rawlins, a friend and talented designer who read this manuscript, sharing his creativity and attention to details and the spirit of the book and developing the cover design. He grew up in Idaho, in a world about as far removed as was possible from the world my parents inhabited. Yet he came to understand their world. We had just returned from our visit to Israel, Poland and Germany, and I related to him just how difficult and sad, yet also extraordinary and uplifting our time had been. He wisely observed: "I'm told that the highest honor in Judaism is to be remembered well," and so encouraged me to continue. By the way, he too likes chocolates and deserves more.

To the many colleagues to whom Giles introduced me, who work tirelessly at Holocaust research centers in Germany and at concentration camp memorial sites across Europe, who shed new light and invaluable information and insights about various family members. These generous, talented and compassionate individuals – some authors and scholars in their own right – included: Bernd Horstmann of Bergen-Belsen's memorial site; Andrea Rudorff with her expert knowledge of Bergen-Belsen, Auschwitz, Gross-Rosen and the death marches; and Peter Egger of the Mauthausen Memorial Site.

To Gerald (Jerry) Darring, who created the first profile of my parents as Holocaust survivors in September 2016, demonstrating what was possible and also why their story was important enough to uncover and share.

To the researchers at the United States Holocaust Memorial Museum in Washington, DC, who discovered the first treasure trove of information about my parents, especially Steven Vitto, who in April 2017 provided the first collection of documents that led me to pursue a hundred different and important paths.

To the great dedicated researchers at the Swedish National Archives, Ulrica Hofverberg and Barbro Kvist Kahlstedt, who provided so many details about our years in Sweden, demonstrating both their own sensitivity and empathy for my parents' difficult journey after the war ended.

To Yona Kobo, for sharing her memories of the Kotlicki family, including her aunt and my father's first wife, Chaja, after we discovered each other and met at Yad Vashem in 2018.

To Monika Heimbold, for translating difficult parts of the documents I received from Sweden and who, by asking me to work with her on her memoir and that of her husband Charlie, showed me the way and the need to do a memoir of the lives of those who gave me life.

To Brian Langer of the Jewish Research Institute (JRI), for sharing my parents' Żarnowiec and Sieniawa records, archival documents difficult to otherwise locate.

To Aleksandra Bijak of the Dąbrowa Gornicza Registry Office, who first discovered Ada and Feigla's birth certificates and other critical documents and provided initial translations, while demonstrating great sensitivity in the process.

To the many resources that became available through JewishGen, the major Jewish genealogical site, and for its many critical links to Polish and Holocaust historical data.

To Rosemary Eshel and Elona Avinezer at the National Library of Israel and the Israel Genealogy Research Association.

To the translators of dozens of documents including those discovered in Yiddish (Lawrence Gillig), Polish (Jadwiga Cyparska and Aleksandra Heska) and German (Ute Brandenburg).

To Paula Zuback and Tony Balogh, a belated appreciation for introducing us to Halmstad and for helping make possible a truly meaningful initial journey back into my family's history in Sweden. Meeting Paula was to become the first of many emotional surprises along the way.

To the late Rabbi Sarah Tauber, a dear friend, brilliant writer and Jewish theologian, someone who left us so suddenly and painfully, who pointed me in countless new directions to learn more as she had done herself in exploring her own family Holocaust story. So many of us will sorely miss her remarkable wisdom and her generous friendship.

To Göran Rosenberg for writing *A Brief Stop on the Road From Auschwitz*. While his was just one of many books, articles and other materials I explored and have referenced, his insights about the circumstances and challenges of those first years after liberation in the aliens' camps in Sweden were singularly revealing to me and unique in ways that require a special mention and appreciation. He is also a son of survivors, researching and writing a family story that serves as a model for meticulous research, superb writing and great compassion.

To Judy Altmann, who generously shared her own survivor story with me and with many others as she sought to educate as many people as she could about her experiences in Auschwitz and Bergen-Belsen and the losses that so many endured.

To the late Ada Lewenberg (married name Herskope), for her touching Shoah testimony about Dąbrowa and those war years, including insights about her family, who were members of my father's first family.

To all our family, friends and the readers of this book, for honoring Sam and Frieda Friedman by becoming part of their lives through these memories, and in so doing, returning their humanity to them. Several family members (children of my father's first cousins) who are still with us, Rabbi Aaron Zuckerman and Manny Henzel, kindly shared their memories of my parents for this book. I owe them a special thanks for their thoughtfulness and extremely useful recollections, and my eternal gratitude to them and their families for being there for us over many years.

And of course to Liesbeth Heenk and her colleagues at Amsterdam Publishers, who provided an opportunity to share my Holocaust family story with a wider audience by publishing this book. I had intended to create a memoir only for my family and close friends until Liesbeth recognized the possibility that my parents' story could touch other readers and provide new insights into the experience of survivors of the Holocaust as well as what came before and after. I will be forever grateful to Liesbeth and Amsterdam Publishers for the important work they continue to pursue on behalf of survivors of the Holocaust and their families and generations still to come. As a result their stories and what they teach us can live on.

BIBLIOGRAPHY

As you can imagine, I consulted a great many sources and discovered a great deal of useful information, some of which I used directly (and when possible footnoted), and all of which provided an important context for what I was to cover in this book. Here are some of those sources:

A Brief Stop on the Road from Auschwitz by Göran Rosenberg, Other Press, New York, 2017 (English Edition). Originally published in Sweden, 2012.

A Narrow Bridge to Life: Jewish Force Labor and Survival in the Gross-Rosen Camp System, 1940-1945 by Bella Gutterman, Berghahn Books, 2008.

A Small Town near Auschwitz: Ordinary Nazis and the Holocaust by Mary Fulbrook, Oxford University Press, Oxford, 2012.

Beyond Despair by Aharon Applefeld, Fromm International, New York, 1994.

Children of the Holocaust: Conversations with Sons and Daughters of Survivors by Helen Epstein, GP Putnam's Sons, NY, 1979.

Encyclopedia of Camps and Ghettos, 1933-1945, Seven Volumes, General Editor: Geoffrey P. Megargee, United States Holocaust Memorial Museum, Indiana University Press, Bloomington, IN, 2009-2018.

From Bendzin to Auschwitz: A Journey to Hell by Arnold Shay, The Christopher Publishing House, Hanover, MA, 1996.

From Black Dust to Diamonds by Izzy Randel and Maryann McLoughlin, The Richard Stockton College of NJ, ComteQ Publishing, Margate, NJ, 2011.

Image Before My Eyes: A History of Jewish Life in Poland before the Holocaust, Yivo Institute for Jewish Research, 1980.

Inhumanity: Death March to Buchenwald and the Last Jews of Bedzin by John Ranz, AuthorHouse, 2007.

Lives Remembered: A Shtetl through a Photographer's Eye, edited by Louis D. Levine, with essays by Jonathan Rosen and Jeffrey Shandler, Museum of Jewish Heritage, New York, 2002.

Man's Search for Meaning by Viktor E. Frankl, Beacon Press, Boston, 1959, 1962, 1984, 2006.

Maus: A Survivor's Tale: My Father Bleeds History by Art Spiegelman, Pantheon, 1986.

Memoirs of a Holocaust Survivor by Icek Kuperberg, Universal Publishers, Florida, 2000.

Neighbors: The Destruction of the Jewish Community in Jedwabne, Poland by Jan T. Gross, Princeton University Press, 2001.

On the Edge of Destruction: Jews of Poland between the Two World Wars by Celia S. Heller, Columbia University Press, New York, 1977.

Sala's Gift: My Mother's Holocaust Story by Ann Kirschner, Free Press, 2006.

Shtetl Memoirs: Jews in Galicia under Austria and in the Reborn Poland, 1898-1939 by Joachim Schoenfeld, KTAV Publishing House, Hoboken, NJ, 1985.

Social and Political History of the Jews in Poland, 1919-1939 by Joseph Marcus, Mouton Publishers, Berlin, New York, Amsterdam, 1983.

Survival: The Story of a Sixteen-Year-Old Jewish Boy by Israel J. Rosengarten, (translated from the Dutch), Syracuse University Press, 1999.

Tell Ye Your Children by Stephane Bruchfeld and Paul Levine, The Living History Forum, Stockholm, 2012.

The Forgotten Memoirs: Moving Personal Accounts From Rabbis Who Survived the Holocaust by Esther Farbstein, Shaar Press, Brooklyn, NY, 2011.

The Holocaust; An Encyclopedia and Document Collection, Vol. 3, Holocaust Testimonies. Paul R. Bartrop and Michael Dickerman, editors, ABC-CLIO, Santa Barbara, CA, 2017.

The Jews of East Central Europe: Between the World Wars by Ezra Mendelsohn, Indiana University Press, Bloomington, IN, 1983.

The Jews of Poland between Two World Wars, edited by Yisrael Gutman, Ezra Mendelsohn, Jehuda Reinhartz and Chone Shmeruk, Brandeis University (University Press of New England), Hanover & London, 1989. (Includes papers from the International Conference on the Jews of Poland Between Two World Wars, held April 12-15, 1986 at Brandeis University, Waltham, MA.)

The War After: Living with the Holocaust by Anne Karp, WT Heinemann Ltd., 1996.

ABOUT THE AUTHOR

Max J. Friedman realized early in life that the world he lived in was very different from what most others his age would ever experience. He was born in Sweden to Sam and Frieda, Polish-Jewish parents who met and married there after their liberation from Bergen-Belsen and then emigrated to the US in 1952.

Max and his sister learned very little from their parents about their parents' lives before WWII or what they had gone through during the Holocaust, and much of what they did learn from them, it would turn out, did not really happen. What was real were their parents' years of ghettos, slave labor and concentration camps like Auschwitz and Bergen-Belsen, which Sam and Frieda endured while suffering the horrific loss of their families: spouses, parents, siblings and children.

Max's family experienced the after-effects that flow from parents who have survived such horrors. When it came time to care for their elderly survivor parents, Max and his sister well understood that they too would have to become survivors. This book is the story of this family's journey of discovery, transformation and acceptance.

It was a long time coming. After getting a BA from Columbia College and a Master's of Journalism from UC Berkeley, Max spent the next five decades first as a journalist and then in related writing fields, including public television, leading a communications group for a major pharmaceutical company, and operating his own editorial consultancy. He married and has twin sons and two grandchildren. After spending a career discovering and then sharing the stories of so many others, and more recently completing the memoirs of two complex personalities, he found himself reexamining his own past, spurred by a question from his grandson. The result is *Painful Joy*, an effort to finally uncover the truth of his parents' extraordinary journey of survival and the effects it had on others.

Traveling to Poland, Germany, Israel and Sweden, he sought to help restore his parents' humanity by uncovering who they really were, apart from damaged survivors: where they came from, the lives they once led, their lost hopes and dreams. He learned how all that had unraveled, leaving dual legacies of pain and resilience for future generations. This retelling of what he discovered and what remained hidden was more complicated than he could have imagined. It is a story that goes beyond his own family to explore larger questions about the nature of survival, the tricks our memories can play on us, how hate can destroy and how love can restore. In the process he transforms Sam and Frieda, who start out as strangers, into people who merit our attention, empathy and respect.

NOTES

Preface

1. Attributed to Rabbi Chaim Stern (1930-2001), Brooklyn, NY. Also attributed to Yehuda (Judah) HaLevi (1075-1141) and to Emmanuel of Rome. This poem was probably first published in *Gates of Prayer*, the original Reform Siddur/prayer book, which was authored by Rabbi Stern. It was also found – appropriately, it would seem – in the Mourner's Kaddish section of that Siddur (Meditations before Kaddish). It is furthermore attributed to Yehuda HaLevi, one of the great medieval Jewish poets and an accomplished Spanish physician and scholar. He was born in Spain and lived there from 1075 to 1141, when he traveled to Palestine and then died in Jerusalem that same year. Whatever its origins, in some ways it encapsulates the story of Sam and Frieda, two souls who found love but then lived to discover the changed nature of love – and life altogether – as they were touched again and again by death and other immutable tragedies. Pain remains and touches every aspect of love and life, or at least it did for these two fortunate – and unfortunate – people. They were my parents.

2. I should say at the outset that in this book I use my father's Polish given middle name, Szlama, during the years when he used that name as his first name, basically before he came to the United States. He was born Israel Szlama Frydman, but my mother often called him Szlameck, his Yiddish name. He also went by Sam, Shlomo and Salomon. Although his family surname was Frydman at birth, it became Friedmann, Fridman and Friedman at various times in his life. What he lacked in riches, he made up for in variations on his name. In 1957, when the four of us became US citizens, he officially changed his full name, including his and subsequently our surname, to Salomon Friedman. I've also seen his family name in some post–World War II Polish-sourced records as Friedman or Friedmann. For the purposes of this book, as you will see starting with the US section, I have changed his given name to Sam, the name he usually went by in the United States. Most of his acquaintances and many members of his family called him Sam.

3. About $30 at the time.

4. When you see a reference to "we" or "our" elsewhere in this book, please read it as "my sister Rachel and me" unless stated otherwise.

5. The letter was sent to the Swedish/Jewish Aid organization in early 1946, a month or so after my father met Frieda in Mölle.

6. "What Is the Origin of the Term Holocaust," *The Encyclopedia Britannica Online*, Britannica.com.

7. Readers here will see many, sometimes horrifying, statistics in reports on estimated numbers of deaths or of survivors during the course of the Holocaust in Poland. In general, I have relied on sources that primarily include The United States Holocaust Memorial Museum and especially its Holocaust Encyclopedia,

and the archives of the Yad Vashem World Holocaust Remembrance Center. Other sources of statistics concerning Jewish populations in the shtetls and other cities in Poland came primarily from The Virtual Shtetl pages of Warsaw's POLIN Museum of the History of Polish Jews, as well as from the JewishGen.org genealogical site.

Introduction

1. Gopnik, Adam, "Measuring Man," *The New Yorker*, June 22, 2020, page 79.
2. These especially concerned Poland during the interwar years.
3. By his age and well before, Rachel and I had already heard from my mother, chapter and verse, over and over again about Auschwitz, Płaszów and Bergen-Belsen.

Żarnowiec and Będzin

1. Also called and spelled Żarnowiecze, Zarnowice, Sarnowice.
2. His birthdate was sometimes listed as October 3, 1911, October 10, 1911 or October 11, 1911, with the discrepancy perhaps resulting from the dates of his bris (ritual circumcision eight days after birth), the Gregorian versus Julian calendars with their peculiarities and a civil apparatus with generally poor record-keeping, especially of Jews. Any mix-up in his birthdate, as my father admitted to a Jewish aid agency worker in Sweden right after the war, was also due to his sometimes forgetting his actual birthdate. Indeed, he had lost track of all time whatsoever after years of imprisonment in slave labor and concentration camps. Furthermore, he rarely if ever used Israel as his given name, except in some official documents before World War II. He preferred Szlama.
3. There happens to be another Żarnowiec in northern Poland on the Baltic Sea.
4. Blima's marriage to Kalma Mandelbaum was recorded in 1940 in Będzin, but by then they already had three children: Sura, b. 1935, Perla, b. 1938 and Mailech, b. 1940.
5. That Swedes attacked Żarnowiec is ironic, since it was the Swedes who would later help rescue my father (and mother) after World War II.
6. On February 8, 12, 20 or 21, 1853. These inconsistencies were in part based on whether one followed the Gregorian or Julian calendars, and can be attributed as well to poor record-keeping, especially for or about Jews at that time.
7. Jochim's father, Kalma, b. 1803, and his mother, Judyta Idessa Herzfeld (1805–1871), stayed in Będzin and died there. Tauba's father, Salomon Szwarcmer, and her mother, Bona, were both from Żarnowiec. Jochim's siblings included Gitla (1831–1832), Jakob Hersz, b. 1835, Dawid, b. 1837, Baruch (1841–1844) and Estera Bluma, b. 1845. Estera Blima (Bina, Bluma) married Kopel Londoner in 1862 in Będzin. Their children were Abram Szlama, b. 1868, Josek Chaim, b. 1870, Anszl, b. 1872, Idesa, b. 1875, Lewek, b. 1877 and Icek, b. 1879. Lewek married Blima Cukierman in 1899 at age 22. Jochim also had one other younger brother, Nuchym Wolf, b. 1849, who married Atal Wislicka in 1868. Together they had at least three children: Idessa, b. 1872 in Będzin, Ita, b. 1875 (who married someone named Szpajzer and was buried

in the Będzin-Czeladź cemetery, which we visited during our trip to Poland in 2018), and Jachweta, b. 1883.

8. Also spelled Mailich, Majlech.

9. Also spelled Lajter, Leichter or Larhten.

10. Chana's parents had also been married in Włoszczowa, in 1858. Genealogical records trace the Lajchters and their children and siblings back to 1816. Chana was one of eight children, six of whom survived into adulthood. They included Naftuli, born in 1859, Mosiek, born in 1862, Haskiel, born in 1864, Josek, born in 1868, Chana, born in 1869, and Judka, born in 1874. Many of them and their children ended up living in Będzin, attracted by the relative safety of that city during World War I, compared to the situation in Włoszczowa, their birthplace. Many of them also lived in or near Blima (née Mandelbaum) Frydman's apartment building in Będzin, where Chana lived after Mailech's death in 1915. They became part of a large extended family that helped guide my father and his siblings while they were still small children and after they lost their father at very early ages. Much like neighboring Żarnowiec, their hometown of Włoszczowa had a large Jewish population representing about 50 percent of the town in 1925. Earlier, in the 1800s, the Jewish population had been even larger. Its roots date back to the 1500s, so it was a slightly younger town than Żarnowiec. Not until the beginning of the 19th century did it recover from the destruction caused by the Swedish invasion in the 1650s, various other foreign incursions and even earlier attacks that had also plagued Żarnowiec. By 1860, a synagogue had been built there, where some well-known rabbis of the time were active, including some aligned to the Hasidic movement that was beginning to grow in the region. Young Zionists were also active there in the early 20th century. For a brief time in the 1920s, a rich cultural life developed; there were Jewish sports clubs and classes in Hebrew and Jewish history were available. The Germans took command of the town in 1915 and stayed there till 1918. Subsequently, almost all the Jews who remained there were murdered in the Holocaust, most of them in the Treblinka and Majdanek concentration camps. Today visitors can see ruins of a castle of local nobles and a layout of streets tracing back to the 16th century.

11. March 12 or possibly February 28, 1895. I'm not sure why two dates are indicated in the translation of the marriage certificate from the Cyrillic. Perhaps the existence of two dates relates to a discrepancy between the use of Julian and Gregorian calendars in that part of what became Poland, or perhaps the earlier date was when vows were exchanged in the synagogue and the other was the official marriage date as recorded by civil authorities.

12. It's not clear why Berek was born in Józcfów, a town about nine miles southeast of Warsaw, rather than in Żarnowiec. The area around Józefów became a kind of summer retreat, but that happened later, spurred by the construction of a rail line from Lublin to Warsaw that didn't yet exist in 1872/3. It may have been that Jochim and Tauba were visiting Tauba's younger sister Zofja Szwarcmer, who lived with her husband (whose surname was Neufeld) in Warsaw. Żarnowiec was about 200 kilometers to the south, but it had access to a railway, possibly built by the Russians at the time. Regardless, in those days it would not have been an easy trip for an older pregnant woman. The only other information I could find about Berek was that he married Itla Rajzia Kuperberg in Będzin in 1903, and may have become a religious teacher in Dąbrowa Górnicza, where my father lived with his

first wife and children. (See further endnotes in this chapter for other possible siblings.)

13. More about Mailech's siblings, i.e. my father's aunts and uncles: Mosziek (Motel) Szmul (Szaul) was born in Żarnowiec on September 6, 1859. According to the records, Jochim turned 20 seven months after he married Tauba, who was 24. Her recorded age was likely incorrect, as another record indicates that Tauba was about 18 when she was married seven months earlier. In 1883, at age 24, Mosziek married Szyfra Szaulowicz. They had three kids: Sura, b. 1898, Kalma, b. 1903, who in 1931 married Bluma Frajdla Feldberg in Będzin, and their own Szlama Israel, b. 1905, who married Cerla Sara Malc in 1942 in the Będzin Ghetto. Mosziek died in 1928 in Będzin at age 69. Another sister, Idessa, married Icyk Cukierman (Zuckerman) in 1900 at age 23. They and their children ended up emigrating to the US, and it was Idessa and Icyk's children who sponsored my father and his second family (my mother, my sister and me) in the process of coming to the US in 1952. The Zuckerman relationship is described in the chapter on Sweden. Yet another sister, Estera Bina, was born April 8, 1857. She married Mosziek Hersz Blat in 1886. Mailech's older brother Berek (Barnard Berl) was born to Jochim and Tauba in 1873 (or possibly 1867) in Józefów, not Żarnowiec; he then married Itla Rajzia Kuperbergt at age 30 in 1903 in Będzin. (See previous endnote in this chapter for more about Berek's birthplace.)

14. The record keepers in Żarnowiec (and I) had a tough time keeping track of marriages, births and deaths because there was another Jochim Frydman, not at all related, who had become a widower at age 42 and then married a 22-year-old widow and raised a family in Żarnowiec during this same period. That Jochim had raised a number of children with his first wife, and started yet another family with his second wife, creating even more little Frydmans to confuse researchers like me. Furthermore, the records, such as they were for Jews in Poland, were rarely accurate or consistent. Jews often did not register births or marriages with the civil authorities at all, or if they did, it was sometimes not until years later. So it is quite possible that there were more brothers and sisters for Mailech and more uncles and aunts for my father than the records might have indicated, or more than I could discover. Records also show other possible relatives of Mailech's – perhaps siblings, perhaps cousins or other relatives. Alternatively, they may have been relatives of the other Jochim, either with his first or second wife, and their offspring: Josek Dawid, possibly an older brother of Mailech's, and his wife Sura Bijla (Bajla) Lewit, bore Naftula in 1905, Frajdla Ita in 1909, Abram in 1913, Alta Mordka in 1915, Ellijasz in 1918, Haja in 1920 and Estera in 1926. They lost a baby girl, Szprinca Jacheta, who died in 1909 at 18 months, and Szuml Majer, who died in 1910, possibly in Działoszyce, at age nine. Another possible older brother, Josek, married Krajndla Trajman, who delivered their own Jochim in 1913 (or 1914). Then there was a possible brother-in-law, Szulim Kopel, born in 1871 (Szulim signed Mailech's death certificate in 1915 in Będzin), and two other possible siblings who died young: Izrael in 1877, and Chaja Perla in 1879. Another of Mailech's possible younger brothers, Herszlik (maybe Cherszlik) Fridman and his wife, Chana Cywia Liberman, gave birth to Mosziek Josek in 1898, Sura Perla in 1899, and Rywka Laja in 1904. Herszlik and his wife married off Mosziek Josek (Mojzesz) in 1918 at age 20. Another possible older sister, Chana Gitla Fridman, and her husband, Majer Wajsnsztok, had a girl, Sura Perla, in 1910. Yet another possible younger brother, Izrael Icyk Fridman, and his wife, Estera Mindla Biedak, had a girl, Liba, in 1902.

Another of Mailech's possible older sisters, Ruchla Fridman, and her husband, Szmul Szaulewicz, (perhaps the brother of Szyfra, who was married to Mosziek Fridman, above), gave birth to Baila in 1909 and Chana Fejgla in 1911. Another possible sister, Elka Rachla (Ruchela), who was married to Chaim Lederman, gave birth to a boy, Josek Dawid, in 1911, Chaja in 1913 (who died in 1922, aged nine), Icek Majer in 1914 (or 1915), Abram in 1916, Naftula in 1923 and Mosziek in 1926.

15. Rubin, I., ed., *Visoka-Mozovietsk-Wysokie Mazowiecki, Early History.* Translation of Memorial Book. Wysokie-Mazowiecki Society, Tel Aviv, 1975, page 280. Yizkor Book Project, JewishGen.org.

16. Some records even indicate that my father lived with his first wife for a time in the same building or nearby, perhaps very early in their marriage.

17. We visited the Będzin-Czeladź cemetery in 2018, and while we couldn't find Mailech's gravesite, we saw the graves of someone who may have been his brother, Nachum Zev, and one of Nachum's daughters.

18. There were at least 28 cheders to choose from at the time in Będzin.

19. The next time he would attend any formal classrooms was in Sweden, when he studied English for a few weeks at classes held in a refugee camp in late 1945 or early 1946 in Furudal as he sought to emigrate to the US. After that, he saw the inside of a classroom again in 1955-1957, when he and my mother attended "night school," a program for adults held at a neighborhood elementary school (PS 225) in Brooklyn's Brighton Beach section where they learned English and American history as they prepared to become American citizens.

Dąbrowa Górnicza

1. Also possibly spelled Kotlicka, Kotlitski or Kotlitzki.

2. Some details about Chaja's siblings: Leah, her oldest sister, was mentioned earlier in her daughter Ada's story. Leah was murdered during the war. Another sister, Szaia, b. 1901, married Szandla Szwimer and had a daughter named Zierla in 1932. All three were murdered during the war. A brother, Israel, b. 1908, married Ruchla Grinszpein in 1931. Their son, Chaim Lejb, was born later that year. Ruchla and the child were murdered; however, Israel survived the war and remarried a German Christian named Klara, who converted to Judaism. They emigrated to Israel in 1948. There they had a daughter named Yafa, b. 1960. Israel, Klara and Yafa all passed away in Israel. Another sister, Chana, married Emial Lejbus Krymokowski in 1927. That year they had a boy named Efroim Zelik and then, in 1936, a girl named Genedla. They were all murdered by the Nazis. A brother, Icek, was born in 1909 and married Chawa Wolfowicz in the Dąbrowa Ghetto in 1941. Both were murdered. A sister, Ajdla, b. 1913, passed away at the age of three months. Another sister, Hela, never married and was murdered during the war. Chaja's oldest brother, Pinchas, b. 1905, emigrated to Palestine in 1920. A brother, Herszel, b. 1912, married Pesla Ganeles in 1937. They had a daughter, Masza, in 1939. Pesla and Masza were murdered in Belzec. Herzsel survived Auschwitz, remarried and emigrated to Israel in 1948. He had two children, Jacob, born in Germany in 1947, and Yona, b. 1952. We met Yona in Israel in 2018.

3. When the Germans occupied the town they changed the Kotlicki home's street name to Fabrikstrasse.

4. Londner, Juda, *Jewish Trade as reflected in the Telephone Book: Dąbrowa*, page 191. Translated by Lance Ackerfeld. Yizkor Book Project, JewishGen.org.

5. Ury, Scott, *Zionism and Zionist Parties*, The Yivo Encyclopedia of Jews in Eastern Europe, November 15, 2010.

6. Dobrowolska, Joanna, *A Complicated Peace: Nationalism and Antisemitism in Interwar Poland*. Graduate Theses and Dissertations, Utah State University, 2018.

7. Goda, Norman, *The Holocaust: Europe, the World, and the Jews, 1918–1945.*

8. Ben-Ami, Yitshaq, *Perspectives on the Holocaust*, pages 71-91. Also, *The Irgun and the Destruction of European Jewry*, pages 75–76.

9. Rovner, Adam, "Madagascar: An Almost Jewish Homeland," *Moment Magazine*, May-June 2009.

10. Randel, Izzy and McLoughlin, Maryann, *From Black Dust to Diamonds*, The Richard Stockton College of New Jersey, ComteQ Publishing, Margate, NJ, 2011, page 8.

11. *The History of the Dąbrowa Górnicza Jewish Community before the Holocaust: The Dąbrowa Górnicza Jewish Community in the Interwar Years*, Exhibition: The Valley of the Communities, Yad Vashem, yadvashem.org.

12. My father reported the year of his wedding as 1936 while in Sweden, but the marriage certificate said otherwise. The year remains an open question since there may have been a reason for my father pointing to a year earlier than records would indicate.

13. Or perhaps even in the ultra-Orthodox tradition, as my father would sometimes assert.

14. *Jewish Views on Premarital Sex*, My Jewish Learning Newsletter (Online), 70/FACES Media.

15. Gray, Helen T., *Living together: What various denominations say*, The Wichita Eagle, February 5, 2011.

Będzin

1. Będzin was later renamed Bendsburg by the Germans.

2. In German: Auschwitz.

The Slave Labor Camps

1. *Op cit.*, Randel, page 13.

2. German for labor camp Gräditz.

3. Interview with David Schnitzer, July 17, 2913, RG-50.106.0209, Collections, Ushmm.org.

4. Bachrach, Zvi, "Worked to Death" Review of 'A Narrow Bridge to Life' by Bella Gutterman, *Haaretz,* June 6, 2018.

5. During the course of numerous postwar interviews, my father would sometimes say he arrived in Bunzlau in July 1941, and sometimes, he would recall, not until May 1942.

6. Her married name was Herskope.

7. Rozen, Israel, *Dąbrowa: In the Hell of Auschwitz*, translated by Avi (Abraham) Stavsky, The Yizkor Book Project, JewishGen.org., page 428.
8. Of course, they were told they were going to take showers and get new clothes.
9. *The Dąbrowa Górnicza Jewish Community during the Holocaust: Aktions in the Dąbrowa Górnicza Ghetto and the Murder of the Ghetto's Jews*, Exhibition: The Valley of the Communities, Yad Vashem, yadvashem.org.

Bunzlau

1. In English, the Protective Unit.
2. *The United States Holocaust Memorial Museum Encyclopedia of Camps and Ghettos, 1933-1945, Volume 1*, pages 720-722. Volume Editor: Geoffrey Megargee, 2009, Indiana University Press.
3. There is no telling how long or short that was, since he did say that most of his time at Bunzlau was doing excavation work in the quarries.
4. Urbach was born on December 11, 1913 in Chrzanów, a town in southern Poland that had once been an important hub of Jewish life. One record from Chrzanów lists members of a family named Urbach who were murdered by the Germans. They included Abraham, Shloyme, Chai, Gitl, Perez and Itzchak. Yet Itzchak did survive, likely thanks to my father.

The Death March and Bergen-Belsen

1. *Op cit., Haaretz.*
2. Grünberg, Kurt, "Contaminated Generativity: Holocaust Survivors and their Children in Germany," *The American Journal of Psychoanalysis* 67, pages 82-96, February 26, 2007.
3. Kornfeld, Israel, *The Martyrdom of the Jews in Death and Concentration Camps*, translated by Gloria Berkenstat Freund, The Yizkor Book Project, JewishGen.org., page 407.
4. Levi, Primo, *Survival in Auschwitz*, Simon and Shuster, 1995.
5. Yona's father's name is sometimes spelled: Hersszel (Zvi), Herzsl or (Herszel)-Henri-Zvi Kotlicki (Kotlitzky).
6. The other two were Pinchas, b. 1905, who had both the foresight and the courage to emigrate to Palestine in 1920, where he married Naomi Halevy and had six children, and another brother, Israel, who also emigrated to Israel with Yona's father.

Sieniawa

1. Over the years, her first name was also listed as Fryda, Frymet, Fryma, Frida and Frieda. In this book, I will use Frimet for her until after World War II, when she seemed to move to Frida (or Frieda) beginning with her DP interviews.
2. Some of these spellings had to do with the exigencies of record keeping in Poland, and with how names were spelled, especially Jewish names. Sometimes it was

intentional on her part – for reasons unknown.

3. Another official record in the Kraków City Archives listed her mother as Ruchela Huta (perhaps a middle name), b. 1881, and her father as Jakob Goldman, b. 1866, a difference of 15 years. Most other records list their birth years as 1876 and 1872, respectively.

4. As if to purposely render this genealogy still more confusing, my mother first married someone named Friedmann and took his last name. As you now know, her second husband, my father, was also named Friedman (Frydman, Fridman). This was likely another source of confusion, or confused identity, later in her life. In any case, once she married my father she became Frieda Frydman. They used the surname Friedman informally but then, in 1957 in the US, legally changed our surname to Friedman. Other spellings I found for her surname over the years were Friedmann, Fridmann, Frydmann, Fridman, Singer-Friedmann and Singer-Fridman.

5. The record was actually of the death of a baby named Hersh in 1905.

6. See 1919 map of Sieniawa and house numbers circled. Marim (Miriam), born in 1900, and Chaja, born in 1901, were both delivered in house #174. Chaim, born in 1901 (twins with Chaja?), died in 1902. Golda (Golde) was born in 1903. Hersh, born in 1905 at #51, died at nine months of an unspecified inflammation on August 10, 1905 at #59. (He was the only child whose father was officially listed as Jakub Goldman.) That same year, according to the available records, Genia was born on November 8, 1905 (perhaps also one of a set of twins). Leib was born at #30 on June 3, 1906; Leon was born on October 5, 1907; Moses was born in 1909 at #86; Abraham was born on March 12, 1910 and Frimet was born on December 14, 1910 at #82. It is unlikely that both Abraham's and Frimet's birthdates were correct. That may have to do with when their births were registered. There was no record in which house Naftali was born on October 8, 1913. And of course, Jozef was born in Prague on April 7, 1917.

7. We don't have any specific records of deaths, except for Chaim and Hersh.

Refugees from War

1. Radio Prague International described what it called a "Forgotten Chapter in History: Jewish Refugees in the First World War" in a broadcast on September 2, 2014, from an exhibition at the Jewish Museum in Prague, which featured an interview with the exhibition's creator, Michal Frankl.

2. Ibid.

3. There is no record of any of the Goldman/Entenbergs attending schools in Prague.

Settling in Kraków

1. Meilech Goldman was originally from Kanczuga. It is possible that Meilech's father's name was Jacob Schuja Goldman and his mother's name was Estera (Goldman). Estera may have died in 1929 at age 75. Her father's name was Chaim Beer Singer, and her mother was Marim (no father is listed for Marim). Perhaps

my mother's grandparents were deceased and their names were given to several of my mother's siblings. Or maybe all these names were confused in the retelling or the odd record keeping.

2. Kazimierz was named after the benevolent (as far as Jews were concerned) Casimir (Kazimierz) the Great.

3. Alternatively, she may have gone to one of a network of Bais Ya'akov schools for girls, founded by a seamstress named Sarah Schenirer in Kraków in 1917, which provided Orthodox Jewish educational alternatives for girls and young women.

4. Leib also lived for a time in Podgórze at Koszykarska 13 on the other side of the river from Kazimierz.

5. Sussel Beitscher (Beitsoyer, Bejczer) was born July 7, 1903 in Nisko (Nisko Mielec). Initially, Genia and Sussel lived at Daszynskiego 26 in Pradnik Czerwony, a district in the northern part of Kraków. Later, his sister Eugenia also lived with them at Meiselsa 22. Their apartment building today features a highly rated local Polish restaurant on the ground floor. It is just a block or so from Jozefa 12.

6. Frymeta might have been born in 1933; records show that year as well. Genia and her family also lived for a time at Jozefagasse 18 (which was Jozefa 18).

7. Also Friedman, Frydman, Fridman.

8. Another record claims the marriage took place on April 15, 1939, and my father himself once wrote in a letter that my mother had married only eight months before the war began. Still, I am sticking to 1938.

9. Perel's given name might have also been Perli or Perla. Abe's mother was born on May 23, 1870 or December 19, 1879. Her parents were Salomon and Mindel. Abe had two sisters, Frymat, born in 1901, and Rozalia, born in 1902. Perel Friedmann was from a large town called Tarnów, just east of Kraków and not very far from where Frimet was born. We know nothing more about Abe's father; only his mother was listed on Frimet and Abe's marriage certificate.

10. A data table from the Bundesbank – the German Central Bank – dated January 2021 – called "Kaufkraftaequivalente-historischer-betraege-in-deutschen-waehrungen" (available through Google searching) looks at the value of Reichsmarks (two złotys to one Reichsmark multiplied by the factor in Euros.) In that calculation, Abe Friedmann's monthly wages in the late 1930s and early 1940s might have equaled US $200 in 2005. However, that does not account for the scarcity of goods at the time, or the high inflation rates, so his purchasing power was considerably reduced from that amount. His wages would have bought very little and would instead have primarily supplemented the food ration cards provided to Jews after the German invasion. The cards themselves were valued so as to once again discriminate against Jews versus other Poles. For instance, they covered fewer items than those given to other Poles. Ultimately, the value of his work was more about his job being considered a productive activity supporting the Nazi effort. Thus, for a time it protected him and his family (my mother) from deportation to concentration (or later extermination) camps. Of course, all that had changed by 1942, and in subsequent years neither Abe, Frimet nor any other Jew was truly protected.

Frimet's Kraków Home: Jozefa 12

1. Famed pre-Holocaust photographer Roman Vishniac came to Kazimierz in the 1930s, believing that what he saw in this prototypical, very large Jewish quarter was the essence of Jewish civilization in the Ashkenazi heartland of Galicia. He sought to create a picturesque form of Jewish authenticity, including his widely reproduced, mistitled masterpiece *Entrance to the Old Ghetto*, which in fact opened only onto a courtyard passageway between Meiselsa and Jozefa Streets. It appeared in Vishniac's landmark collection of photos about Eastern European Jewish life before the war called *A Vanished World*. It is where my mother and her family lived.
2. Wasserman, Henry, "Tailoring," Jewish Virtual Library, American-Israeli Cooperative Enterprise, 1998-2021.

Deportations

1. The General Government was the name given to the German zone of occupation not incorporated into the German Reich.
2. Apenszlak, Jacob et al., *The Black Book of Polish Jewry*, American Federation for Polish Jews, Association of Jewish Refugees and Immigrants from Poland, Brohan Press, 1999, pages 79–84.
3. I have tried my best to identify family members by name. It is important to consider each of those murdered as individuals. Naming them, if possible, restores just a tiny bit of their humanity. When I first learned the names of my father's children, Ada and Feigla, I wept. They became much more real, with personality and histories. I began to think of them as people, linked by our blood and genetic codes, as well as family ties.
4. They had just moved to Koszykarska 13 in Kraków from the suburb where they were living.
5. Also called death camps or killing centers.

The Kraków Ghetto

1. Polanski, Roman, *Roman*, Morrow, 1984, page 22.

Płaszów and Auschwitz

1. "Płaszów Concentration Camp in Krakow," *Essential Krakow*, September 4, 2012.
2. Brecher, Elinor J., *Schindler's Legacy: True Stories of the List Survivors*, Plume, 1994, page 151.
3. Peter Egger, Mauthausen Memorial Site.
4. The 92-page *Book of Block 22B* lists my mother as Prisoner A-9898. Auschwitz-Birkenau Memorial and Museum/Memories, Auschwitz.org.
5. *Behind Every Name a Story: Irene Safran*, United States Holocaust Memorial Museum, Ushmm.org.

Bergen-Belsen

1. There are other records that indicate my mother was transferred from Auschwitz-Birkenau to an Auschwitz subcamp called Lichtewerden in North Moravia. Her name was on a list of female prisoners there, arriving on or about December 30, 1944 along with 300 other women. Lichtewerden was a slave labor camp housed in a thread factory for G.A. Buhl und Sohn. From there she would have gone on to Bergen-Belsen. However, various other documents where she listed her "camp" imprisonments made no mention of Lichtewerden. Possibly another Frieda Friedmann was at Lichtewerden and had arrived there from Auschwitz, and then also went on to Bergen-Belsen on a death march.
2. "Bergen-Belsen in Depth," United States Holocaust Memorial Museum: Holocaust Encyclopedia, Ushmm.org.

Before Leaving Poland

1. We talked about Schindler days earlier, when we were at Yad Vashem with Yona Kobo and the kids. As it turned out, we learned then that in the final days of the war, having been liberated by US Army soldiers, the woman who became Yona's mother, Anny (Hana) Keller, born in Germany and also a survivor, was approached by a group of liberated Polish Jews who asked her to help them rescue Oskar Schindler and his wife. These Poles had been Schindler Jews, rescued in Kraków and who had worked at his factory. As a Nazi, Schindler would have been shot if he were captured by the approaching Soviets. Her mother accompanied some American soldiers, whose help she had enlisted, to Schindler's hideout. After hearing his story, the GIs brought him and his wife back under US protection, saving his life.

Searching for Life after Death

1. After the war my mother started using Frida or Frieda as her given name, so from with this chapter on, I will do the same when referring to her.
2. Bornstein, Ernst Israel, *The Long Night*, Toby Press, 2016. Excerpted from: Holocaust Matters: The Story of Ernst Bornstein, The Holocaust Selection Process Explained, Holocaustmatters.org.

A New Kind of Camp

1. Martinez, Victoria, "History dies deep in the Woods: The forgotten Nazi concentration camp survivors in the forests of Småland," *The Local*, July 4, 2017, News@the local.se.
2. Rosenberg, Göran, *A Brief Stop on the Road from Auschwitz*, Other Press, New York, 2017, pages 162–163. (Originally published in Sweden, 2012.)
3. Ibid, page 180.

4. Definition of repatriandi, *Svenska Academiens Ordbok*, a dictionary published by the Swedish Academy in English, Column R 1196, Volume 22, 1957.

5. Rosenberg sometimes writes this memoir of his family as though he is talking/writing to his father.

6. *Op. cit.*, Rosenberg, pages 181-182.

7. Ibid.

8. Ibid.

9. Ibid, page 184.

Szlama: Alone

1. Esther Zuckerman Henzel was born in Mińsk-Mazowiecki, Poland, the site of another famous pogrom against the Jews in 1936. Her siblings may also have been born there. She was the first cousin of my father to whom he was closest and with whom we lived for a short period after coming to America. She, her siblings and her parents, Isaac Zuckerman and his wife Yehudis Friedman, had emigrated from Poland to the US in 1923 after a series of pogroms were launched in and around their small hometown east of Warsaw during and after World War I. Isaac seems to have been fairly well off in Poland. He owned either a successful grocery or a number of sugar mills. It seems that a brother-in-law (but definitely not my grandfather Mailech) swindled Isaac out of his wealth, and when he arrived in the US, he had to work in a sweatshop for most of the rest of his life. I have heard several versions of the extent to which my father's family was observant. Certainly my father's aunt, Yehudis, was a very religious Jew, so much so that she initially refused to join her husband and children in the US because she felt the move would cause her to lose her religion. She eventually asked a panel of three leading Hasidic rabbis in Poland for permission to leave. Although the ultra-Orthodox Jewish leadership generally tried to dissuade Polish Jews from leaving during the interbellum years (for precisely the same reasons behind Yehudis' reluctance) they gave their permission. Actually, they told her that irrespective of religious concerns, her place had to be with her husband and children. God would always remain by her side no matter where she lived.

2. *Op. cit.*, Martinez.

3. He would eventually settle on October 3, 1911, as his official birthday.

Frieda: Alone

1. After doing some research about Fania, I increasingly came to suspect that a mistake in documentation caused my mother to be mixed up with another Frieda Friedmann. I discovered a similar, perhaps even parallel confusion in researching my mother's journey from Auschwitz to Bergen-Belsen. Again, another Frida Friedmann was discovered leaving Auschwitz after first going to the Lichtewerden slave labor camp at the end of December 1944 and from there to Bergen-Belsen sometime later. My mother had entered Bergen-Belsen earlier, in November or early December 1944. Perhaps this other Frieda Friedmann was on that ship to Sweden as well, but I have a feeling she was on a ship that arrived later, in mid-

July 1945, and that was the ship that Fania traveled on, though both Friedas and Fania started their respective journeys in Bergen-Belsen. The other Frida Friedmann, born on April 4, 1913, came from Hungary. In fact, she actually stayed in Malmö after arriving in Sweden and died there on November 22, 1962. Her husband was listed as Abe Friedman in the records of the Jewish Community of Malmö, which seems extraordinarily odd – and also wrong. As it turned out, Fania's mother's surname was Swidler. I could not discover how my mother was related to her, or if they were related at all. Other records show her arriving via Lübek from Bergen-Belsen on the *SS Kastellholm* on July 15 or July 26, 1945. My mother reported that she had left from Lübek on the *SS Karskaer* on June 27, 1945. Fania, who was from Wilno (Kobylinki, now Vilna in Lithuania), was born on October 15, 1920, or May 1, 1920, and would marry another survivor, Moses Kornbluth (an electrician), and become a Swedish citizen in 1953. They settled in Malmö at Kistianstaelgatan 21. She died on February 11, 1972. Her husband, who was 20 years her senior, had died earlier on July 20, 1966.

2. *Op. cit.,* Rosenberg, pages 163-164.

3. The Crisis Time Organization was a Swedish authority that was responsible for rationing various foods and other supplies in the First World War and then during and after the Second World War.

Coming Together

1. In fact, Abe died there soon afterward.

2. Halmstad, about 80 kilometers north of Mölle, was also on Sweden's west coast, famous for its port, beach and castle.

3. 50 kronor were worth about US $12 at the time.

4. Hebrew Immigrant Aid Society (HIAS), the American Jewish Joint Distribution Committee (JDC), as well as the United Service for New Americans (USNA).

5. Built in 1925, the *MS Gripsholm* was the first diesel-powered cruise ship to cross the Atlantic. Its luxurious interiors were modeled after one of Sweden's most famous castles. Though seafaring vessels were in high demand during World War II, the US government was able to charter the *Gripsholm* and its sister ship, the *SS Drottningholm*, to use as "repatriation" vessels. The ships were painted white and lit up with bright lights at night to broadcast their protected status. Enemy governments agreed to give the ships safe passage. The *Drottningholm* was used in exchanges between the US, and Germany and Italy. The US government chartered the *Gripsholm* to transport civilians and POWs caught behind enemy lines during World War II. Between 1942 and 1946, these "Mercy Ships" participated in a dozen exchanges between the US and its wartime enemies Germany, Italy and Japan. (Source: Iritani, Evelyn, "The Gripsholm WWII Exchanges," *Densho Encyclopedia*.)

The Coney Island Years

1. I have decided for most of the rest of this story to use the "Americanized" names they had come to adopt shortly after their arrival – at least when others would ask

who they were. My father was Salomon – Sam to those he worked with and any other Americans who might ask. My mother was Frieda, which she had decided on back in Sweden. My father's given name, Szlama, as well as their married family name, Frydman, would remain as they were until they became naturalized citizens five years later in 1957. Then his first name officially became Salomon and our family name was transformed to Friedman.

2. Coincidentally, years later I worked for public television's Channel 13, which was headquartered on several floors of that same hotel.

3. Eventually my father would one day return some of that kindness, finding a job for Abe Henzel at his workplace years later.

4. The laundry was operated by a family whose son Roy was the only one who came to the only birthday party I recall having as a child.

5. The only time I ever ate there was when my high school graduating class held its 50th reunion at Gargiulo's in 2017.

6. Johnson, George, "Who's Afraid of the Evil Eye," *Jewish World*, September/October 2014, Arts & Culture section, September 29, 2014.

7. We would later move to that neighborhood.

8. I had written Jacob at first (the American spelling), but then changed the *c* to a *k* as befit my European heritage and my grandfather's spelling of his name.

9. Her craziness, in Yiddish.

10. I should amend that slightly. One of my closest friends growing up was David Louie, whose family owned the only Chinese restaurant in Coney Island. In the afternoons I would sit with him and sometimes with his family while dumplings were made and filled, Chinese cabbage chopped and egg rolls stuffed and rolled. All the other preparatory work that went into making that food was ultimately offered to take-out customers, who had the chance to select one item from Column A and one from Column B. At least, that's how it was done in the old days, or so I think, since I never had the opportunity to actually do that. When David would invite me to stay and eat with his family, as happened on a few occasions, I would instead take out the tuna sandwich my mother had prepared from my brown paper bag and feasted on it, or just simply watched.

11. This included a particularly unnerving experience in which I ended up in the sub-basement of the Associated Press Building in Rockefeller Center.

12. I don't recall his first name.

13. I suppose "Greener" was a Yiddish term for greenhorn.

Brighton Beach Family Memories

1. The platform at the center of the synagogue where the Torah is read.

Sam and Frieda: By Themselves Again

1. This was all before cell phones, so communication, which was difficult and disturbing anyway, was downright primitive.

Psychological Effects of the Holocaust through the Generations

1. Such documents were no doubt precious few, given my own extreme difficulties reconstructing even a small sample of their records for this book.
2. Barel, E., Van IJzendoorn, M. H., Sagi-Schwartz, A., & Bakermans-Kranenburg, M. J., "Surviving the Holocaust: A meta-analysis of the long-term sequelae of a genocide," *Psychological Bulletin, 136(5)*, 2010, pages 677–698.
3. Rodrigues, Tori, "Descendants of Holocaust Survivors Have Altered Stress Hormones," *Scientific American Mind*, March 1, 2015.
4. Goldman, Daniel, "Holocaust Survivors had Skills to Prosper," *The New York Times*, October 6, 1992.
5. Yehuda, Rachel, *How the Effects of Traumatic Stress Are Transmitted to the Next Generation,* Glasgow Center for Population Health: Seminar Series, March 5, 2013.
6. I'm using my mother's actual birthday here.
7. *Op. cit.,* Goldman.
8. Ibid.
9. Ibid.
10. Kaplan, Fara, *Holocaust Survivors and Their Children: A Search for Positive Effects,* American Academy of Experts in Traumatic Stress, 2020.
11. Dutton, Emily, "Survivorship and Shame; Tracing the Affective Afterlife of the Holocaust," *Constellations,* Volume 5, No. 2, University of Alberta, May 12, 2014.

From Auschwitz with Love. The Inspiring Memoir of Two Sisters' Survival,
Devotion and Triumph Told by Manci Grunberger Beran & Ruth Grunberger
Mermelstein, by Daniel Seymour

Remetz. Resistance Fighter and Survivor of the Warsaw Ghetto, by Jan Yohay
Remetz

My March Through Hell. A Young Girl's Terrifying Journey to Survival, by
Halina Kleiner with Edwin Stepp

Roman's Journey, by Roman Halter

Beyond Borders. Escaping the Holocaust and Fighting the Nazis. 1938-1948,
by Rudi Haymann

The Engineers. A memoir of survival through World War II in Poland and
Hungary, by Henry Reiss

Memoirs by Elmar Rivosh, Sculptor (1906-1967). Riga Ghetto and Beyond, by
Elmar Rivosh

The series **Holocaust Survivor True Stories** consists of
the following biographies:

Among the Reeds. The true story of how a family survived the Holocaust, by
Tammy Bottner

A Holocaust Memoir of Love & Resilience. Mama's Survival from Lithuania
to America, by Ettie Zilber

Living among the Dead. My Grandmother's Holocaust Survival Story of Love
and Strength, by Adena Bernstein Astrowsky

Heart Songs. A Holocaust Memoir, by Barbara Gilford

Shoes of the Shoah. The Tomorrow of Yesterday, by Dorothy Pierce

Hidden in Berlin. A Holocaust Memoir, by Evelyn Joseph Grossman

Separated Together. The Incredible True WWII Story of Soulmates Stranded
an Ocean Apart, by Kenneth P. Price, Ph.D.

The Man Across the River. The incredible story of one man's will to survive
the Holocaust, by Zvi Wiesenfeld

If Anyone Calls, Tell Them I Died. A Memoir, by Emanuel (Manu) Rosen

The House on Thrömerstrasse. A Story of Rebirth and Renewal in the Wake
of the Holocaust, by Ron Vincent

Dancing with my Father. His hidden past. Her quest for truth. How Nazi
Vienna shaped a family's identity, by Jo Sorochinsky

The Story Keeper. Weaving the Threads of Time and Memory - A Memoir,
by Fred Feldman

Krisia's Silence. The Girl who was not on Schindler's List, by Ronny Hein

Defying Death on the Danube. A Holocaust Survival Story, by Debbie J. Callahan with Henry Stern

A Doorway to Heroism. A decorated German-Jewish Soldier who became an American Hero, by Rabbi W. Jack Romberg

The Shoemaker's Son. The Life of a Holocaust Resister, by Laura Beth Bakst

The Redhead of Auschwitz. A True Story, by Nechama Birnbaum

Land of Many Bridges. My Father's Story, by Bela Ruth Samuel Tenenholtz

Creating Beauty from the Abyss. The Amazing Story of Sam Herciger, Auschwitz Survivor and Artist, by Lesley Ann Richardson

On Sunny Days We Sang. A Holocaust Story of Survival and Resilience, by Jeannette Grunhaus de Gelman

Painful Joy. A Holocaust Family Memoir, by Max J. Friedman

I Give You My Heart. A True Story of Courage and Survival, by Wendy Holden

In the Time of Madmen, by Mark A. Prelas

Monsters and Miracles. Horror, Heroes and the Holocaust, by Ira Wesley Kitmacher

Flower of Vlora. Growing up Jewish in Communist Albania, by Anna Kohen

Aftermath: Coming of Age on Three Continents. A Memoir, by Annette Libeskind Berkovits

Not a real Enemy. The True Story of a Hungarian Jewish Man's Fight for Freedom, by Robert Wolf

Zaidy's War. Four Armies, Three Continents, Two Brothers. One Man's Impossible Story of Endurance, by Martin Bodek

The Glassmaker's Son. Looking for the World my Father left behind in Nazi Germany, by Peter Kupfer

The Apprentice of Buchenwald. The True Story of the Teenage Boy Who Sabotaged Hitler's War Machine, by Oren Schneider

Good for a Single Journey, by Helen Joyce

Burying the Ghosts. She escaped Nazi Germany only to have her life torn apart by the woman she saved from the camps: her mother, by Sonia Case

American Wolf. From Nazi Refugee to American Spy. A True Story, by Audrey Birnbaum

Bipolar Refugee. A Saga of Survival and Resilience, by Peter Wiesner

Before the Beginning and After the End, by Hymie Anisman

Malka Owsiany recounts, by Mark Turkow (editor)

I Will Give Them an Everlasting Name. Jacksonville's Stories of the Holocaust, by Samuel P. Cox

The series **Jewish Children in the Holocaust** consists of the following autobiographies of Jewish children hidden during WWII in the Netherlands:

Searching for Home. The Impact of WWII on a Hidden Child, by
Joseph Gosler

See You Tonight and Promise to be a Good Boy! War memories, by
Salo Muller

Sounds from Silence. Reflections of a Child Holocaust Survivor, Psychiatrist
and Teacher, by Robert Krell

Sabine's Odyssey. A Hidden Child and her Dutch Rescuers, by
Agnes Schipper

The Journey of a Hidden Child, by Harry Pila and Robin Black

The series **New Jewish Fiction** consists of the following novels, written by Jewish authors. All novels are set in the time during or after the Holocaust.

The Corset Maker. A Novel, by Annette Libeskind Berkovits

Escaping the Whale. The Holocaust is over. But is it ever over for the next generation? by Ruth Rotkowitz

When the Music Stopped. Willy Rosen's Holocaust, by Casey Hayes

Hands of Gold. One Man's Quest to Find the Silver Lining in Misfortune, by Roni Robbins

The Girl Who Counted Numbers. A Novel, by Roslyn Bernstein

There was a garden in Nuremberg. A Novel, by Navina Michal Clemerson

The Butterfly and the Axe, by Omer Bartov

To Live Another Day. A Novel, Elizabeth Rosenberg

A Worthy Life. Based on a True Story, by Dahlia Moore

The series **Holocaust Heritage** consists of the following memoirs by 2G:

The Cello Still Sings. A Generational Story of the Holocaust and of the Transformative Power of Music, by Janet Horvath

The Fire and the Bonfire. A Journey into Memory, by Ardyn Halter

The Silk Factory: Finding Threads of My Family's True Holocaust Story, by Michael Hickins

Hidden in Plain Sight. A Journey into Memory and Place, by Julie Brill

Winter Light: The Memoir of a Child of Holocaust Survivors, by Grace Feuerverger

The series **Holocaust Books for Young Adults** consists of the following novels, based on true stories:

The Boy behind the Door. How Salomon Kool Escaped the Nazis. Inspired by a True Story, by David Tabatsky

Running for Shelter. A True Story, by Suzette Sheft

The Precious Few. An Inspirational Saga of Courage based on True Stories, by David Twain with Art Twain

The series **WWII Historical Fiction** consists of the following novels, some of which are based on true stories:

Mendelevski's Box. A Heartwarming and Heartbreaking Jewish Survivor's Story, by Roger Swindells

A Quiet Genocide. The Untold Holocaust of Disabled Children in WWII Germany, by Glenn Bryant

The Knife-Edge Path, by Patrick T. Leahy

Brave Face. The Inspiring WWII Memoir of a Dutch/German Child, by I. Caroline Crocker and Meta A. Evenbly

When We Had Wings. The Gripping Story of an Orphan in Janusz Korczak's Orphanage. A Historical Novel, by Tami Shem-Tov

Jacob's Courage. Romance and Survival amidst the Horrors of War, by Charles S. Weinblatt

Join the AP Review Team

Reviews are very important in a world dominated by the social media. Feedback for Holocaust books is more than just a customer review; it also shows the relevance and importance of such books in today's society.

Please go over to the AmsterdamPublishers.com website (top of page) if you want to join the *AP review team,* showing **at least one review on Amazon** for one of our books. You will get updates about new releases and will get the chance to read and review.